Private Lives
Public Voices

Private Lives Public Voices

Drama for the Classroom

JOHN T. RAMSAY

Toronto
OXFORD UNIVERSITY PRESS
1994

Oxford University Press

70 Wynford Drive, Don Mills, Ontario M3C 1J9

Toronto Oxford New York
Delhi Bombay Calcutta Madras Karachi
Kuala Lumpur Singapore Hong Kong Tokyo
Nairobi Dar es Salaam Cape Town
Melbourne Auckland Madrid

and associated companies in
Berlin Ibadan

Oxford is a trademark of Oxford University Press

All rights reserved. No part of this book may be reproduced in any form without written permission of the publisher. Photocopying or reproducing mechanically in any other way parts of this book without the written permission of the publisher is an infringement of the copyright law.

Canadian Cataloguing in Publication Data

Main entry under title:

Private lives/public voices

ISBN 0-19-540996-5

1. Canadian drama (English) – 20th century.*
2. Drama – 20th century.   3. Radio scripts.
4. Television scripts.   5. Motion picture plays.
I. Ramsay, John (John T.)

PS8307.P75 1994   C812'.5408   C93-095250-2
PR9196.3.P75 1994

Copyright © Oxford University Press (Canada) 1994

Editor: Laura Edlund

Design: Jeffrey Tabberner, Marie Bartholomew

Illustrators: John Etheridge, Kevin Ghiglione, Glen Hanson, Peter Lacalamita, Larry Limnidis, Kent Monkman, Susan Todd, Leon Zernitzky

1 2 3 4 5 98 97 96 95 94

This book is printed on permanent (acid-free) paper ∞.

Printed and bound in Canada by Best-Gagné Printing

Contents

To the Reader   vii

Acknowledgements   viii

Identity

Eve A stage play by Larry Fineberg,
based on the novel *The Book of Eve*
by Constance Beresford-Howe   3

The Interview A stage play by Peter Swet   44

The Man Who Turned into a Dog A stage play by
Osvaldo Dragún, translated by Francesca Colecchia
and Julio Matas   71

The Exhibition (Scenes from the Life of John Merrick)
A stage play by Thomas Gibbons   81

Relationships

Medicine River A radio play by Thomas King, based on
his novel   107

A Marriage Proposal A stage play by Anton Chekhov,
translated by Theodore Hoffman   145

On the King's Birthday A stage play by Hilda Mary Hooke   160

To Set Our House in Order A teleplay by Anne Wheeler,
based on the short story by Margaret Laurence   171

Power

Compensation Will Be Paid A stage play by
GWEN PHARIS RINGWOOD   197

Frankenstein: The Man Who Became God A stage play by
ALDEN NOWLAN and WALTER LEARNING, based on the novel by
Mary Shelley   203

Death Seat A stage play by JOAN MASON HURLEY   259

Glossary   275

Additional Selection Groupings   277

Credits   279

To the Reader

Drama is life with the dull bits cut out.
Alfred Hitchcock

WHETHER a Hitchcock film, a television series, your own improvised scenes, a stage play, or another form, drama at its best is concentrated, powerful, and immediate. Drama focuses, often very intensely, on the human condition and the complex issues which affect human beings in all their variety.

Through the lives and voices of diverse characters, the dramas in this collection address relevant and compelling issues. Eleven scripts are presented in three broad themes—identity, relationships, and power—with additional groupings suggested at the end of the anthology. These selections offer an exciting variety of drama—ranging in inspiration, setting, form, style, tone, and length. Original works and adaptations of familiar literature explore long-standing issues and themes in both contemporary and historical contexts. Among the plays for stage, radio, and television, you'll find serious and comic dramas in a variety of styles—realistic, symbolic, and experimental. Together, the plays are a rich collection for you to choose among and read.

Your readings will encourage you to respond, question, and explore. For each script, an introduction to the author and dramatic work gives you a starting point. Then, "Prelude" sets the scene with pre-reading activities, and "After Words" offers follow-up activities. With these follow-up activities, you will give personal responses in your journal, explore and examine the play, develop critical responses, and extend creatively beyond the text. You might, for example, write character sketches or stories, role-play, script, explore other media and representations, work collaboratively to report, present, or debate, independently research themes or references, read further, or create sequels.

Whichever dramas you read, whichever activities you pursue, the editor and the publishers of this anthology hope that you will use it to discover and enjoy, as Alfred Hitchcock said, "Life with the dull bits cut out."

JOHN I. RAMSAY

Acknowledgements

Thanks to the following educators for their constructive comments in reviewing the manuscript:

Nora Allingham, Teacher, City Adult Learning Centre, Toronto, Ontario

Barry Buckler, Head of English, Albert Campbell Collegiate, Scarborough, Ontario

Glen Kirkland, Coordinator of English, Edmonton Catholic School District, Edmonton, Alberta

Wayne McNanny, Senior English Consultant, Waterloo County Board of Education, Kitchener, Ontario

Elaine Snaden, Teacher, Riverside Secondary School, Windsor, Ontario

The author expresses his thanks to Tony Luengo, Laura Edlund, and the staff at Oxford, Canada for their invaluable assistance and support.

1

IDENTITY

Eve

A stage play by LARRY FINEBERG,
based on the novel *The Book of Eve* by
Constance Beresford-Howe

CONSTANCE BERESFORD-HOWE'S tale of Eva—a feisty pensioner determined to live her own life—was an immediate success when it was published in 1973. Two years later, the Stratford Festival in Ontario, which specializes in the classics of theatre, made a rare commission by asking Larry Fineberg to write a stage play based on the novel. The play was under tremendous pressure to succeed. Eventually it played to sold-out houses at Stratford, won the 1976 Chalmers Award for an Outstanding Canadian Play, and went on to acclaimed performances in England, the United States, and Holland. The original starred Jessica Tandy, who has since won an Oscar for *Driving Miss Daisy*. In 1993, the distinguished Canadian author and broadcaster Pierre Berton confirmed plans for a film adaptation.

Born in Montreal in 1920, Constance Beresford-Howe published her first novel at age 28. She has since written eight other novels, taught creative writing at Ryerson Polytechnical University in Toronto, and raised a family. The CBC has produced a film based on her novel *A Population of One*. Beresford-Howe's writing reflects her belief that life, despite its demands, can be terribly funny.

Larry Fineberg was born in 1945, also in Montreal. He first worked as an assistant director on Broadway and in London, England. He returned to Canada in 1972 when *Stonehenge*, the first of his many plays, was produced in Toronto.

Prelude

1 Write a journal entry about what you think you will be like at age 65. Consider your surroundings, daily activities, relationships, and concerns.

2 What images of the elderly, both men and women, are presented in the media? Discuss and, if possible, display images (e.g., in magazine clippings) on a classroom bulletin board. How do these images compare with your experiences of the elderly?

Eve

Characters

    EVA: sixty-five-year-old woman
    BURT: sixty-seven, Eva's husband
    NEIL: forty, son of Eva and Burt
    JOHNNY HORVATH: fifty-four, Eva's neighbour in rooming house
    KIM: fifteen, Eva's granddaughter

Setting

    EVA's *flat; a squalid room, cot, table, sink. Around her, the city of Montreal. This should be evocative but sparse. Several garbage cans. Note: In "memory scenes" the people never enter* EVA's *room itself, although they may appear in close proximity.*

Act One

Dark. No sound. BURT *coughs. He is seen, an old, ill man, in pajamas and a bathrobe.*

BURT: (*Weakly*) Eva. Eva.

(EVA *appears, in a different area, in a plain housedress. There is a coat over a chair, and a suitcase nearby.*)

EVA: (*Softly*) No.

BURT: Can't you even—can't you—

EVA: No.

BURT: Spilling the cocoa, mess, and slop and *can't you even—*

EVA: (*Softly*) It is messy.

BURT: Pain all night, hardly call it sleep, wake up to mess and—

EVA: All right, Burt.

BURT: Look at your hair.

EVA: (*Surprised*) My hair?

BURT: Grey and straggly. When I first met you—

EVA: Please, Burt.

BURT: You're old.

EVA: You're young?

BURT: I'm an invalid, I hate it, but you, you've—

EVA: Are you saying I haven't aged gracefully?

BURT: Don't even seem to care how you look any more.

EVA: Do I care. Do I?

BURT: You were beautiful.

EVA: So were you. If I remember—

BURT: That's cruel.

EVA: Sorry. I'm feeling testy or— Burt . . . I never told you I thought *you* were beautiful.

BURT: Stop it. Leave me alone.

EVA: Is that what you want?

BURT: Don't want to hear about what I was . . .

EVA: . . . What do I want . . .

BURT: Clean up the mess and let me alone.

EVA: All right dear, I'll clean up the mess and get your breakfast and tidy the porch and do an extra laundry and see if the preserves are . . . are . . .

BURT: What are you babbling?

EVA: I won't. Enough . . . *no*. What it is, what I'm doing, is going away.

(*She puts on coat, takes her bag, and walks into the street area.*)

I have left my husband. Left breakfast outside his door, took my first pension check, my first one, packed a few things and left that house! I've gone away!

BURT: Eva!

(*He vanishes.*)

EVA: I don't feel guilty. Air. Where to go—what to do—don't think. Get that taxi. Drive, just drive. *Away*. Keep moving, *move*, know these houses, away, farther, now that's more like it, we cross St Lawrence Main, turn right, turn left here, god knows why. Now it's all strange, I'm in the French section, it's poor, rundown, and there isn't anybody here who knows me. Alone. Rue de la Visitation. House. Room for rent. Landlady suspicious. But she sees my coat, takes my cash. First month paid in advance. I'm about two miles and three galaxies away from Notre Dame de Grace.

(*She enters her room for the first time.*)

Dirty. Not well-lit. Nobody I know'll ever come down here. Wouldn't think to. Not to Rue de la Visitation. It's mine. (*Sits on cot*) The furnace grumbles. (*Starts to unpack*) What is it I'm doing. Don't care. Just go with it. Noise, basement, window needs cleaning, to heck, been cleaning all my life. Who needs Windex? Sleepy. I can nap. Now, later, whenever I like. Don't have to get up in the night for anyone. No worries about if Burt's in pain, if he needs something, if my son, if this needs fixing, if that needs—it's me. Just me. Alone. State of rest. Of grace, of shock. Feels like I've given birth and the baby died, shock, *empty*. Is that bad. What's bad? It's just me, only me.

(*Pause*)

Bug in the sink—let it stay. No nightmares, no guilt . . . And a whole week's gone.

(*Pause*)

And a whole week's money too. Not much left and the pension cheque doesn't come again until—how long has it been since I worried about funds? I mean, really worried? *Am* I worried? Lack of money. Means no new clothes, bought this coat as a treat with the last of my savings. Last of my treats. Didn't pack my slippers or a warm dress or winter boots. Or my bits of jewellery in case finances get really desperate since I can't very well ask Burt to—or would he? I've left him—Money can't be a connection. I'll have to call Neil, call my son and ask him to get some of my things. That's contact. That's a worry.

(*She slips her coat on.*)

Still, it's been a fine week, a calm week, of myself, only a phone call and I can come right back. Still.

(*She goes to a "phone" area.* NEIL *appears, at his office.*)

NEIL: Dad's in a state and I've been worried sick. Where are you, Mum? What's happened?

EVA: I thought it would be obvious. I've left your father.

(*Pause*)

NEIL: Tell me where you are and I'll come and drive you home.

Eve 7

EVA: Neil, I'm not going back.

NEIL: That's completely impractical, Mother.

EVA: I only called to ask if you could collect a few of my things for me, Neil. They're all at the house. I want some warm dresses. My slippers, the *wool* underwear, my bits of jewellery—

NEIL: Look, I know that things between you and Dad haven't been exactly—but you must realise—

EVA: Why even talk about it.

(*Pause*)

NEIL: Lunch at the Ritz.

EVA: Not today.

NEIL: Why not?

EVA: Too much still to do. New place and all.

NEIL: Friday then. At one. You'll meet me there, Mum. We have to settle this.

EVA: It is settled.

NEIL: Mother, please. Totally irrespective of the—the situation—you've got me worried sick. How can you say you won't meet me for lunch.

EVA: All right Neil darling, but there's no cause for worry. But I will meet you on Friday. Just don't forget my things, my slippers and the—

NEIL: Until Friday, Mum, at one.

(*Lights out on* NEIL)

EVA: Mistake to call Neil. He's so practical. But I need those things if I'm going to learn to be self-sufficient again. *How am I going to protect myself against my son.*

(*She slips, catches herself on a garbage pail.*)

Or myself against puddles. I need my boots. Anyway, Neil isn't going to hurt me, just urge me back to the old cell, the practical way, the useful way, the way to do it right. I did it right for years and I still don't have a pair of my own boots.

(*She pulls herself up, looks into the can.*)

Is there a pearl in this oyster? Light's catching something. (*Takes a worn brooch from the can*) An old brooch. Grimy, pretty in a way. Who needs it.

(*She tosses it back in the can.*)

After a week by myself what a state—family, my son—dear God, he's not a stranger. It's his love that would pull me back— that's why he scares me! Why not take this brooch? Might be nice to wear? Might even have to pawn it one day, for a perm, since my bankbook won't stretch to a beauty salon. And if I can't pawn it maybe I can wear it. Simple solution. Clasp doesn't work but still, why not have it?

(*She is in her room.*)

One and a half days to fix myself up for Neil, so he won't think I'm destitute. I am not destitute. Not by my new standards. Whatever they are. A long bath, no bubbles and the tub has little claws for feet. Brush to my hair, so messy, can't do it properly—wonder what I look like.

(*She takes out a pocket mirror.*)

Crumpled. All of it. Doesn't matter what I look like here but for Neil. Is my suit in season? It was fine last month but the month turned. Leaves all blown off the trees, in clumps, bare branches, wind blowing me. Leaves aren't off this tree just yet thank you. I'll keep my coat on for the Ritz, and *buttoned*, then I won't look like I need a good pressing. Wouldn't it be nice to have an iron though. I'll do for the Ritz won't I? Grey sky, not a bird anywhere. Hell, I'm meeting my son for lunch and I'm put in the position of feeling I'm about to ask for an advance on my allowance. Won't do. State of mind won't do. Onward Christian soldiers. Marching to the war. Marching to the Ritz for lunch, I can do it, I've been there before.

(NEIL *rises from the table to greet* EVA.)

NEIL: You look tired, Mother.

EVA: I'm not, dear.

NEIL: How's your back?

EVA: Actually, it's much better.

NEIL: I ordered for us, do you mind? I know your favourites.

EVA: Thank you dear. You know son, I'm a bit worried. You're looking terribly thin.

NEIL: No, it's . . . I've joined a gym, to keep in shape. It's high time.

EVA: Aren't you feeling well, dear?

NEIL: Mum, come on now. We aren't here to discuss my health.

(*Pause.* EVA *attacks her food.*)

Haven't you been eating?

EVA: It's very good, dear. Aren't you hungry?

Eve

NEIL: Not really.

EVA: How's Kim?

NEIL: Same, rebellious. It's her age, I guess.

EVA: And Rosemary?

NEIL: She sends her love.

EVA: That's nice.

NEIL: Mum . . . do you realize how worried we've all been?

EVA: You don't have to be.

NEIL: Why won't you tell us where you're staying?

EVA: So I can remain staying by myself.

NEIL: Why did you do this? I mean, I do know that things between you and Dad—but after forty years of marriage—

EVA: Exactly why I did it. I knew it was high time.

NEIL: Now, Mother . . . let's get down to it, please. I've had two or three talks with Dad about the whole thing and there's no doubt that he's . . . very badly upset.

EVA: You mean he's being extremely disagreeable.

NEIL: I think he feels this more than you realize.

EVA: I'm not going back. To the house or to your father.

NEIL: What was it he did? Was there a fight or—

EVA: Nothing specific. Just all those years I guess.

NEIL: But my god, Mum—that's just marriage.

EVA: It isn't. Just.

NEIL: Well, can you tell me more about . . . whatever the problem is.

EVA: There isn't a specific problem. I don't expect you to understand.

NEIL: At least try me.

EVA: I've started a new life.

NEIL: What are you talking about?

EVA: I'm trying to tell you. It's a permanent thing, Neil.

NEIL: The shock nearly killed Dad.

EVA: I'll bet it did.

NEIL: I had to get in a nurse, and he's getting shots and his pain—

EVA: He's had shots and pains for the last twenty years. You aren't giving me new information.

NEIL: Mum . . . I can't believe you. What you're doing is heartless.

EVA: Try to understand. It isn't your father so much, Neil. It's me, really. I simply won't live that way any longer. I don't want to. I can't. I know what I'm doing is selfish. It also isn't easy. But that's what I want. Not to see anyone. Not even Kim. Not you.

NEIL: Look Mum, Rosemary thinks—

EVA: I don't give a goddamn what Rosemary thinks.

NEIL: Now Mum, let's try to be practical.

EVA: I'm trying to be.

NEIL: What about money? How can you manage on what you've got. You can't have much saved, the pension cheque's a joke, dear. How much do you have in the bank?

EVA: I've found a cheap comfortable place to live.

NEIL: Well you can hardly expect Dad to give you an allowance.

EVA: Why not? I worked for him all those years. A cleaning lady and a nurse, which is what I was, would have at least gotten wages.

NEIL: You aren't being realistic.

EVA: What makes your facts more real than mine?

NEIL: How can you ignore a marriage, Mum?

EVA: People get divorces. And move away.

NEIL: Not at your age.

EVA: Why not?

NEIL: It's just not done.

EVA: I'm doing it. Why can't I do what I want to? I only want to live alone, and in a different way than I have before.

NEIL: Let me say something. At the very least I can agree that you need a vacation. You haven't been anywhere in such a long time. Let me give you a little present. Take a month. Go to New York, or Florida, or anywhere you like. We'll go from here to the airline office and make a reservation. Then, when you come back—

EVA: Peru.

NEIL: I beg your pardon.

Eva: May I go to Peru? I've never been there.

Neil: Let me drive you to wherever it is you're staying.

Eva: No.

Neil: I just want to be sure that you're all right.

Eva: And I've told you that I am.

Neil: Are you feeling in top shape? You look a bit—

Eva: I'm fine. I don't need a checkup.

Neil: I wasn't suggesting—

Eva: Yes, you were. I haven't gone senile.

Neil: It's hard for me to have any respect for what you're doing.

Eva: I don't care. It's not you that's doing it. It's me.

(*Pause*)

Neil: Take two weeks. This will pass. Whatever it is. Meanwhile you're going to need money. Dad obviously won't—

Eva: Have you asked him?

Neil: No. He was too—

Eva: Try.

Neil: I'd rather give—

Eva: I won't take money from you, Neil. That isn't what I want. Just the bag of things I asked you to collect.

Neil: I forgot them.

Eva: You thought I'd come home.

Neil: I did think that you'd—

Eva: What I want are winter boots, a warm dress. I want my slippers. My jewellery. Just go to the house and pack them. Your father can't object to that. They're all my things.

Neil: I'll bring them to you. *Where?*

Eva: We'll find a neutral place.

Neil: Tell me where you live!

Eva: A baggage locker at the bus terminal.

Neil: Mother, I will not take a bag of clothes to a bus terminal.

Eva: Why not?

Neil: It smells of poverty.

EVA: Oh Neil. Neil. That's funny. No, I guess you can't take a suitcase to . . . no.

NEIL: And please stop saying "no".

EVA: Why? It feels rather good.

NEIL: Mother, promise me you'll come home by Christmas.

EVA: Neil, promise me that you'll listen to this. You're talking about seasons. I'm talking about what's left of my life.

(EVA *leaves the Ritz and goes into the "street area".*)

Good for me. Didn't take a dime from him, not even taxi fare. I can walk. Got some pride. Where'd that wind come from though. I can take it. Montreal winters can't be worse than Siberia. Hell, what about me, this isn't proper. I'm an old lady. I've only gone about six blocks and I'm blue and my joints creak. An hour walk home. Because I forgot to bring change for the bus. Learn to be like your son, learn practicality. That's almost better, those big gusts are the best ones. They almost completely anaesthetize you. Use anger, that's good, that'll get me home. Pride should take me another foot or two. Add the fact that your pride stems from irritation that he treated you like a child. All right, I'll add that. He won that game even if he doesn't know it. I'm acting like a damn fool kid, games with my son. It's only that . . . I fortified myself ahead, I planned, I wanted to be useful to myself, to me, and I wasn't. All I got was concern and a free meal. *One more block and I'm home.* Three cheers for pride.

(EVA *is in her room.*)

Why do I feel I have to be of use? (*Pours herself a large sherry*) Fortification! Major discovery. Cheapest liquid refreshment— rotgut sherry. *More.* It'll make me fat. I am a bit fat. Well, who cares? I haven't joined any gym for anyone. Should I have? Nonsense. Talking nonsense. Who cares what I look like? Not now. Actually, I haven't cared for some time. I was bored. Whose fault was that. Bored at home for years. Burt had lost, oh hell, fond memories, Burt had lost interest in me. And I went through hell to get him, caught him, and then, so quick, he lost interest. But he'd married me. How many years of marriage add up to a pyrrhic victory? Mine.

(*She sits bolt upright.*)

Wearing my clothes in bed. Watch isn't ticking. Hell with it. Maybe noon, maybe eight, I care a lot. All sherry and no food, stomach's like a fat animal. When did I start becoming a compulsive eater?

(BURT *appears, young, more robust, preoccupied.*)

BURT: Did you finish the cookies?

Eve

Eva: I don't think so. Burt, couldn't we go somewhere tonight?

Burt: I wanted to have something to nibble on while I finish this report—where'd we go? You hate hockey and I don't care for movies.

Eva: If there are no more cookies in the breadbox, Burt, look in the tin in the pantry, beside the jams and preserves.

Burt: I looked there too. Aren't you putting on a little weight, Eva?

Eva: It's the baby.

Burt: I think it's too early for the baby to show. (*Gently*) I see you nibbling all the time. You never used to do that.

Eva: It's just because there's food around the house. If I'm baking I have a piece of—

Burt: Well. Doesn't matter. I'm going to get back to work.

Eva: I'll make you some more cookies. So we'll have them in case you get hungry.

Burt: Doesn't matter. Don't bother on my account. (*Goes*)

Eva: It's no trouble, Burt. It's something to do—

> One thing I don't miss down here is conversation. But I did become a very good cook. Hated it, finally. Mixing, beating, set the oven, grease the pans, smother my mind with dough—anything but think. Food. Get something in here besides soup and sherry. Maybe tinned spaghetti. Cheap *and* fattening. Might as well keep some habits. Don't have to look thin for anybody now.

> (*Her coat on, she steps outside.*)

> Why it's almost dawn. Nothing'll be open. Everyone's asleep except me. That's all right. No wind at least. Might as well walk. Listen. Stupid yowling cats. They're not asleep. Slaves, always in heat. Yowl. Yowl. Thank god I'm past all that. What a relief. Yowl, you poor bastards. Poor slaves, no freedom for you. Find your toms. Yowl. Now who'd throw this out?

> (*She discovers a small pot of ivy near a garbage-pail.*)

> Pot's cracked but the ivy inside might be alive. Might be. Get it home. Shut up, cats. What ninny'd throw out a good plant. Save everything, that's the trick. Always has been, hasn't it. Hold on to what you might be afraid to lose. Hold on. Collect. Store. Keep. Just to be safe, I'll do some repotting.

> (*She's home. She transfers the plant to an empty coffee tin.*)

There. That'll do it. Bit of water. Now it'll pollinate, or whatever plants do. They're not neutered, not like me. God alone knows when a man last looked at me.

(BURT, *at his youngest and best, passes her, not looking.*)

Hello.

Do I want to remember this?

BURT: Sorry. Didn't see you. You must be the daughter.

EVA: Are you Dad's accountant?

BURT: Yep, and you're the schoolteacher.

EVA: You needn't say it as if it were a disease.

BURT: Guess you feel good, out working and earning and all.

EVA: Yes, I do. After the first year it bored me. Don't you think women should work?

BURT: Not really.

EVA: What do you think women should do?

BURT: I'm a Baptist, see, there are certain—

EVA: You don't look like a Baptist.

BURT: What are we supposed to look like?

EVA: Stern!

BURT: I can be stern.

EVA: I'll bet you can.

BURT: But that's not my nature.

EVA: (*Genuine*) Talk to me.

BURT: Tell me about yourself kid.

EVA: I'm not a kid. I'm only a few years younger than you.

BURT: Go on.

EVA: And I love teaching because I'm helping—don't you ever want to help?

BURT: I think I do that by being good at what I do.

EVA: Accounting sounds so dull.

BURT: What's dull about money?

EVA: Everything, if money's all you care about.

BURT: If you *don't* care about it, you're in big trouble. I've never had a lot, you see, and I mean to have. Anyhow, I do care.

Eva: What else do you like?

Burt: I like sports.

Eva: Bore me to death.

Burt: Yep. You'd play maybe . . . badminton.

Eva: I do as a matter of fact.

Burt: It's a woman's game.

Eva: I'll bet you like boxing.

Burt: I did some in school—lightweight of course.

Eva: Were you any good?

Burt: Good enough. I placed second in the—

Eva: But if money's so important to you, you must love the competition in getting it.

Burt: You're right. I do.

Eva: Then placing second must have irritated the heck out of you.

(*Pause*)

Burt: Nice meeting you, kid. See you around.

(*He is gone.*)

Eva: And I'd scared him off. I could always second-guess Burt from the word go. But he irritated the hell out of me with his notions about women—he thought we were a separate species— necessary but strange—and I didn't understand that our mutual irritation was plain simple sex appeal. We competed from the word go. I fought to get Burt's attention when he visited Dad. Who wasn't so dumb himself. Dear Dad, you didn't want me to be an old-maid schoolteacher and you knew a young up-and-coming accountant. So he came to the house as much as to the office.

Burt: That's a new dress.

Eva: No. You just haven't seen it before.

Burt: Come for a walk. It's nice out Eva. It's spring.

Eva: Oh I can't really.

Burt: Why not. Grading papers?

Eva: Yes. That's my work.

Burt: Take twenty minutes.

Eva: All right.

Burt: Nothing like a spring night, is there?

Eva: No. Really there isn't.

Burt: Stars, and the earth smelling so fresh, and hope. It's good to be young, to have your life ahead of you. To know that it's all out there, waiting for you.

Eva: I don't see it quite that way.

Burt: How else could you see it?

Eva: There are things that I have to do, that are expected of me, and—

Burt: Know what I'd like to do? I'd like to make a fortune, and raise a family, and invest in things that I love, that excite me. Like a baseball team.

Eva: A baseball team!

Burt: Sure. It can be done. This country's so young, almost anything's possible. Why can't I be rich? Why can't I—

Eva: I'd just like to raise a family.

Burt: You're not so hard, are you.

Eva: Hard. What makes you think I'm hard?

Burt: Well, not that exactly—afraid? It took me a while to figure you out. See, you're warm really, but you're also shy, and you try to hide that behind being clever and smart.

Eva: What if I am clever and smart? Should I be worried about that?

Burt: If it stops you from feeling.

Eva: It doesn't!

> All we did that night was kiss, but Burt found me out, and that hooked me. He knew it, and it gave him what he wanted. The upper hand, control, to win the game. And he won me. We swept each other off our feet, saw those spring stars, and they blinded us from the fact that we didn't truly like each other, that the irritation came out as jokes, jokes that turned less funny, a young love that went vinegar dry, and years later when Burt hadn't made his million and fell ill and I had to take care of him—and I tried to show that care could be love but he wouldn't accept it or maybe saw through it—
>
> (Burt, *older now, slumps onstage, or is found weary in a chair.*)
>
> What did the doctor say?

Burt: (*Softly*) It's a good thing that Neil's grown now, that he's a man, can take care of himself.

Eva: What is it, Burt?

BURT: My lousy stupid back. It's going to hurt, give pain, for the rest of my life.

EVA: Can't they do—

BURT: As Doctor Cobb says, it's a pain I'll learn to live with. I can work, I'll have maybe two bad days a month, it'll get progressively worse as I get older.

EVA: Isn't there anything—

BURT: An operation. If it works—and it works on one out of five—I'll be better, not perfect, but better. If it doesn't, I'll be a cripple. That's the future. I'd rather have pain than be a cripple. Does that mean I'm a coward?

EVA: No. I understand. (*Pause*) Maybe there's a way that we—together we might—

BURT: Are you better than the doctors?

EVA: Let me try, Burt. Burt, it isn't your fault. I agree the operation is crazy, but you mustn't hide behind your pain.

BURT: You think I want to wind up having you wait on me—it'll come to that eventually—you think that's what I want for my wife!

EVA: (*Softly*) I *am* your wife. Let me help you.

BURT: (*Directly*) Do either of us have a choice?

EVA: And so poor Burt lost his nobility in his own eyes, and all we had to sustain us was the memory of our courtship, the first year, let's be honest Eva, good sex, and a marriage that simply went on like a boat floating on a lake, an occasional storm, but mostly just floating. We both made our own shells and hid. It wasn't sad. It was waste.

Enough strolling down memory lane. Hungry. Famished. What's for lunch today, assuming it's lunch time? Stroll to the grocery and get a nice chicken pot pie. And at the rate I walk, it'll be defrosted before I get it home. Even if it is winter.

(*Coat on, she's outside.* JOHNNY HORVATH *is shown briefly, far upstage.*)

That one there—up ahead, he lives in the house too. A foreigner. Asked if he could help me the other day, I had parcels—shook him off quick, last thing I need in my life now is people. More people. Lunch is better than people—good, foreigner grabbed a bus, no need to natter to him. I can natter to myself. Hello you, what's new. Well, it isn't snowing; in fact, there's a nice thaw. Dangerous on two counts because it lulls you into thinking spring might be around the corner when it's further than Mars, and also makes the ice melt of course which means you can slip and crack a shin—there's a warming thought—or you go getting damp by falling into what you thought was hard and secure. Oh security. Sweet security. Where you hiding today security. No answer huh? Security is not a lady, security is a bitch. Dear me, filthy mouth, learn to watch my tongue. And also the neighbourhood. A little brat, maybe ten, a little lout grabbed at my purse and tried to run off with it. 'Cause I'm an old lady. Fooled him though, he didn't get it, I kicked *his* shins, but problem is, my strap broke, so my purse doesn't carry itself in the proper fashion. And what would the proper fashion be? Luck!

(*She stops beside a garbage can and in the rubble lying near it picks up a small change-purse.*)

Bless my sharp eye. Bless it. (*Shakes change-purse*) I hear money. There is money. Twenty-seven cents. Today that'll almost get me a cup of coffee. Somewhere. This is a lure. Means I have to see what's inside the treasure chest. (*Peers into the garbage can*) There's nothing in here today but real garbage. Long walks are fine until water seeps through your shoes, stockings, into the skin of the foot. I'm damp, mildewed, and cold. I'm going to freeze. This just won't do. I have to call Neil and persuade him I need my winter boots. Prospect of lunch palls if I catch pneumonia before I catch my lunch.

(NEIL *appears, again at his office. His dapper appearance is now in sharp contrast to* EVA.)

NEIL: Mum . . . what the hell have you been doing! It's been weeks.

EVA: Sorry about so much time passing Neil, but in a way that's why I called. Winter's here son and I—

NEIL: Knew you'd come to your senses. That's what I told Rosemary. She's been after me to find you, even a detective or—

EVA: I suppose the police would have been indelicate. What if it made the newspapers. You know what I like about Rosemary, Neil? Her consistency.

NEIL: Anyway Mum, since you do know it's winter we can pick you up, find a way to tell Dad that you've decided to do what's right—

EVA: I want to talk to you about boots.

NEIL: What?

EVA: We both agree it's winter. Can we agree that I'm going to need my boots? Please.

(*Pause*)

NEIL: Mum, I don't want you to take this the wrong way but what you're doing isn't normal. You aren't really yourself. You've had some kind of mild breakdown. Mum?

EVA: I'm here.

NEIL: Why even your voice sounds different.

EVA: That's the telephone connection, dear.

NEIL: We want to take care of you, that's all. A psychiatrist . . .

EVA: Nice of you Neil, *no*. I do feel different, but maybe it's a good thing to be broken down. Maybe that seems less than normal to you—I find it necessary.

NEIL: Mum, I have to speak frankly.

EVA: I don't mind that, dear. It's exactly what I've been trying to do.

NEIL: You can't, at your age, spend December and January alone. Not in this climate. Not away from your family.

EVA: Experienced winters before, Neil. I'm not a baby in a crib. That's why I need my boots!

(NEIL, *frenzied, fades.*)

It's no good trying to get things from him. I do have to do it all myself.

(*She's at a garbage can.*)

All right then, I will! What's in here today? Bib lettuce with frozen dressing. God, my throat feels raw. Well-chewed bone from a steak. I hate feeling damp. Crunched ping-pong ball. Well, never a ping-pong champion.

(*She discovers a battered pair of running shoes.*)

Oh, ugly. Ugly. Can't use these. (*Throws them back*) Mind you, they'd keep my feet dryer than shoes. (*Retrieves them*) Ugly. But the price is right. (*Putting them on*) And if they hold out until summer, I'll join the Racquet Club and play tennis. Ooops, no white shorts. What do you mean I can't have a court? To hell with you Miss Priss! Maybe I can't play tennis, but I've got traction. I can walk again like other people. Well why's he moving away so fast? Don't you like my outfit? I'm in training for the next Olympics. Hundred-yard dash. Over-sixties division.

(*She's home again.*)

Training time over. Approved official beverage. (*Pours a huge glass of sherry*) It aches when I swallow. Getting a damn fool cold. Raw, groggy, and feverish. I know those symptoms. Practically been a nurse for twenty-five years. And before Burt, Neil. Sturdy now, but as a kid he caught everything. Poor

Neil. Don't shake, darling, it's Mother. I'm wiping your head. I'm holding you so you can drink your juice. Don't shiver, darling, here's a blanket.

(*Shivering, she wraps one around her own body.*)

Oh poor baby, can't you get well?

(**Burt** *appears, far upstage in pajamas. Now middle-aged, he's repressing a torrent of emotion.*)

Doctor says he's got whooping cough.

BURT: How many more things are there for him to catch?

EVA: I can't help it if he's weak.

BURT: You worry him too much. Let him get out more, like a normal kid.

EVA: He's sick. Can't you hear it?

BURT: Of course I can. What I'm saying is, when he gets well, you've got to let him get outside, play more.

EVA: Of course I let him play.

BURT: More sports and he'll get stronger. I did.

EVA: He doesn't have your constitution.

BURT: He'll develop it if you only let him—

EVA: I'm just going to get him a glass of apple juice.

BURT: Fifty times a day. It's a bit much.

EVA: He is my child.

BURT: I'd like to sleep one night through.

EVA: So would I.

BURT: I spent all night up with him last week.

EVA: What's one night to my—

BURT: You like it.

EVA: Oh what's the matter with you? Can't you even understand normal concern?

BURT: I work bloody hard to give you what you have. I live here, but it's as if I don't see you. How can you talk to me about concern?

EVA: Would you mind not crowding me?

BURT: Sorry I touched you. Let's divide the bed.

EVA: I'm tired, Burt. Normal consideration.

BURT: Consideration for you. What about me?

EVA: My lord—I take care of the house and the child and I'm weak and tired and I don't ever get out—

BURT: All right. Just relax.

EVA: I can't relax when you hold me. (*Softer*) I mean I can't sleep.

BURT: Guess I don't count for anything.

EVA: Count, count, count. I'm not a lousy balance sheet.

BURT: Why treat me like one. At least talk to me!

EVA: That isn't talking.

BURT: What about him Eva? Always him. What about me? Never me? Never. Never. Never?

(*He fades. She's on the floor, wrapped in a blanket wrecked.*)

EVA: Never mentioned it again. Not him. Not me. Blocked it away. But he cried after he forced himself upon me. We still slept in the same bed, but we slept miles apart. We sealed ourselves off. We talked and we didn't speak. For years, until I left. My wonderful tender marriage. And not even Burt's fault. He didn't force the ring on my finger.

(*Pause*)

Who did, then? Oh shut up Eva. I believe I am ill. Not Neil. *Me.* Something just turned in my stomach.

(JOHNNY HORVATH *is seen in the street area making for home. He wears a worn, useful greatcoat. He is very drunk, but not without a certain dignity.*)

It's a touch of flu. I know that's all it is. I hope. Dear heaven, I'm delirious, I can tell that. There's a new horror. Alone, feverish, and getting worse. I don't even have an aspirin. Please let it be just a little flu.

(JOHNNY *falls on the stairs, and tumbles into* EVA'S *room.*)

Good Christ! Who the hell are you?

(*He doesn't move.*)

Can't you get up.

(*She edges towards him.*)

Are you hurt?

(JOHNNY *is indignant as only the inebriated can be.*)

JOHNNY: Who the hell are you?

EVA: I live here. You've fallen into my flat and you're dead drunk as a bonus.

JOHNNY: You look terrible.

EVA: I'm sick. I've been up half the night with flu. I'm not dressed for company. Drunken company.

JOHNNY: I'm not drunk. A little trip on the stairs. It's dark.

EVA: I'll bet it is to you.

JOHNNY: Landlord won't put a bulb in the stairwell. It's hard to see.

EVA: You're standing. You must be all right.

JOHNNY: I am definitely all right!

EVA: Good. Go away.

(JOHNNY *vomits*.)

Oh Christ, don't encourage me. (*Tosses a washcloth to him.*)

JOHNNY: No really. Please don't trouble yourself. I'm fine. (*Falls again*)

EVA: I'll wipe your stupid mouth but I will not clean up your swill.

JOHNNY: You're a very good woman. Will you marry me?

EVA: (*Weaving*) Could you go away now. I'd like to die by myself. I know it's selfish.

JOHNNY: I will carry you to your bed as a favour.

EVA: I don't want a favour. You'll fall on me and break something. Please—just go away.

JOHNNY: Are you really sick?

EVA: No. It's just a little novelty turn I perform for unexpected drunks.

JOHNNY: I am not a drunk!

EVA: Fine. I believe you. You're cold sober. Keep your driver's license. Now—will you go away.

JOHNNY: (*Hauteur*) John Horvath never forces himself on a woman.

EVA: That's a comfort to know.

JOHNNY: But I owe you a favour. I will repay you.

EVA: Go sleep it off, will you.

JOHNNY: (*Exiting*) I shall come back.

EVA: He's coming back! And I have no door to lock off those back stairs. (*Staggers to the cot*) Crazy loony foreigners in a rooming house—it's come to that. Wipe up a drunk's vomit, and plan raids on the neighbourhood garbage. My useful college degree. I've just got to have some water. I'm too dizzy. My entire useful life.

(*Pause*)

I am going to die. Alone. Oh who gives a good goddamn anyway. I'm fat, I'm old, I'm sexless. It's been a stupid life. It's been wasted. And God, if you don't like my attitude, there isn't much left you can do to me. Thanks God, all the same. I've never had any control over my life, why should I have any over death. But it's ludicrous. I've never had control over anything. And I've done exactly what I was supposed to do. Always. I was good. I don't know anything more now than I knew when I was born. *What the hell has it all been for?*

(*Pause*)

I do know one thing. Maybe one. After Burt, Neil, after all that I have been through, it doesn't make any sense to die down here alone without somebody to bring me a glass of water. That just doesn't make any sense.

CURTAIN

Act Two

    Eva *sits up, wipes her forehead.*

EVA: Fever's gone. That's a blessing. I feel so much better. I feel like an old paper bag. I want a wash. And a meal. (*Crosses to sink*) Clean some of this sweat off me first. Oh God, I love water.

    (JOHNNY HORVATH *enters, sober and relaxed.*)

JOHNNY: Aaaahhh. At last you're up.

EVA: Who are you? Get away.

JOHNNY: But we're friends.

EVA: I don't know who you are.

JOHNNY: John Horvath. You wiped my face, remember? I fell on your stairs.

EVA: You're the drunk.

JOHNNY: Wipe yourself missus. Don't catch a chill.

EVA: What do you want?

JOHNNY: I'm glad you're better. I looked in here every day.

EVA: You looked in here?

JOHNNY: Two, three days. You must have been very sick.

EVA: I was sleeping.

JOHNNY: (*Dubiously*) Long rest.

EVA: I go at my own pace Mr.—

JOHNNY: Horvath, John Horvath.

EVA: Mr. Horvath, I'd like to finish washing.

JOHNNY: I can wait.

EVA: Not here, please.

JOHNNY: I bring you a little gift.

EVA: I don't want your little gift.

JOHNNY: Look missus, I wasn't well. You helped me.

EVA: I had no choice. You were dead drunk and fell into my flat.

JOHNNY: And I come only to apologize.

EVA: Thank you. The apology's accepted.

JOHNNY: I cleaned up the mess I made.

EVA: Well now I would like to clean up my own mess.

JOHNNY: I apologized missus. It's silly to hold a grudge.

EVA: I'm holding no grudges. I just want to tidy myself up in the privacy of my own flat.

JOHNNY: Here. I leave you a little present anyway.

EVA: Leave anything you want.

JOHNNY: I made it myself.

EVA: Fine. Thank you.

JOHNNY: Homemade strudel. Poppyseed.

EVA: Thank you.

JOHNNY: Later, when you've had enough privacy, I live just upstairs.

EVA: Thank you.

(*He exits.*)

The curse of the rooming house neighbour. Barging in here like the proverbial bull in a china shop. Well, this isn't a china shop and I'm damned if I'll put up with uninvited company. I'll complain to the landlord. I need my privacy.

(**BURT** *appears, older now, and in a state of some excitement.*)

BURT: We've done it!

Eva: Oh Burt, you mustn't come in on me like that when I'm in the bathroom.

Burt: Why not? We're married.

Eva: I just like my privacy.

Burt: Well forget about your damned privacy for once. We've got cause to celebrate.

Eva: Celebrate what? Just let me finish drying, Burt.

Burt: I'll dry you off.

Eva: Thanks. I can manage.

Burt: We've paid off the house. It's ours. We finally own this house.

Eva: Is that what you're so excited about? My goodness, you are excited, Burt.

Burt: I'm nearly fifty but I've got my own house. I thought we could call the McLeans and go out for dinner.

Eva: Oh. Whatever you like.

Burt: You're such a damper Eva. Why don't you ever take an interest—

Eva: I do Burt. I'm very happy. I'd just forgotten. After all, we have lived here now for—

Burt: But the difference is it's ours.

Eva: I guess I'd always thought of it as ours somehow.

Burt: Aren't you feeling well.

Eva: Of course I'm feeling well.

Burt: It's just that you're always tired. Nothing seems to interest you any more.

Eva: I take a lot of interest in—

Burt: Hell Eva, forget about problems. We don't have any. Let's celebrate. Let's be happy. What would you like to do? We can have a night out with the McLeans, go somewhere nice for dinner.

Eva: Well I think that's fine Burt if that's how you want to celebrate.

Burt: I'll do anything that you fancy.

Eva: I saw the most beautiful Queen Anne table. It would be lovely in the hall— instead of that old—anyway, a decent dinner would cost so much—

Burt: You never want to do anything any more.

Eva: Then call the McLeans, Burt. Just let me finish drying myself off in peace.
 (*He fades.*)

Eva: Guess I wasn't much fun by then. Burrowed in like a groundhog and

Eve 27

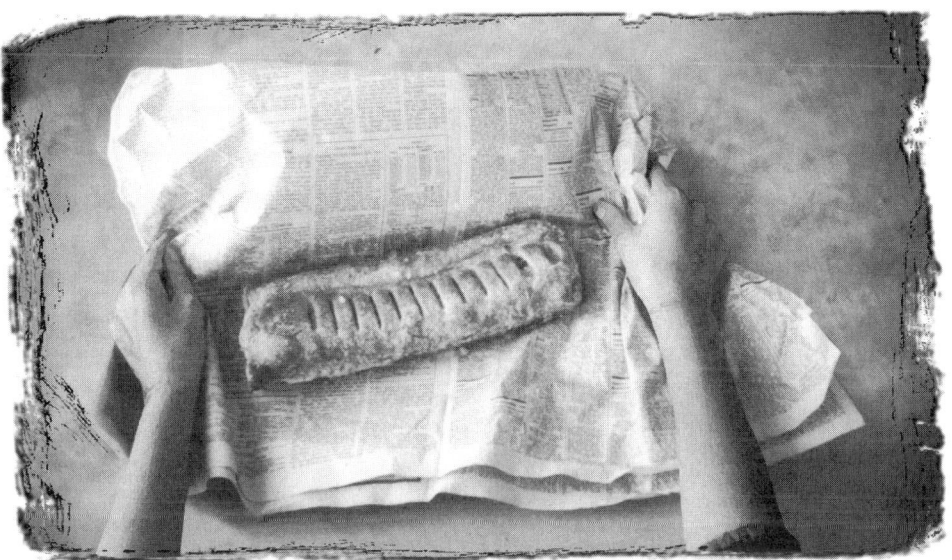

collecting acquisitions like a squirrel with nuts in its teeth. Strange. I hated that home—it trapped me, and I did everything I could to fortify the prison. I want my soup.

(*She sees the "gift" from* JOHNNY.)

Now what's this? I haven't had a newspaper in here since— Ah! It's the gift from Central Europe. Let's just what—why it's strudel. It's very stale. When was he here. Yesterday or the day before? Eva, you are going dotty. He probably brought it fresh. I've just let it sit. Well. I can take it for walks as protection from muggers. What's the paper say, probably *days* old.

(*She sits down to read, the lights go out.*)

Hell's bells. Bulb's blown. Where's the candle? I won't save it for my birthday. (*Searches uselessly*) Mr. Horvath? Mr. Horvath, no. That would be making a big mistake. (*Goes to stairwell*) Mr. Horvath! Probably gone out for a gallon of inspiration. Oh what the hell, I'll throw my coat on and go out for a lousy bulb.

JOHNNY: (*Enters*) You called, missus. Do you need a doctor?

EVA: I haven't been sick for days. I want to borrow a light bulb.

JOHNNY: Very impractical to be without necessities.

EVA: I agree. I'm not practical. Having agreed, do you suppose I might borrow one?

JOHNNY: But of course. Let me get you what you need. (*Exits*)

EVA: Now we'll have hours of social chit-chat. Mind broadening and time consuming. I've got to learn to be practical or privacy's out the window. Along with everything else.

JOHNNY: (*Returns*) Bulbs and fuses!

EVA: Wonderful.

JOHNNY: Why are you so cranky?

EVA: I'd planned a meal and a quiet read.

JOHNNY: You like to read?

EVA: Yes. I like to read.

JOHNNY: What?

EVA: Jane Austen.

JOHNNY: Boring. Prim and sterile.

EVA: I like her.

JOHNNY: I loan you Goethe.

EVA: Another time thank you.

JOHNNY: (*Fiddling with bulb*) The incredible thing about Goethe is his independence of spirit, the desire to preserve solitude. But that is something only Europeans can fully understand.

EVA: You think so, do you?

JOHNNY: Your problem is not the bulb. Where is your fusebox located?

EVA: I don't know. I never thought to look.

JOHNNY: That's very stupid.

EVA: I agree. Look Mr. Horvath, thanks very much for your help. We'll forget the whole thing.

JOHNNY: Unless it's behind all this junk.

(*He goes to the collection of garbage and debris she's acquired.*)

EVA: Leave that where it is please. It's all in a certain order.

JOHNNY: You can rearrange it later. Aha. It hides the fuse box. You collect all this? It must mean something to you.

EVA: I don't know.

JOHNNY: Has to. Otherwise you are a crazy woman.

EVA: I am *not* crazy.

JOHNNY: (*Amused*) No no. You are a collector.

Eve 29

(*He's replaced a fuse during this. The light comes back on.*)

EVA: Thanks ever so much Mr. Horvath. I'll return your fuse the next time I shop.

JOHNNY: Forget it, a small thing.

EVA: No really. I'll leave it outside your door.

JOHNNY: Why not come inside for a little visit? I'll give you schnapps.

EVA: Thanks very much. I'll do that.

JOHNNY: When?

EVA: After I shop.

JOHNNY: You're going shopping now?

EVA: I have to. There's no food in the house.

JOHNNY: I can make you something. I love to cook.

EVA: You're much too kind. Thanks, but no.

JOHNNY: Fine. You have your light. Thank you. I'll go.

EVA: I don't mean to be rude.

JOHNNY: Then why are you rude?

EVA: I just want a little privacy.

JOHNNY: I leave you with your privacy, and your light. Good night to you, missus. (*Exits*)

EVA: Now his feelings are hurt. (*Puts on her coat*) Who cares about his feelings. Social gaffe on poverty row. God, life's a bugger. So easy to hurt people. Who'd hurt anyone on purpose? People come and go and it's hard to help saying the wrong things, especially if you think they're right. Thing is, though, the hurt gets buried, and it festers like a cancer.

(*She is rummaging at a garbage pail.* NEIL *appears upstage, younger and buoyant.*)

NEIL: Mum, I've wanted to talk to you for a while.

EVA: Your father said you had something on your mind.

NEIL: Well, but I need your advice.

EVA: My advice dear. Whatever for?

NEIL: I think I'm in love.

EVA: But that's wonderful, Neil. Who is it?

NEIL: It's Rosemary, Mother. You remember her?

EVA: You wouldn't let her stay very long—

NEIL: We were already late for our party. I just wanted you to say hello.

EVA: She was very pretty. Tell me about her.

NEIL: Well, her parents are the Martins—her father owns that chain of hardware stores.

EVA: Of course. But tell me about her.

NEIL: She's unlike anyone—anyone I've ever met. Been to a private school in England, worked for a year in the States as a nurse—

EVA: Why she can hardly be twenty.

NEIL: She's twenty-four. And I can't tell you what I feel. I take her home, come back here, and I miss her. I'm thinking about her all day Mum, even when my mind should be on a brief. I can't concentrate on work—it's all Rosemary.

EVA: Does she feel the same way?

NEIL: Even more than I do. She's started to talk about how we should spend our lives. How many children we might have, where to live—Mum, she's soft and beautiful and yet somehow so organised. I'm in love with her, Mum. And her dad can get me a job at that law firm that works for him—hell, he's their principal client. Why it won't be long before I'm—

EVA: You've got it all planned.

NEIL: Mum—I'm just coasting. I don't have to plan. Rosemary's doing that for us.

EVA: How long have you been seeing her, dear?

NEIL: Eight weeks, Mum.

EVA: My goodness. Your father and I saw—or courted for—

NEIL: Things happen more quickly now, Mum. Times are different.

EVA: She seems lovely, Neil. It's just that eight weeks isn't— and you're talking about a lifetime.

NEIL: Why don't you like her?

EVA: I do like her darling. She seems lovely. I hardly know her.

NEIL: Mum, it's settled. We're going to get married.

EVA: Then my advice is that you're making a terrible mistake!

(NEIL, *hurt and shocked, fades.*)

And I'd lost a part of him forever. Something we lived with and never talked about. Probably for the best.

(*She discovers a mangled, broken doll.*)

Here's a find! Without strings. I can look at it, stroke it, toss it aside. It won't fix my electricity and it won't make a single demand. I want it.

(*She's back home.*)

Why can't I live without collecting? Or at least find a way to shut my memory up. And my conscience. Keeps nagging. (*At the stairwell*) No sign of the neighbour. Good. Maybe he's moved.

(*Out she goes again.*)

Wasting gathering-time. Why there's been a blizzard. Hardly a sound. Sun's bright and clear but nobody's stirring. All holed up in their homes. Fine by me. One thing's certain, though—garbage collection, come rain, come snow, more regular than the mail. (*Discovers an alligator purse*) And this must be alligator. I'll bet it's alligator. Far from the swamp. Off it goes to Sam at the pawnshop and he won't get it for less than five dollars or I'll keep it myself. Keep shining, sun, it's turning into a good day.

(KIM *enters, exuberant, young.*)

KIM: Gran . . . Gran! It is you!

EVA: Hi Kim. Dammit.

KIM: I wasn't sure at first. Why didn't you say hello?

EVA: I was just, you know, walking and not seeing.

KIM: Gran, you saw me. (*Pause*) Are you living around here?

EVA: Just out walking.

KIM: It's so cold. There's a Chinese restaurant over on Viger.

EVA: Near the pawnshop.

KIM: That's the one. We'll have tea.

(KIM *takes* EVA*'s arm and hustles her to the restaurant.*)

EVA: How's everything, Kim?

KIM: How's you?

EVA: Terrific.

KIM: I'm so happy to see you. It's been a year. (*Hugs* EVA, *stares.*) But you don't look terrific. You look kind of—

EVA: Ratty? It's because my coat ripped.

KIM: I'll sew it for you.

(*They enter the restaurant and sit down.*)

How'd you rip it?

EVA: In a fight.

KIM: Gran, we always tell each other the truth.

EVA: With a dog.

KIM: Sure Gran, sure. I need mum's sewing machine for this.

EVA: It isn't Westmount here Kim. I dropped a bag of groceries, they ripped, and a mangy mutt tried to run off with my steak. I have steak once a week so I chased him. I tripped and fell and the coat ripped. But I saved my steak!

(KIM *stops pouring tea*.)

KIM: Gran, this is crazy.

EVA: I'm open for suggestions.

KIM: You could come home.

EVA: That sounds like your father.

KIM: Don't do this Gran. I'm not like Dad. I only want to help. Also, I miss you. I miss you a lot.

EVA: And seeing you I— (*Takes* KIM'S *hand*) I can't come home. Not now. I've turned a corner. I'm growing up. A little late maybe, but . . .

KIM: Help me understand. Is it Grandpa?

EVA: It was at first. But it's more. It's everything. The whole life. What I was living. I'm flushing it out.

KIM: That's incredible. But if you don't have any money . . .

EVA: Burt and I had money for years. We had the house, and that was a prison for me. And I had a budget. Now I live in a different place and it isn't a cage, and if I can't get my hair done I can do other things. I can go and get maybe ten dollars for this purse at Sam's!

KIM: That's the pawn shop. Sometimes I go there.

EVA: It's good to know you're carrying on the tradition. But don't tell your mother.

KIM: Tell her. Are you kidding?

EVA: It'll be our secret.

KIM: But Gran, it's kind of hard to think of you pawning stuff.

EVA: I like it. Keeps me off the streets.

KIM: This is terrible. You aren't ever going to come home.

EVA: Never.

KIM: What if you get sick?

EVA: I'm old, darling. I can get sick in front of a fireplace drinking tea or on Viger Street.

KIM: I think I understand. I think.

EVA: (*Soft*) Bless you, Kim.

KIM: Can I come home with you? And talk?

EVA: We're talking here.

KIM: But I've got a boyfriend, and school and, and— All that's kind of far away from you now isn't it, how I'm doing in school . . .

EVA: Part of me wants to hear, and another part . . . is kind of removed from that. I think you're growing up well. That makes me happy.

KIM: I promise not to tell Mum or Dad I saw you. But I want to keep seeing you. How.

EVA: You're too clever by half. I don't have a phone and—

KIM: But I do. Mum finally let me get one. (*Takes out scrap paper*) And here's its number.

(EVA *takes it and rises.*)

You can't go so soon. *Please.*

EVA: I have to. I have an appointment.

KIM: Gran . . . doing what?

EVA: Getting on with things!

KIM: You'll call me. Gran, you have to.

(KIM *embraces* EVA.)

EVA: I love you, Kim.

(EVA *leaves* KIM *at the restaurant and hustles away, muttering.*)

And she's the one person that *could* drag me back to the old ways, because I do love her so much. And she's growing up fine. And she'd want to see me, and I'd want to see her—

(*She's in front of a garbage can.*)

—and I'm still not strong enough to resist that temptation. I can't take that risk.

(*She drops* KIM'S *number into the garbage.*)

There goes another piece of my life. Strange, when you think you've given everything up how much there still is to lose. I'm obviously a bottomless pit. And I want my doll.

(*She goes home, sits on her cot still wearing her coat, and cuddles the doll.* JOHNNY *enters, watches. It takes a moment before* EVA *sees him.*)

You again? Don't you work, Mr. Horvath?

JOHNNY: I try not to on Saturdays.

EVA: Is today Saturday?

JOHNNY: This is none of my business I know, but why are you playing with a broken doll?

EVA: Because I haven't got a baby bottle to suck on. Because I had a shocking day. And because I seem to like it. Is that reason enough for you?

JOHNNY: Yes.

EVA: And I never got your fuse. I went out shopping but I got sidetracked. Bumped into someone and didn't even get to a grocery. Can't you wait until tomorrow for your fuse?

JOHNNY: Sure. But groceries all closed on Sunday.

EVA: Monday then. Surely you can wait one more day.

JOHNNY: Sure. But what will you eat?

EVA: Oh Jesus! I— I'll open a tin of soup.

JOHNNY: You were sick last week. Need to keep up your strength. A tin of soup is not enough until Monday. I don't understand you missus. You sure act crazy.

EVA: I am not crazy.

JOHNNY: You go out shopping, forget your food, and come home with junk. You are crazy.

EVA: Whatever I am is none of your goddamn business.

JOHNNY: Why are you so rude?

EVA: Because you take it for granted that you can barge in here and ask me all kinds of personal questions.

JOHNNY: You come home without food. I wonder why. How is that a personal question. Don't most people eat?

EVA: Of course they do.

JOHNNY: So what will you eat?

EVA: I don't know. You're confusing me. There. That's what I mean. What I eat isn't your concern.

JOHNNY: You want to starve?

Eva: Of course I don't want to starve.

Johnny: So. It's all settled. I'll make you a little dinner.

Eva: Nothing's settled. I don't want your dinner.

Johnny: I'll make you a coquilles.

Eva: I couldn't possibly eat it. It's too rich. No thanks.

Johnny: Coquilles isn't easy. It's hard to make.

Eva: I don't want it.

Johnny: And I won't even make it for you unless you tell me your name.

Eva: What does my name have to do with a dinner I don't plan to attend?

Johnny: John Horvath invites no nameless women to dinner!

Eva: I don't want your dinner!

Johnny: And you won't get it. I cook for myself. And if you're lucky, I save you leftovers. (*Exits*)

Eva: Don't bother. My god. Now that one wasn't my fault. I didn't collect that. Can't get away from people. They won't let you be. Do I have to move away? I won't take his dinner. I'll have the last tin of soup, drink sherry, and sleep until Monday. Good for me. I'm being practical.

(*She settles on the cot with her sherry.*)

My this goes down smoothly. Well, Monday for groceries, a fuse, and a paper for a look at the new room listings. Who says I'm impractical? I'm captain of the leakiest barge around, and I'm still floating.

(*She nods off. In a moment,* Johnny *reenters with a steaming skillet, begins to set the tiny table in a makeshift way.* Eva *gives a start.*)

Johnny: You miss cocktails but still time for the main course.

Eva: You've woken me up. You don't listen. No dinner.

Johnny: A little nap is good for the appetite. I see you like to drink too.

Eva: On occasion.

Johnny: I brought more. You see?

Eva: You're not going to go away, are you?

Johnny: After dinner I'm meeting a friend. Retired music critic. We sing operas together.

Eva: Sorry I can't make the recital.

Johnny: Who asked you? We don't let anyone hear us sing.

EVA: Why not?

JOHNNY: We're lousy singers.

EVA: Do I dress for dinner?

JOHNNY: Please. Be comfortable in your own home. Come along, it gets cold. Up, up.

EVA: Don't rush me.

JOHNNY: But not coquilles. Instead—bourguignon.

EVA: Why the change.

JOHNNY: Actually, it's leftovers from yesterday. Add this, add that. My bourguignon improves with age.

EVA: I don't.

JOHNNY: Why so hard on yourself?

EVA: Force of habit or something. Where'd you learn about opera?

JOHNNY: At university in Pest.

EVA: You're Hungarian.

JOHNNY: What else?

EVA: Couldn't quite place your accent.

JOHNNY: Gets worn away year by year. I'm in Canada since fifty-six.

EVA: You like it?

JOHNNY: Except for the winters. Cold, numbing winters. Makes people reserved. Keep themselves at a distance.

EVA: Why not go home?

JOHNNY: You don't listen to me. Here since fifty-six. I was dispatch rider for Nagy. I am political exile. I can't go back home. Never mind. How do you like the bourguignon?

EVA: It's very tangy.

JOHNNY: What is tangy?

EVA: It's . . . distinctive.

JOHNNY: You hate it.

EVA: Wonderful.

JOHNNY: More salt maybe?

EVA: Don't worry. I'm so hungry I could eat literally anything. Oh, I'm sorry Mr. Horvath—

Eve 37

JOHNNY: I'm used to you now missus. A little rudeness from you is like a good morning from a normal person.

EVA: Mr. Horvath . . .

JOHNNY: Old Hungarian custom. Call dinner guests by first name. Mine is Johnny. You are—

EVA: Force it out of me, will you?

JOHNNY: Is there another way?

EVA: It's Eva.

JOHNNY: Where you from, Eva?

EVA: I'm Canadian.

JOHNNY: Montreal.

EVA: Yes.

JOHNNY: How long you widowed?

EVA: I'm not a widow.

JOHNNY: Divorced?

EVA: No. Not exactly. I've been . . . separated from my husband since last fall.

JOHNNY: And that's when I first noticed you around. Why you come here?

EVA: It seemed like a good place.

JOHNNY: A rooming house? I don't think you plan to stay. You must want to go back to him.

EVA: That's entirely wrong.

JOHNNY: Is he much younger than you?

EVA: Wrong again. Older. That is possible.

JOHNNY: So you didn't leave him because he was unfaithful?

EVA: Look. Dinner doesn't entitle you to play detective.

JOHNNY: All right. No more questions. Your cheeks are pinker from the wine.

EVA: My cheeks are pink because I'm annoyed that you're a nosy busybody.

JOHNNY: Pretty too.

EVA: I'm not pretty.

JOHNNY: Who told you that? Your husband?

EVA: I don't think he ever said one way or another.

JOHNNY: Lousy waste to live with a woman and not tell her when she's pretty.

EVA: Well he just never talked about things like that.

JOHNNY: Stupid man.

EVA: He wasn't stupid.

JOHNNY: You still love him.

EVA: I never loved him. Will you leave me the hell alone with your questions!

JOHNNY: Stupid to be afraid of questions.

EVA: It isn't your affair.

JOHNNY: But it's crazy to live with a man you don't love.

EVA: I lived with him because I was married. Because I had a family. Because that's how I was supposed to live and so I did it. Because you have to keep things together—keep things.

(*She breaks.* JOHNNY *goes to her, kisses her gently.*)

What are you doing? Stop that. I'm old.

JOHNNY: I don't see you like that.

(*Another kiss.*)

EVA: Please don't do that.

JOHNNY: Why not?

EVA: I understand you're just being friendly.

JOHNNY: Not just that. Let's lie on the bed.

EVA: Johnny, it's enough. Really. You're frightening me.

JOHNNY: Why?

EVA: I'm too old.

JOHNNY: Don't talk. Hold me back.

(*He embraces her, passionately. Finally, her arms go around him. He leads her to the cot. They lie on it. Blackout. Lights up and* EVA *is now seated at the table, alone.*)

EVA: So still. Satisfied. Two whole days. Oh Eva, Eva, what have you been up to? Well, I can be loved—love back. I'm a woman. He kissed my feet, said they were beautiful. He's crazy. After work he's coming home to cook me dinner. Why these are perfectly good hands. I just have to take better care of them. Johnny's at the market by now. Maybe a new dress at the Sally Ann, and my hair could—wish I had a watch that worked. Where is he? Having second thoughts? It's not possible. He kissed my feet. But if he's thinking about me what will he think? That we were drunk, that we made a mistake?

Eve   39

That I'm old . . . he can't be thinking that. He felt what I felt. I know he did . . . Well, why is he late? Very late. He's had worries by now—goddamn him—I didn't start it. He isn't going to come. What's to do? No damn room in here, place is like a prison, this poor plant is bone dry. What am I going to do? I feel such a fool. I'll have to move, can't risk running into him in the hallway. Oh goddamn him. I felt so alive. Well, pull together Eva, pull together, you're too old for a breakdown. My back hurts. No wonder. It's my mistake, my stupidity. I'm an incurable romantic. I bought it all the way down to my feet being pretty. You buy what you're after and what you're after is always on sale. And it's getting tiring and humiliating and I am a bit too old to be running away. At sixty-plus I need a self-contained bathroom, not stars and romance, unlimited hot water. Sherry was nice, lots of it was nice, how can I say to Neil that I've given up?

(*Her coat on, she's outside.*)

Find a way Eva, it won't be the first time. There. Church clock says after ten. He's with some lousy waitress. Fine for him. I'll go back to my Chippendale prison in Notre Dame de Grace.

(NEIL *appears, at home, tie off, relaxed.*)

NEIL: I'm really glad you called, besides the fact that it's good to hear from you. It's been almost two months.

EVA: I got a little involved in things.

NEIL: Well I've got good news.

EVA: Good news . . .

NEIL: Dad's getting much better. I mean, he's almost cheery compared to the way he was. And it's all due, really, to Mme Lévesque.

EVA: Who?

NEIL: Sorry Mum. Of course you don't know. She's a retired nurse we finally found after a series of horror stories. Anyway, she agreed to take care of Dad on a trial basis and it worked out. She's moved in. And Dad's bought a dog.

EVA: He's bought a dog.

NEIL: Well of course she has to take it for walks but the thing is I've finally been able to broach the subject of money to Dad.

EVA: And Burt agreed?

NEIL: Not yet. But I'm working on it. Also, I finally got to the house and collected that bag of your things you wanted. I shouldn't have taken so long but now that I do have it, how can I get it to you?

EVA: It's almost spring, Neil. I don't really need—just let everything sit. I've gotten used to managing without at this point.

NEIL: Mum, are you okay?

EVA: I've been going through a kind of . . . confusing period.

NEIL: Why confusing? I'd expect you to be happy, and you say you've gotten used to not having your old things, so you must be settled. You've got what you wanted, Mum, and I know how hard you had to fight to get it. You've got more independence than, I guess than anybody I know.

EVA: (*Softly*) And what do I do with it?

NEIL: I imagine you're doing whatever you like.

EVA: Neil, say hello to Kim for me, and I'm glad you father's better, and I'll call again soon.

NEIL: What are you up to now?

EVA: Whatever I like I guess. Whatever that is.

(NEIL *fades,* EVA *starts home.*)

It really isn't my day. They won't even let me be a martyr. I can't be Joan at the stake. It's incredible. I'm not even allowed to do the right thing. I'm a damned woman. There's a touch of humour in all this but what I want most is a bottle of sherry and a good cry. Well, I'm home. Hello empty house, hello bug in the sink. Hello sagging cot. Damn, damn, damn.

(JOHNNY *comes in.*)

JOHNNY: I have to talk to you.

EVA: Look Johnny, let's not talk. I'm bone tired, I'm scraping bottom. Let's just be adult enough to accept the fact that we both made a mistake.

JOHNNY: I know I didn't show up Monday night. I went away. I got frightened.

EVA: Do we have to go through this? I understand. I understand you got frightened because I'm an older woman.

JOHNNY: That's exactly what frightened me.

EVA: Terrific. Now we both know.

JOHNNY: But not only that.

EVA: Do you have to tell me I'm gnarled and wrinkled too?

JOHNNY: Shut up! Listen, I didn't plan what happened with us. It just happened.

EVA: I know that.

JOHNNY: But you know how I've been living since I came to Canada?

EVA: Wine, women, wine.

JOHNNY: What else. Why not. I have a wife, two children—men now—in Hungary. I'll never see them again. You think that's easy. Everything I had I now don't have—so I made a rule. Here, in this country, no ties and no knots. This is a free country? Fine. I'll be free. And so I sleep with a lot of women and everything's terrific. Then suddenly you grabbed me—an older woman.

EVA: You grabbed me. I was just holding on.

JOHNNY: Suddenly we had a date. How'd that happen?

EVA: You made it.

JOHNNY: You did.

EVA: Look Johnny, here's the easiest thing. I don't have much stuff really. I'll move.

JOHNNY: Don't move.

EVA: Well what do you want me to stay for—you big ox?

JOHNNY: I don't know.

EVA: Then I'll move.

JOHNNY: You shouldn't do that.

EVA: What the hell do you want from me!

JOHNNY: How the hell do I know. I'd like you around. Sometimes.

EVA: I won't be your sometime whore.

JOHNNY: Are you so stupid that you want another marriage?

EVA: I certainly don't.

JOHNNY: Then stay here.

EVA: I don't want your occasional favours.

JOHNNY: Right now, we're in the same rooming house. What are you doing for dinner?

EVA: I'm busy.

JOHNNY: Crap.

EVA: I'm damned if I'll eat with you.

JOHNNY: I cook better than you can.

EVA: Tomorrow night.

JOHNNY: I don't want to plan for tomorrow night.

EVA: You're a big scared aging kid.

JOHNNY: And you're a dumb crazy woman who still wants ties and knots.

EVA: Don't bully me.

JOHNNY: I don't want ties. So what's so terrible?

EVA: You make me angry. You always make me angry.

JOHNNY: Because you never know what you ought to do.

EVA: You mean what you think I ought to do.

JOHNNY: I know better.

EVA: Crap!

JOHNNY: If you want dinner, you can come upstairs and get it.

EVA: Tomorrow night.

JOHNNY: You're hungry tonight!

EVA: All right!

JOHNNY: I'll be upstairs. I've got two bottles of wine.

EVA: We'll need them!

(*Pause*)

Now what have I done to myself. I'm free, but I'm tied. I left a home, I've got another one. I left a man, but another's around. How in the name of Christ are you supposed to live your life? It's all complications. Confusions. I simply don't know what I'm doing from one day to the next. But wait—Johnny's upstairs, I'm down here. And I'm not tied—that's the point, I'm not married, so I'm on my own. I can come and go where I like, when I like and do what I like. I've learned something—at last. Give it time. Don't rush into anything. It's high damn time I learned to love time. If I use it well, then I'm giving myself my life. And that's something I never did before. I've kind of given birth to myself, even if I am sixty-five. And whatever time left to me is mine—not anybody else's. And now . . . I want my dinner.

(*She leaves to go upstairs.*)

CURTAIN

Eve 43

After Words

1 In your journal, respond with your thoughts and feelings about Eva—her past, relationships, motivations, and development in the play.

2 In a small group, discuss Eva and make notes for a character sketch. Then each group member chooses one other character in the play to consider independently. How does the character add to Eva's development and to our understanding of her? Is the character a foil or a chorus character? Share your findings with the group; then add to and refine the character sketch of Eva.

3 Identify an important theme in the play. Choose one portion of dialogue that expresses that theme (e.g., "I've kind of given birth to myself . . . " in Eva's final speech).

4 Extend the play in one or more of the following ways:

   a) Write a journal entry from Eva's viewpoint two years later.

   b) Brainstorm other reactions to Eva's quest for independence (e.g., Neil and Rosemary demand a social worker place Eva in a home for the aged). Choose one situation to script as a dialogue; then present it to the class.

   c) Improvise, refine, and present a future scene in which Eva and Burt meet.

5 Stage a formal debate about Eva's actions on the proposition "Eva is an admirable character."

6 Examine the structure of the play. In general, what functions do the "memory scenes" serve? How do they relate to the scenes preceding and following? Focus on one or two scenes. Adopt the role of a drama critic to present your analysis.

7 Identify and discuss the stereotypes and biases the characters in the play voice, accept, and/or defy.

The Interview

A stage play by PETER SWET

According to *The Best Short Plays 1975*, only Peter Swet's hard work and some quirky fortune allowed *The Interview* to be produced commercially in New York. Swet, born in 1942, grew up in an area of New York City known as Ozone Park, Queens—so removed from the bright lights of Manhattan and Broadway that he first saw live theatre only at age 15. The play was a flop. However, it did stimulate Swet's interest. He finished his first draft of *The Interview* in 1967 but had to put it aside due to financial and other pressures. In 1971, when Swet and his wife both lost their jobs on the same day, he returned to the script at her insistence. Following exposure at a small theatre and a very positive response, the play was to reopen on a commercial basis. On opening night, the Broadway Central Hotel—the building that housed the theatre—collapsed. The show went on at other venues. Swet's second play was titled *Debris*.

Prelude

1 In your journal, write about an interview you've seen (e.g., on TV) or one you've experienced yourself (e.g., for a part-time job, in counselling, or for a research project). Describe the interview—its goal, questions and answers, tone, emotional impact, outcome.

2 This play involves insurance. Discuss what you know about insurance, its various kinds (e.g., automobile, crop, life, home, unemployment), how one gets it, why one gets it, insurance claims, insurance fraud, and so on.

The Interview

Characters

    ABRAHAM MOSCOWITZ: Tailor
    SHANNON: Insurance investigator

Scene

The tailor shop of Abraham Moscowitz, New York City.

A small, rather tattered-looking shop in the Canal Street area of Manhattan. There is a cluttered work table with an old-fashioned sewing machine, the kind formerly operated by foot treadle but now fitted with an electric motor. Behind the table, a plain wooden chair facing out toward the audience. Beneath the table, a large waste paper basket filled to overflowing with garment scraps and, just to the left, a large pile of additional scraps. These are all of the same dismal tones of grey and black as the cheap old secondhand suits that fill the many garment racks which crowd the room everywhere except for the sewing area and a small working area at center. The working area consists simply of a cleared space where ABIE *can sit on the comfortably padded straight back chair that is located there, a good place for doing any handwork that may be necessary. From the work area, a path of sorts cuts to the front of the store located at stage left. Here we see the entrance to the shop, a narrow door, glass, but covered by a ragged shade drawn throughout the proceedings. Beyond the door, there is a large window, with shades similarly drawn. At the side of the window, clearly visible to the audience, there is an old faded sign, which reads:*

A. MOSCOWITZ
— FINE ALTERATIONS —

Immediately beneath this is another sign, also old and faded, and obviously hand-lettered at one point by ABIE *himself. This sign reads:*

SECONDHAND CLOTHING
Fitted Like New

Broad pools of light from ancient shaded fixtures located overhead illuminate the work area, the entranceway and some racks of clothing. With the lighting concentrated as it is toward the center, we have just a notion of the true dimensions of the room and what old, forgotten objects and materials may be lying in its hidden, dusty corners.

ABIE is sixty-three years old, although he actually appears to be somewhat older. He is slightly stooped from so many years of bending over garments and, though he tries to keep up appearances by wearing a shirt and tie, his pants are wrinkled and baggy and the collar points of his rather dingy shirt are bent upwards and frayed.

ABIE is at work, running a garment through the sewing machine. Soon, however, he takes the garment (a pair of men's trousers) to the chair at center for some handwork. As he sits there with needle and thread, we hear a knock at the door. Behind the door is SHANNON, the insurance investigator, a man of average build and height, about forty-five years old, with dark, thinning hair. He is brusquely efficient at his job, facing it with a kind of forced pleasantness that occasionally serves to make his own sense of discontent that much more apparent. He wears a suit, an overcoat and business hat, all of which, although fairly neat, are not of the best quality and are several years out of fashion. He carries a timeworn briefcase.

NOTE: The name "Moscowitz" is pronounced quite differently by the two characters throughout the entire play. SHANNON uses the Americanized MOS-cowich, with strongest emphasis on the first syllable, while ABIE insists on the correct pronunciation, Mu-SCO-veetz, with strongest emphasis on the second syllable.

ABIE: (*Approaching the locked door*) Who? (*We hear a muffled reply.*) Who? (*He opens the door a crack, leaving the chain lock on.*) Who is it? We are closed now.

SHANNON: Mr. Moscowich?

ABIE: What is it?

SHANNON: Are you Mr. Moscowich?

ABIE: (*After a brief pause, during which he eyes* SHANNON *up and down*) You want to buy a suit?

SHANNON: No. I'd like to talk to Abraham Moscowich.

ABIE: Mos-*co*-vitz. Abraham Mos-*co*-vitz. What is it?

SHANNON: I want to talk to you about your insurance.

ABIE: Insurance? I got plenty of insurance. I don't need no more.

(*He tries to close the door but* SHANNON *forces it back.*)

The Interview

SHANNON: All I want is a few minutes of your time to talk to you about . . .

ABIE: Talk? You want to talk?

SHANNON: Yes.

ABIE: Good. Make a left and two doors down there's a florist shop with two women in it with one mouth bigger than the other. They'll talk. But me, I'm too busy now. (*He tries to close the door.*)

SHANNON: Hey, I'm not a salesman, Mr. Moscowich. I'm here to talk to you about your insurance policy.

ABIE: What's this?

SHANNON: Didn't you just apply for an extension on your life insurance policy a couple of weeks ago?

ABIE: Could be. So?

SHANNON: Well, I have to talk to you before it can be approved.

ABIE: (*Annoyed, opens the lock and* SHANNON *stands in the doorway*) What is it?

SHANNON: My name is Jim Shannon, Mr. Moscowich. (*Offers his hand, which* ABIE *weakly accepts*) I'm an insurance investigator.

ABIE: Insurance investigator?

SHANNON: Yes.

ABIE: Mr. Shannon?

SHANNON: That's right. Do you mind if I come in for a few minutes? (*He moves further into the shop.*)

ABIE: So what's an insurance investigator? I don't know nothing about investigators.

SHANNON: Well, sir, your policy is now being considered for approval, you see. And before it's approved, I have to talk to you for a few minutes. Just to check out a few things, you know, your background, your health, make sure you haven't robbed any banks lately. (*Laughs, but stops at* ABIE'S *sour expression*) That sort of thing. (*He draws* ABIE'S *chair over to the sewing table and sits down at the chair that's already there, indicating that he wishes* ABIE *to sit, too.*)

ABIE: (*Drawing his chair back to its original position*) Hey, mister. I have to tell you. I'm not so sure I like this. I'm a busy man. You couldn't call first and make an appointment? That's not a common courtesy?

SHANNON: (*Removing a clipboard, pencil and questionnaire from his briefcase, prepares to take down information*) Sorry if I caught you at a bad time, but I can't work from appointments. I just have too many cases to handle.

ABIE: So, you just drop in on people. And, that way, maybe you'll catch them doing something they shouldn't be, uh?

SHANNON: Well . . .

ABIE: And what did you think you'd find a sixty-three-year-old man doing in a tailor shop at seven o'clock at night? Having a hot time? Smoking some of that LSD? Come on, mister. I don't think I like this. You better leave.

SHANNON: Mr. Moscowich, look . . .

ABIE: Mos-*co*-vitz.

SHANNON: You're going to have to go through this some time, so it might as well be right now.

ABIE: Mr. . . . Shannon, is it? (SHANNON *nods*.) There are some things a man must do. A man must live. A man must die. A man must suffer for his sins. But a man does not have to be at the beck and call of his insurance company any time of night or day. That's where you're from, right? From the insurance company?

SHANNON: Right.

ABIE: So tell me. What is the name of my insurance company?

SHANNON: Look. All I'm going to do is ask a few questions, do a little background check on you, and if everything is all right, your policy will be approved. No problem.

ABIE: Yes. Mister. But I ask you the name of the insurance company.

SHANNON: All right. I'm not from the insurance company directly. I'm from the National Investigations Bureau. We're a company that specializes in doing insurance investigations, and that's why I'm here, Mr. Moscowich, to do an investigation on you.

ABIE: Investigations?

SHANNON: Right.

ABIE: On me?

SHANNON: Yes. All we want to do is determine the risk, that's all.

ABIE: Risk? What risk? I already got one policy with this company, mister. They know me for a long time. All right, so I'm sixty-three years old, so for that I have to pay an extra bigger premium, but what risk? I pay my bills, is that what they want to know? I pay my bills! No risk!

SHANNON: Come on, Mr. Moscowich. Risk involves more than credit, you know that. Now, all I want you to do is answer a few questions and verify some information for me, all right?

ABIE: Just a minute. So maybe you are from this investigations company. Still, you must tell me the name of my insurance company!

SHANNON: Here. Let me show you my credentials. (*Removes wallet, showing* ABIE) You see, don't you, where it says "James T. Shannon, Insurance Investigator"?

ABIE: Yes, yes. (*Points to his sign*) And you see, don't you, where it says "A. Moscowitz, Fine Alterations"? That sign don't make me what I am. What I have here in my hands—what I do with this suit—the things that I have buried deep in my head—*these* are the things that make me what I am. If you are who you say you are, don't show me a business card. Tell me the name of the company!

SHANNON: I work by account number. That's all that I need.

ABIE: You mean, you don't even know the name of the company? Look, I'm sorry, mister . . .

SHANNON: Mr. Moscowich we're a big company. We have hundreds of customers, and this is just the best way for us to do business, that's all.

ABIE: So you don't even know who you're doing this for. (*Urging* SHANNON *out*) No. Come on.

SHANNON: Look, I don't make up the rules. These things are figured out way ahead of time by people who know a lot more about it than you or me. And people like you and me, we just have to follow it.

ABIE: This you believe?

SHANNON: Sure I do.

ABIE: This you accept?

SHANNON: What else can you do?

ABIE: Well, in my language there is a perfect word for men who believe this way.

SHANNON: What's that?

ABIE: Schmuck.

SHANNON: *What?*

ABIE: You want me to translate?

SHANNON: (*Quietly threatening*) Look here, Mr. Moscowich, there's an awful lot I have to put up with in my line of work, but if there's one thing that I will not stand for, it's abusive language!

ABIE: What's abusive? Every man is entitled to an opinion. This is my opinion about this crazy system of yours. So you just go now and leave me alone!

I'm working and I'm busy and I got a deadline on this suit for tomorrow morning and you make me nervous, and you make my head like I don't know what. (SHANNON *has begun to take notes.*) What's this? What are you writing?

SHANNON: Never mind, Mr. Moscowich.

ABIE: What's this you are writing?

SHANNON: Just doing my job.

ABIE: So tell me what you write about me!

SHANNON: All right. You said you were nervous, didn't you?

ABIE: No! No! I am not a nervous *man*. What I mean is that *you, you* make me nervous, you and this crazy system of yours, mister! So leave! *Tell* them that I am a nervous man, I don't care! If this is what the company wants to do for a little insurance, then I take my business someplace else! So go! (SHANNON *packs his things.*) That's it!

SHANNON: You know, of course, that I'll have to finish this report on you, anyway.

ABIE: So . . . go. Do it, I don't care what you do. I don't like you snoops coming around here trying to find reasons why I can't have my policy.

SHANNON: I never hand in a partial report, you see, never. When my customers order a report, they get what they pay for. So don't think I'm going to stop here. There are other ways of getting information, you know, other people to talk to.

ABIE: What are you saying?

SHANNON: Those talkative little ladies in the florist shop, for one thing.

ABIE: No. No, you don't want to talk to . . .

SHANNON: I don't miss a trick, Mr. Moscowich. I think you should know that. I've been very reasonable up to now. But business is business.

ABIE: I stop you. They don't tell you anything.

SHANNON: Stop me from talking to an informant? Then you have something to hide?

ABIE: Hide? Me? What have I got to hide?

SHANNON: That's exactly what I'm going to find out. You wouldn't be in such a hurry to see me leave, would you, if you thought I was the kind of man who'd automatically approve your policy.

ABIE: I don't need you. I go to another company.

SHANNON: (*At the door*) Oh, sure, go ahead. But I'll tell you something. The company you change to will probably be just another one of our customers, and in that case . . . I'll be back.

ABIE: No.

SHANNON: And by the time I get back, my file on Abraham Moscowich isn't going to look too good.

ABIE: (*With a start*) File?

SHANNON: (*Stops abruptly, and slowly turning around*) Yes. A file. Of course.

ABIE: I . . . I don't understand you with your questions and your . . . files. I never go through anything like this for insurance before.

SHANNON: Oh, you don't think so?

ABIE: What?

SHANNON: Your original policy. 1957. You remember that, don't you?

ABIE: Yes . . . yes.

SHANNON: A ten thousand dollar policy.

ABIE: Yes.

SHANNON: And it was approved.

ABIE: Yes, yes. But nobody ever came around for questions and information.

SHANNON: Oh, yes, Mr. Moscowich. We were there, all right. I have your old file right in my office. Oh, we didn't speak to *you* at the time. We spoke to your neighbors.

ABIE: My neighbors? You spoke to my neighbors?

SHANNON: Oh, no, not me! I didn't handle that case myself. That was a very simple investigation. It didn't even require a personal interview. All the investigator had to do on that case was just ask around a little bit, you know, just to make sure you were alive. I wouldn't handle a case like that. I only handle the really big cases, the ones that require the most thorough investigations, the ones that involve a lot of money. That was a much smaller policy than the one you're applying for now.

ABIE: Smaller? Why smaller? I'm applying for another ten thousand.

SHANNON: Oh, no. That's not what *I* show.

ABIE: What? How much do they say?

SHANNON: One hundred thousand dollars.

ABIE: One hundred thou . . . mister, that is crazy. I don't want so much . . .

SHANNON: What are you, changing your mind now?

ABIE: No. I want ten thousand.

SHANNON: You put in for a hundred thousand, didn't you?

ABIE: No. No. I didn't.

SHANNON: Mr. Moscowich, I happen to be the most experienced man in my entire office. They wouldn't waste my time on anything less than a hundred thousand. Why, just an hour ago I interviewed one of the most powerful businessmen in this entire country. Sat there right in his office, a room three times the size of this, Picassos on the wall and everything else. That's the kind of man I'm used to talking to, Mr. Moscowich, the men with the real power, the men who buy a million dollar insurance policy the way you buy a subway token! Now, if all you applied for was another ten thousand dollar policy, there would be a much, much smaller investigation. And they wouldn't need the services of James T. Shannon for that!

ABIE: Oh, so this is it. You are the man they send to talk to all the hot shots, uh? Well, don't you see? Your machines, your computers, or whatever you got there, they make a mistake! One too many zeros they put in! (*Taking a pencil, he marks the correction on* SHANNON's *sheet.* SHANNON *quickly pulls the sheet away and erases the correction.*) So now, instead of saying ten thousand like it should, it says a hundred thousand. (*Conciliatory*) Oh, all this waste of time for nothing, uh? Well. You go now and tell them to send around the kind of man they should be sending out for just a little ten thousand dollar investigation. O.K.? (*Tries to usher* SHANNON *to the door*) So come on.

SHANNON: So you think there's some kind of mistake, do you?

ABIE: Sure. It's not obvious?

SHANNON: Mr. Moscowich, I don't make mistakes.

ABIE: But . . .

SHANNON: All I know is that your insurance company has ordered a thorough investigation based on a one hundred thousand dollar policy. And I intend to give them what they're paying for.

ABIE: What? You mean you can't see this mistake? You can't look around this palace of mine and know that I'm not a man to take out a hundred thousand?

SHANNON: (*With a wry smile, gazing directly at* ABIE) I don't like being called a schmuck, Mr. Moscowich.

ABIE: (*More to himself*) Oh. Oh, so you are a man who believes in . . . retribution.

The Interview

SHANNON: I'm a man who believes in doing his job, that's all. I have this sneaky little feeling that you're trying to put one over on the insurance company, Mr. Moscowich, and I'm just the man to find out what it is. (*He removes his coat, throws it on the chair.*) I am going to finish my investigation right now. And you are going to sit there and answer my questions. I don't think you realize just what kind of man you're dealing with here, Mr. Moscowich.

ABIE: (*Quietly*) I think I do.

SHANNON: (*Removing materials from briefcase*) All right. Now, it's important that you answer all of these questions completely and to the best of your ability, and it's only fair to advise you that any false, misleading or erroneous information can result in the immediate cancellation of your policy. Your name: Abraham Moscowich. M-o-s-c-o-w-i-t-z. Is that correct? (*No answer*) Is that correct, Mr. Moscowich?

ABIE: (*Quietly*) Yes. Mos-*co*-vitz.

SHANNON: And your address . . . 3301 Ocean Parkway?

ABIE: 3301 . . . yes.

SHANNON: In Brooklyn?

ABIE: Yes.

SHANNON: Is that a private home? (*Pause*) Mr. Moscowich, is that a private home?

ABIE: No . . . no . . . an apartment.

SHANNON: How big?

ABIE: Uh?

SHANNON: How many rooms?

ABIE: Oh . . . four . . . four-and-a-half rooms?

SHANNON: Is that four or four-and-a-half rooms?

ABIE: I don't know . . . It looks like four. They call it four-and-a-half.

SHANNON: Four-and-a-half. Is that rented or cooperative?

ABIE: Rented.

SHANNON: How much rent do you pay?

ABIE: Sixty-five dollars a month.

SHANNON: You're a widower, is that correct?

ABIE: Yes . . . yes, that is correct.

SHANNON: You live alone, then?

ABIE: I live alone.

SHANNON: You have one son, is that right?

ABIE: Yes. A son.

SHANNON: And he's married?

ABIE: That's right.

SHANNON: Any other children . . . (*No answer*) . . . Mr. Moscowich, *do you have any other children?*

ABIE: (*Pause*) No, no . . . no.

SHANNON: How tall are you?

ABIE: Tall? I don't know. Five foot, six inches.

SHANNON: Five-six. You must be sure, Mr. Moscowich. Are you sure?

ABIE: Yes, yes. Five-foot-six.

SHANNON: How much do you weigh?

ABIE: Uh . . . one-fifty, one-sixty.

SHANNON: Is that one-*fifty* or one-*sixty?*

ABIE: Uh . . . around there . . . between there.

SHANNON: All right, one-fifty-five. Have you ever been hospitalized? (*Pause*) I *say*, have you ever been hospitalized, Mr. Moscowich?

ABIE: Huh?

SHANNON: *Have you ever been in a hospital?*

ABIE: Hospital? No . . . no.

SHANNON: Describe your health. Are you in good health?

ABIE: . . . Yes, yes . . . yes.

SHANNON: (*Rapidly*) In yourself, your family or any other blood relations, has there ever been any history of heart disease, cancer, tuberculosis, diabetes, mental trouble, or any hereditary, contagious, or communicable disease?

ABIE: Uh, no . . . no . . . no.

SHANNON: All right, then. Your date of birth, 8/17/10. Could that be right?

ABIE: 1910 . . . 1910 . . . I am sixty-three. So you think I look older? Life works harder on some people, that's all. But I am in good health, knock wood.

SHANNON: Are you superstitious?

ABIE: You make me laugh, mister. Superstition is for fools. That was an expression only. I am . . . I try to be . . . a religious man.

SHANNON: Have you had any military experience?

The Interview

ABIE: Military. No . . . no.

SHANNON: Have you ever been rejected for the draft?

ABIE: So now you think I'm a teen-ager?

SHANNON: Mr. Moscowich, the Selective Service Act was passed in this country in 1940, which means that you could have been eligible for the draft, since you were only thirty years old at the time. Now, have you ever been rejected for the draft?

ABIE: When I was a young man, mister, I was not in this country.

SHANNON: And where were you, then? Are you from . . . Russia?

ABIE: Yes. I am from Russia originally. I was born there.

SHANNON: I'll bet you're wondering how I knew that. It's your name. Moscowich.

ABIE: Mos-*co*-vitz.

SHANNON: It has "Moscow" in it. Like my name's Shannon, so my family's originally from Ireland. Oh, yeah, I *notice* little things like that, Mr. Moscowich. Every little detail. Now when did you leave Moscow?

ABIE: It wasn't Moscow.

SHANNON: Oh?

ABIE: You see? You took a guess. You ask a question that's not on your form, and you are wrong. No. It was just a little town, called Afimievsk.

SHANNON: Affie . . .

ABIE: A-f-i-m-i-e-v-s-k.

SHANNON: When did you leave?

ABIE: I was very young, maybe six years old.

SHANNON: So that would put it at about, uh, 1916. Why did you leave?

ABIE: But this is so long ago.

SHANNON: I want to know why your family decided to leave this, uh, Affimivek.

ABIE: Afimievsk. We didn't decide, mister. The officials, the soldiers, they decided for us.

SHANNON: Oh. It was the, uh . . . the . . .

ABIE: The pogroms. Yes, of course, that's what it was. They kicked us out.

SHANNON: Where did you go then?

ABIE: Well, my whole family had to split up. And me . . . they sent me to live with relatives, in Poland . . . in Warsaw.

SHANNON: And when did you come to our country?

ABIE: Your country? (*A small laugh*) 19 . . . 46. Mr. Shannon, you are a Catholic?

SHANNON: What of it?

ABIE: Do you go to confession?

SHANNON: Look, it's not part of my job to discuss religion. Now you came here . . .

ABIE: I am only asking, that's all. You go to confession?

SHANNON: Well, when I was a kid, maybe . . . listen, what is this?

ABIE: You went when you were a child. But now . . . now more sins to confess?

SHANNON: Now, you said you came here in 1946 . . .

ABIE: Just one question. I have always wanted to know. When you go to the confession, does the priest draw your sins from you?

SHANNON: Mr. Moscowich. 1946.

ABIE: Does he ask you questions and make you confess?

SHANNON: Well, sometimes, if you can't remember everything you did, he might . . .

ABIE: And when you leave, you know that you are forgiven? Your conscience is clear?

SHANNON: Well, that's the whole idea, isn't it? Come on, now. 1946. You came here in 1946. What did you do then?

ABIE: I had an uncle. He was able to escape from Poland, and he took my son with him. I came to join them here. Yes. 1946. After the war. After I got out of the . . . hospital.

SHANNON: Hospital? Hospital? You told me you were never hospitalized. I'm going to have to start getting the *truth* here, Mr. Moscowich. Now, *when* were you in the hospital? For how long?

ABIE: For . . . for seven months . . . after the war.

SHANNON: Seven months? What was your condition?

ABIE: It was . . . it was the war.

SHANNON: Mr. Moscowich, you just told me that you never had any military experience, right?

ABIE: Yes.

SHANNON: Then how can you say you were hospitalized because of the war? Were you recuperating from something? Were you recuperating from a . . . oh, no. But you have to say it.

The Interview 57

ABIE: Yes . . . that's what it was.

SHANNON: *You* have to tell me.

ABIE: Yes. I'm telling you? That's what it was!

SHANNON: Say it.

ABIE: You are right! You are right!

SHANNON: Come out and say it! What was it?

ABIE: A . . . concentration camp!

SHANNON: Well. You should just come right out and tell me these things. Now, how long were you there?

ABIE: Two years.

SHANNON: And what was the reason for your hospitalization?

ABIE: Mister . . . it was . . . it was . . . How can you ask?

SHANNON: Well, I have to know if there was anything that might affect your policy.

ABIE: Starvation, mister? Does that affect my policy? (*With sarcasm*) No, it was nothing, nothing for your files. When they released me, I was just like a new man, just like nothing ever happened. All right?

SHANNON: How long have you had this shop?

ABIE: Twenty, twenty-one years.

SHANNON: Is that twenty or twenty-*one* years, Mister Moscowich?

ABIE: 1950, about.

SHANNON: 1950! That's twenty-three years. And what were you doing from 1946, when you came here, until 1950, when you opened this shop?

ABIE: I was a tailor. I worked for my uncle. I learned the business from him, in his shop on Grand Street.

SHANNON: What address?

ABIE: Near Orchard Street. I don't remember.

SHANNON: What was the name of the shop?

ABIE: "Moses' Fine Alterations." That was my uncle . . . Moses Abrams.

SHANNON: Where is he now?

ABIE: Dead. He died in 1950. Then I took my own shop. Here.

SHANNON: What was the cause of his death?

ABIE: I don't know. Old age. Heart attack, I suppose.

SHANNON: You said before that there was no history of heart disease in your family. Didn't you? Well, *didn't you?*

ABIE: I did?

SHANNON: You did!

ABIE: I . . . don't . . .

SHANNON: All right, I'll ask again. In your family, in your blood relations, any history of cancer, tuberculosis, mental disease, diabetes, heart disease, or hereditary, contagious or communicable disease?

ABIE: . . . Yes. My uncle . . . Moses. He died from a heart attack . . . I think.

SHANNON: Do you work alone?

ABIE: Yes.

SHANNON: Then this is a private proprietorship?

ABIE: Yes.

SHANNON: Then it's not a corporation or a partnership?

ABIE: Correct.

SHANNON: And you do not hire help?

ABIE: No.

SHANNON: Describe the work that you do.

ABIE: Look! See what I do! Look at the sign. Look in my hands, I am a tailor of men's clothing. Can't you see that? You have eyes?

SHANNON: Come on, now, Mr. Moscowich . . .

ABIE: And say Mos-*co*-vitz!

SHANNON: Is there anything hazardous about your job?

ABIE: Hazard. What hazard. I sit here and I sew. And I use a sewing machine, and I make chalk marks on clothes. *What* hazard. I prick my finger with a pin sometimes. Am I dead? No. Look.

SHANNON: What is your religion?

ABIE: Religion? I look like a cardinal?

SHANNON: Just answer the question, please, Mr. Moscowich.

ABIE: Mister, I am a Jew. Can't you put together even two and two for yourself?

SHANNON: Hebrew. All right. Are you an American citizen?

ABIE: Yes. Yes, I am a citizen.

SHANNON: This question is a formality, Mr. Moscowich. Please answer "yes" or "no": Have you ever advocated the violent overthrow of our present form of government?

ABIE: Here on Canal Street, mister, a man who fixes cuffs is not a rebel.

SHANNON: "Yes" or "no," Mr. Moscowich.

ABIE: No! Of course no! What kind of questions are these?

SHANNON: Just answer them, will you please?

ABIE: But these questions tell you nothing! (*Mocking*) Do you advocate the . . .

SHANNON: Listen, each and every question is obviously important to the insurance company, or I wouldn't have to ask them, don't you understand? They're all figured out way ahead of time . . .

ABIE: Yes, yes, I know. By people who get paid to sit around and think up stupid questions, right? Well, I have a question for *you*, Mr. Shannon!

SHANNON: Look, if there's any questions to be asked around here, I'm . . .

ABIE: Do they laugh at you? (SHANNON *is stunned into momentary silence.*) I mean these big hot shot businessmen of yours, when you go in there with your briefcase and your pencils and these questions, they take you seriously?

SHANNON: (*Controlled*) At the bottom of my form, Mr. Moscowich, there's a question that says, "Do you recommend?" and *I'm* the one who says "yes" or "no." And don't think I'm afraid to say "no," no matter who it might be. I can dig up an awful lot on some of these sons of bitches out there, and they know it. They take me seriously, all right. And I suggest you do the same thing. Now . . .

ABIE: But these sons of bitches, these are the men with the Picassos on the wall, right?

SHANNON: Look, I don't care if they've got the whole damn Sistine Chapel! It's not my job to worry about . . .

ABIE: And these sons of bitches, they're the ones who have the real power, uh? They're the ones who buy a million dollars insurance the way you and me buy a subway token, right?

SHANNON: Yeah, right. So what?

ABIE: So what do *you* get out of it, Mr. Shannon?

SHANNON: (*Pause*) Me? Don't you worry about me, Mr. Moscowich, I do all right.

ABIE: Sure. That's why you have to work overtime, uh? And at the end, Mr. Shannon, after thirty or forty years of talking to your big time hot shots, what do you get then? A little handshake? A nice backslap? Good work, Mr. James T. Shannon.

SHANNON: You want to know? All right, I'll tell you. Number one, we get a pension, Mr. Moscowich, which takes care of us for life. Then we get free medical coverage for life, and life insurance too, which means that when I'm sixty-three years old, I won't have to worry about applying for a policy! And even the home office sends up a little something. Usually, it's a . . . it's a little, uh . . . well, it's a nice big basket of fruit.

ABIE: (*Pause*) That's nice.

SHANNON: All right, that might not seem like much but, well, they do show their appreciation.

ABIE: You lie to yourself, Mr. Shannon. It's all right, it's all right. I lie to myself, too. The only thing that's wrong with it is that it doesn't work. The truth about yourself has a way of, uh (*He indicates completion of the thought by using a rolling hand motion*), right?

SHANNON: I don't lie to myself, Mr. Moscowich.

ABIE: No? You are a clever man, Mr. Shannon, much smarter than this job allows you to be. Smarter, maybe, than some of these hot shots with the Picassos, uh?

SHANNON: Oh, I don't know about *that*.

ABIE: Oh, so you mean that this is all you are capable of, to be an insurance investigator?

SHANNON: I didn't say that.

ABIE: (*Ignoring* SHANNON'S *last remark; with sarcasm*) Well, then you should consider yourself very lucky, Mr. Shannon. It's not every man who realizes his full potential in life.

SHANNON: (*Quickly*) I didn't say anything like that.

ABIE: (*Same*) You are blessed!

SHANNON: (*Same*) No. Look . . .

ABIE: (*Same*) One in a million!

SHANNON: (*Same*) I didn't say I wasn't capable of anything else, I . . . There's a lot of other things I could've done, but . . . Now, don't get me wrong. I mean, there's nothing wrong with being an insurance investigator.

ABIE: No.

SHANNON: I mean, it's all right.

ABIE: Sure. It's a good job.

SHANNON: Oh, there was a time, maybe . . . but I guess those are the breaks, that's all. You should know a lot about the breaks, Mr. Moscowich.

ABIE: Yes. And now you are stuck.

SHANNON: You learn to live with what you've got.

ABIE: So you learn to live with being an insurance investigator, uh, and you don't think you are living a lie? You know, it's very strange that you should be here, Mr. Shannon. More than just a coincidence, I think.

SHANNON: All right. All right. Let's drop this now and just get on with the investigation, okay?

ABIE: Sure, by all means. Investigate. Go ahead. Continue asking these questions for a company you don't even know the name of! (*Rising, moving toward* SHANNON) For a system that makes no sense to you! Continue your lie, go ahead, and if you do your job like a good boy, there is waiting for you at the end of the line a little pension and a nice, fresh basket of fruit!

SHANNON: Hey, just what do you think you're doing, anyway?

ABIE: I have met men like you before, Mr. Shannon. Oh, yes. You say, "What can I do? It's the system," and meanwhile you know better than that. That makes you a *real* schmuck, the worst kind of schmuck, because you're smart enough to know better!

SHANNON: All right, I think I've had enough of this!

ABIE: Face the truth, schmuck!

(*Overlapping*)

SHANNON: You think you're clever don't you?	ABIE: Schmuck.
SHANNON: You think you're going to throw me off track, get me on the defensive, and and maybe I'll forget what I started out to do, uh? *Stop calling me schmuck!*	ABIE: Schmuck! *Schmuck!* Schmuck!

SHANNON: I said that's enough! Now you sit down. (*He shoves* ABIE.)

ABIE: You know it, don't you, schmuck!

SHANNON: (*Pushing* ABIE *back into his chair*) I SAID SIT DOWN! Now I'm warning you, I've taken all I'm going to take from you! I'm going to get to the bottom of this whole shit you're trying to pull, and you are not going to open that mouth of yours unless it's to answer my questions, is that clear?

ABIE: (*Submitting*) Yes.

SHANNON: Yes, Mr. Shannon!

ABIE: Yes . . . Mr. . . . Shannon.

SHANNON: All right! (*The interview now takes on the appearance of an intense interrogation.* SHANNON *does not record the answers.*) Now! How much do you earn a year?

ABIE: Seven, eight thousand dollars.

SHANNON: (*Overlapping*) Seven or eight!

ABIE: It varies.

SHANNON: Seventy-five hundred! Any other source of income?

ABIE: No . . . none.

(*Overlapping*)

SHANNON: No stocks? No bonds?	ABIE: No, no . . . Nothing, no no . . .
No real estate?	No, no, none . . .
No other business interests?	Nothing, only this . . .
No investments?	No . . .
Nothing?	No.

SHANNON: What is the net worth of this business?

ABIE: I don't know.

SHANNON: Your gross annual sales?

ABIE: I don't know.

SHANNON: Your net worth?

ABIE: I don't know.

SHANNON: Don't you even know your *worth*, Mr. Moscowich?

ABIE: No.

SHANNON: Where is your bank?

ABIE: First National City. Mott Street.

SHANNON: How much do you have in the bank?

ABIE: Three, four . . .

SHANNON: Three or four!

ABIE: Three thousand, four hundred, change.

SHANNON: Do you drink?

ABIE: No.

SHANNON: Not even socially?

ABIE: No.

The Interview

SHANNON: Don't you ever have a glass of wine?

ABIE: Sometimes on holidays. A little glass of wine.

SHANNON: Do you ever drink more than one glass?

ABIE: No.

SHANNON: You never have two or three or four?

ABIE: No. Never.

SHANNON: Do you smoke?

ABIE: No!

SHANNON: Do you do any sports?

ABIE: Think for yourself!

SHANNON: Answer my question! Do you do any sports?

ABIE: No! Don't be ridiculous!

(*Overlapping*)

SHANNON: Have you ever flown a plane by yourself? Taken aviation lessons? Flown in a private plane? Use anything other than regularly scheduled airlines?

ABIE: No. No. Of course no. Think for yourself! No. Ask what's important! Stupid questions. No. No! No!

SHANNON: Do you plan to travel?

ABIE: I don't know.

SHANNON: Wouldn't you like to go to Europe?

ABIE: No.

SHANNON: To Russia?

ABIE: No.

SHANNON: Poland? To Warsaw?

ABIE: No.

SHANNON: Who are you naming as beneficiary of this policy?

ABIE: My son.

SHANNON: What does he do for a living?

ABIE: He's a lawyer.

SHANNON: And he's the sole beneficiary?

ABIE: Yes. He's the only one. My Maurie.

SHANNON: Maurie? What's that short for? Morris?

The Interview

ABIE: Yes. Morris. Morris Mos-*co*-vitz. My son.

SHANNON: That's not what it says on the policy, Mr. Moscowich. It says Martin. Martin Moss. The policy reads Martin Moss, *not* Morris Moscowich. Who is Martin Moss?

ABIE: My son, my son.

SHANNON: He changed his name, didn't he?

ABIE: Yes. He changed his name.

SHANNON: Why?

ABIE: For business. He wanted a business name.

SHANNON: What's wrong with Morris Moscowich? Doesn't have that old all-American ring to it, like Martin Moss, does it?

ABIE: No. No. It's for business. Business only.

SHANNON: You didn't change *your* name for business, Mr. Moscowich.

ABIE: No. That's my name. I am a small businessman only. I don't change my traditions.

SHANNON: Why did you name your son, Morris, alias Martin, as beneficiary of your insurance policy? Your son is a lawyer. He probably makes nine or ten times the amount that you'll ever make. He has all the money he needs. Enough money to take care of you. Enough money to get you out of this dump! Why doesn't he take care of you? And why are you naming him as beneficiary of your policy? He certainly doesn't need your money!

ABIE: NO! YOU! WHAT ARE YOU SAYING! MY MORRIS IS A GOOD BOY! I WILL NOT BE A BURDEN ON HIM! WHEN I DIE, HE HAS MY MONEY! I LEAVE HIM SOMETHING! I PROVIDE! HE IS ALL I HAVE LEFT! MY MORRIS! ALL I HAVE LEFT!

SHANNON: All you have left? All you have left from what? You had other children?

ABIE: Yes.

SHANNON: *Had* other children?

ABIE: Yes.

SHANNON: How many? (*No answer*) HOW MANY!

ABIE: Two . . . two. A girl, a little girl . . . and another boy.

SHANNON: YOU TOLD ME BEFORE THAT YOU HAD ONLY ONE CHILD! MORRIS MOSCOWICH, ALIAS MARTIN MOSS! I ASKED YOU IF YOU HAD ANY OTHER CHILDREN AND YOU SAID NO! WHAT ARE YOU TRYING TO PULL WITH ME?

ABIE: I don't think of them. I try not to think of them. They are gone. Gone. I try so hard not to think of them.

SHANNON: Gone?

ABIE: Yes.

SHANNON: You mean dead?

ABIE: Yes.

SHANNON: And your wife?

ABIE: Gone . . . she is gone.

SHANNON: You mean dead?

ABIE: Yes . . . yes.

SHANNON: You came by yourself to join your son Martin and your uncle Moses here in New York after the war in 1946, right?

ABIE: Yes.

SHANNON: The others couldn't join you?

ABIE: No.

SHANNON: Your wife, your daughter, your other son, they couldn't join you?

ABIE: No.

SHANNON: Why did you lie about your other children?

ABIE: For me . . . for me . . . it is better that they never existed.

SHANNON: Your wife? Your daughter? Your son? Well, what happened to them?

ABIE: No! No! You don't know! How I try! I try! Every year, I go to the river, you know what Yom Kippur is? I stand on the pier, and I take my handful of bread, my sins, and I throw them into the water to get buried in the sea. The tide takes my bread, yes, but I find that my sins are still there! They don't go . . . They never go away!

SHANNON: Tell me what happened to them, Mr. Moscowich!

ABIE: No! No!

SHANNON: I can't make guesses. You have to tell me!

ABIE: . . . Gone . . . they are all . . . gone.

SHANNON: Dead?

ABIE: . . . Dead.

The Interview 67

(*Overlapping*)

SHANNON: And what was the cause of their deaths! Was it cancer?

ABIE: No, no, no, No.

Tuberculosis?

NO, NO, NO,

Heart disease?

NO!

Mental trouble?

NO! NO!

Contagious, hereditary, or communicable disease?

NO!

SHANNON: Then what was it? Mr. Moscowich, what was it? I have to know. Your wife, your son, your daughter, why aren't they here? Why did they die?

ABIE: Killed . . . they were killed. (*He begins to breathe with increasing difficulty, occasionally grasping at his chest.*)

(*Overlapping*)

SHANNON: Oh. Accidental death.

ABIE: No!

Was it an auto accident?

No, no, no,

Plane crash?

No,

Derailment?

No,

A ship?

No, no,

Did they drown?

No!

SHANNON: Then what was it? TELL ME! *You* have to tell me!

ABIE: In the street, I saw them . . . Golde . . . little Mendel . . . little Shandel. Standing there, looking, looking everywhere . . . looking for their papa . . . I had run into this doorway, you see, I thought they were right behind me . . . I crouch. I hide . . . then I slowly look out and I see them *still there* . . . STILL THERE in that group of people. I want to shout, "HERE! HERE IS YOUR PAPA! OVER HERE! I AM WITH YOU!" But I cannot! I dare not! . . . There is a guard, with a machine gun. I want to run out, to distract him . . . but no, I cannot move! I stay there, I hide and I watch!

SHANNON: (*Quietly*) Dear God.

ABIE: They take them across the road, where they were lined up and . . . (*He is unable to finish through increased sobbing.*)

SHANNON: (*After a pause*) You mean that they were . . .

ABIE: Yes, yes, yes!

SHANNON: Please you really have to say it.

ABIE: SHOT! Like little pigs, they are mowed down against the wall! I see them falling! I see them . . . die! I see them take their little bodies and my Golde . . . they throw them like garbage onto the truck! Later, when the uprising is all over, they take the survivors and put them into concentration camps.

SHANNON: And you were the survivor. You got away.

ABIE: No! I never get away! I live, yes, but I never get away, don't you understand that? . . . Ahhhhh . . . I cannot . . . breathe . . . Please . . . Golde . . . my heart!

SHANNON: Your heart?

ABIE: I cannot . . . breathe.

SHANNON: Do you have any pills? (ABIE *makes a dismissing gesture, as* SHANNON *goes to the phone and dials 911.*) You knew you had a heart condition all along, didn't you?

ABIE: . . . Yes . . . yes!

SHANNON: (*Into phone*) Yes. I've got an emergency here, a cardiac. Right. (*He turns to* ABIE.) That's what you've been trying to hide from me, uh?

ABIE: Yes. Yes.

SHANNON: (*Into the phone*) I need an ambulance right away. Moscowich tailor shop. M-o-s-c-o-w-i-t-z. 348 Canal Street, near Mott. Right. (*He hangs up.*)

ABIE: (*While* SHANNON *is on the phone*) No . . . No . . . Too late . . . you don't need an ambulance.

SHANNON: How long have you known about your heart condition? (ABIE *shakes his head.*) Well, come on, was it a long time? (ABIE *nods*) Five years? Ten years, longer? Did you know about it when you applied for your first policy? (ABIE *nods*) Great! Here you are applying for another policy, when you're not even entitled to the first one.

ABIE: Mr . . . . Shannon . . . I . . . have . . . one . . . son. I must . . . provide! (*He falls to the floor.*)

SHANNON: Oh, Jesus! (*He rushes to* ABIE.) God, I didn't mean to . . . I didn't want to . . . (*He loosens* ABIE'*s tie, opens his collar button, then rolls up his own coat, placing it under* ABIE'*s head.*) There. Now . . . now, you're going to be all right, Mr. Moscowich. The ambulance will be here in just a minute.

ABIE: No, mister, you still don't understand. Listen . . . you are not here just by chance. I have been waiting for many years. Now . . . I am happy, you see? . . . I die for my children, for my Golde . . . I am forgiven, I have peace, understand?

The Interview

SHANNON: All right . . . Try, try not to talk now. Just relax.

ABIE: But I must ask . . . you will do an old man a favor? I know that you cannot give insurance to a dead man, (*A weak laugh*) it's true? But on my first policy I have paid all my premiums . . . and you must let my Morris have it. I cannot be a burden, understand? . . . You tell them you came in here, you found me like this . . . you never had a chance for your interview, yes?

SHANNON: I, uh, I better check and see if the ambulance is coming yet. You just, uh, stay calm, I'll be right back. (*He moves toward the door.*)

ABIE: A dying wish, Mr. Shannon. (SHANNON *stops*) You must promise me . . . The truth that you know, you keep here (*He points to his head*), uh? You take your forms, you throw them away . . . and for once in your life mark your file . . . incomplete.

SHANNON: Well, I . . . I don't know. I don't know.

ABIE: (*As we hear the ambulance approaching from the distance, its siren growing louder*) No matter. I believe you will do it for me. To show me that you are maybe not such a schmuck, after all. (*He laughs, then groans from a sudden, more severe attack.*)

SHANNON: I, uh, I hear the ambulance coming now. Now, just hold on. You're going to be all right, Mr. Moscowich.

ABIE: (*With a sudden, deep breath*) Mos-*co*-vitz!

(*As* ABIE *falls, with a slight smile, into his final collapse, we hear the ambulance siren growing louder. Slow fade on all but* SHANNON, *who stands motionless near the doorway until we hear the siren immediately outside and can see its red lights flashing through the door and window.*)

CURTAIN

After Words

1 In your journal, note your responses to the script. Consider any feelings, associations, and questions triggered by the script. Then write a brief account of the events from Shannon's point of view.

2 In a small group, discuss any questions you have about the play (such as its historical or contemporary references).

3 Early in the play, how is Abie characterized? How is Shannon a contrast to this portrayal? What aspects and qualities are later revealed about each? Give examples of dialogue that reflect each character, e.g., "That sign don't make me what I am," "Look, I don't make up the rules . . . " (page 49).

4 Using details from the play, create a profile of Shannon as he might be seen by people other than Abie, such as his employers, co-workers, or family.

5 Extend the play in one or more of the following ways:

a) Write or improvise the discussion between Shannon and two police investigators immediately after Abie's death.

b) In role as Shannon, write his formal report to his employer.

c) Script and present a dialogue between Abie's son and a representative of the insurance company.

6 a) In a small group, discuss the manner in which Shannon handled his investigation. Share your group's ideas with the class.

b) In your group, dramatize a portion of the interview. Take turns in the roles of Abie, Shannon, and director(s). Consider voice (clarity, emphasis, tone), pacing, and blocking. Present your dramatization to others for evaluation.

7 Write of an event or a person brought to mind by the play's conflict, associations, and/or themes. This may be a reflection on the past or present, fact or fiction. Your writing might take the form of a profile, poem, or story.

The Man Who Turned into a Dog

A stage play by Osvaldo Dragún,
translated by Francesca Colecchia and Julio Matas

Born in Argentina in 1929, Osvaldo Dragún began his theatrical career while a university student in Buenos Aires. There he became involved with experimental theatre groups which persisted in creating meaningful and critical theatre despite the dictatorship of Colonel Juan Peron. Dragún's first play, a historical work, was produced in 1956, the year after Peron's first dictatorship ended. Through his international award-winning plays, Dragún explores dehumanizing forces, oppressive social systems, corruption, and violence. Bertolt Brecht, the innovative Berlin dramatist, is one of Dragún's main influences. The following experimental piece was written in 1956.

Prelude

1 In your journal, speculate on the implications of the play's title. Why might a man turn into a dog? What would life be like for this dog who once had been a man?

2 To what extent do we determine our own lives? What effects does society have on our lives?

The Man Who Turned into a Dog

Characters

>FIRST ACTOR
>
>SECOND ACTOR
>
>THIRD ACTOR
>
>ACTRESS

SECOND ACTOR: Friends, let's tell the story this way . . .

THIRD ACTOR: The way they told it to us this afternoon.

ACTRESS: It's the tale of "The Man Who Turned into a Dog."

THIRD ACTOR: It began two years ago on a bench in a square. There, sir . . . , where today you were trying to fathom the secret of a leaf.

ACTRESS: There, where stretching out our arms, we held the world by its head and its feet, and said to it, "Play, accordion, play!"

SECOND ACTOR: We met him there. (FIRST ACTOR *enters*.) He was . . . (*He points to the* FIRST ACTOR.) . . . the way you see him, nothing more. And he was very sad.

ACTRESS: He became our friend. He was looking for work, and we were actors.

THIRD ACTOR: He had to support his wife, and we were actors.

SECOND ACTOR: He would dream of life, and he would awaken during the night, screaming. And we were actors.

ACTRESS: He became our friend, of course. Just like that . . . (*She points to him.*) Nothing more.

ALL: And he was very sad!

THIRD ACTOR: Time went by. Fall . . .

SECOND ACTOR: Summer . . .

ACTRESS: Winter . . .

THIRD ACTOR: Spring . . .

FIRST ACTOR: Lie! I never knew spring.

SECOND ACTOR: Fall . . .

The Man Who Turned into a Dog

ACTRESS: Winter . . .

THIRD ACTOR: Summer. And we returned. And we went to visit him because he was our friend.

SECOND ACTOR: And we asked, "Is he all right?" And his wife told us . . .

ACTRESS: I don't know . . .

THIRD ACTOR: Is he sick?

ACTRESS: I don't know.

SECOND AND THIRD ACTORS: Where is he?

ACTRESS: In the dog pound.

(FIRST ACTOR *enters on all fours.*)

SECOND AND THIRD ACTORS: Uhh!

THIRD ACTOR: (*Observing him*)

> I am the director of the pound.
>
> And that's okay with me.
>
> He arrived barking like a dog
>
> (the main requirement).
>
> Even if he wears a suit,
>
> he is a dog, beyond a doubt.

SECOND ACTOR: (*Stuttering*)

> I am the veterinarian,
>
> and th-this is cl-clear to me.
>
> Al-although he s-seems a man,
>
> wh-what is here is a dog.

FIRST ACTOR: (*To the audience*) And I, what can I tell you? I don't know whether I'm a man or a dog. And I believe that in the end not even you will be able to tell me. Because it all began in the most ordinary fashion. I went to a factory to look for a job. I hadn't found anything in three months, and I went there to look for work.

THIRD ACTOR: Didn't you read the sign. There Are No Openings.

FIRST ACTOR: Yes, I read it. Don't you have anything for me?

THIRD ACTOR: If it says There Are No Openings, there are none.

FIRST ACTOR: Of course. Don't you have anything for me?

THIRD ACTOR: Not for you, not for the president!

First Actor: Okay. Don't you have anything for me?

Third Actor: No!

First Actor: Lathe operator . . .

Third Actor: No!

First Actor: Mechanic . . .

Third Actor: No!

First Actor: Secretary . . .

Third Actor: No!

First Actor: Errand boy . . .

Third Actor: No!

First Actor: Foreman . . .

Third Actor: No!

First Actor: Night watchman! Night watchman! Even if it's just a night watchman!

Actress: (*As if she were playing a horn*) Toot, toot, toooot. The boss! (*The Second and Third Actors make signs to each other.*)

Third Actor: (*To the audience*) Ladies and gentlemen, the night watchman's dog had died the night before, after twenty-five years of dedication.

Second Actor: He was a very old dog.

Actress: Amen.

Second Actor: (*To the First Actor*) Do you know how to bark?

First Actor: Lathe operator.

Second Actor: Do you know how to bark?

First Actor: Mechanic . . .

Second Actor: Do you know how to bark?

First Actor: Bricklayer . . .

Second and Third Actors: There are no openings!

First Actor: (*Pausing*) Bowwow . . . Bowwow! . . .

Second Actor: Very good, I congratulate you . . .

Third Actor: We'll give you ten pesos a day, the doghouse, and your food.

Second Actor: As you see, he earned ten pesos a day more than the real dog.

Actress: When he returned home, he told me of the job he had gotten. He was drunk.

The Man Who Turned into a Dog

First Actor: (*To his wife*) But they promised me that as soon as the first worker would retire, die, or be fired, they would give me his job. Amuse yourself, Maria, amuse yourself! Bowwow . . . bowwow! . . . Amuse yourself, Maria, amuse yourself.

Second and Third Actors: Bowwow . . . bowwow . . . Amuse yourself, Maria, amuse yourself!

Actress: He was drunk, poor dear . . .

First Actor: And the following night I began to work . . . (*He gets down on all fours.*)

Second Actor: Is the doghouse too small for you?

First Actor: I can't stoop so much.

Third Actor: Does it crowd you here?

First Actor: Yes.

Third Actor: All right, but look, don't tell me yes. You must begin to get used to the new you. Tell me, bowwow . . . bowwow! . . .

Second Actor: Does it crowd you here? (*The First Actor does not answer.*) Does it crowd you here?

First Actor: Bowwow . . . bowwow! . . .

Second Actor: Fine . . . (*He leaves.*)

First Actor: But that night it rained, and I had to get into the doghouse.

Second Actor: (*To the Third Actor*) It no longer crowds him . . .

Third Actor: And he is in the doghouse.

Second Actor: (*To the First Actor*) Did you see how one can get used to anything?

Actress: One gets used to anything . . .

Second and Third Actors: Amen . . .

Actress: And he did begin to get used to it.

Third Actor: Then, when you see someone come in, bark at me: bowwow . . . bowwow! Let's see . . .

First Actor: (*As the Second Actor runs past*) Bowwow . . . bowwow! (*The Second Actor passes by silently.*) Bowwow . . . wow . . . wow! (*First Actor leaves.*)

Third Actor: (*To the Second Actor*) It's ten pesos a day extra in our budget.

Second Actor: Hmmm!

Third Actor: . . . but the poor guy's so conscientious, he deserves them . . .

SECOND ACTOR: Hmmm!

THIRD ACTOR: Besides he doesn't eat any more than the dead one . . .

SECOND ACTOR: Hmmm!

THIRD ACTOR: We ought to help his family!

SECOND ACTOR: Hmmm! Hmmm! Hmmm!

(*They leave.*)

ACTRESS: Nevertheless, I found him very sad, and I tried to comfort him when he returned home. (*The* FIRST ACTOR *enters.*) We had visitors today! . . .

FIRST ACTOR: Really?

ACTRESS: The dances at the club, do you remember?

FIRST ACTOR: Yes.

ACTRESS: What was our tango?

FIRST ACTOR: I don't know.

ACTRESS: What do you mean, you don't know! "Love, you abandoned me . . . " (*The* FIRST ACTOR *is on all fours.*) And one day you brought me a carnation . . . (*She looks at him and is horrified.*) What are you doing?

The Man Who Turned into a Dog

FIRST ACTOR: What?

ACTRESS: You're on all fours . . . (*She leaves.*)

FIRST ACTOR: I can't bear this any more! I'm going to talk with the boss!

(*The* SECOND *and* THIRD ACTORS *enter.*)

THIRD ACTOR: The fact is that there's nothing available . . .

FIRST ACTOR: They told me that an old man died.

THIRD ACTOR: Yes, but we're on an austerity budget. Wait a little more time, huh?

ACTRESS: And he waited. He returned in three months.

FIRST ACTOR: (*To the* SECOND ACTOR) They told me that one guy retired . . .

SECOND ACTOR: Yes, but we intend to close that section. Wait a little more, huh?

ACTRESS: And he waited. He returned in two months.

FIRST ACTOR: (*To the* THIRD ACTOR) Give me the job of one of the guys you fired because of the strike . . .

THIRD ACTOR: Impossible. Their positions will remain unfilled . . .

SECOND AND THIRD ACTORS: As punishment! (*They leave.*)

FIRST ACTOR: Then I couldn't take any more . . . and I quit!

ACTRESS: It was our happiest night in a long time. (*She takes him by the arm.*) What's the name of this flower?

FIRST ACTOR: Flower . . .

ACTRESS: And what's the name of that star?

FIRST ACTOR: Maria.

ACTRESS: (*Laughing*) Maria's my name!

FIRST ACTOR: The star's too, the star's too. (*He takes her hand and kisses it.*)

ACTRESS: (*Pulls back her hand*) Don't bite me!

FIRST ACTOR: I wasn't going to bite you . . . I was going to kiss you, Maria . . .

ACTRESS: Ah! I thought that you were going to bite me . . .

(*She leaves. The* SECOND *and* THIRD ACTORS *enter.*)

SECOND ACTOR: Of course . . .

THIRD ACTOR: . . . and the next morning . . .

SECOND AND THIRD ACTORS: He had to look for a job again.

FIRST ACTOR: I went around to several places, until in one of them . . .

THIRD ACTOR: Look . . . we don't have anything. Except . . .

FIRST ACTOR: Except what?

THIRD ACTOR: Last night the watchman's dog died.

SECOND ACTOR: He was thirty-five, the poor wretch . . .

SECOND AND THIRD ACTORS: The poor wretch.

FIRST ACTOR: And I had to accept again.

SECOND ACTOR: We did pay him, fifteen pesos a day. (*The* SECOND *and* THIRD ACTORS *walk back and forth.*) Hmmm! . . . Hmmm! . . . Hmmm! . . .

SECOND AND THIRD ACTORS: All right, let it be fifteen! (*They leave.*)

ACTRESS: (*Enters*) Of course the four hundred and fifty pesos won't be enough for us to pay the rent . . .

FIRST ACTOR: Look, since I have the doghouse, move to a room with four or five other girls, all right?

ACTRESS: There's no other solution. And since your salary isn't even enough for us to eat on . . .

FIRST ACTOR: Look, since I've gotten used to bones, I'm going to bring the meat to you, all right?

SECOND AND THIRD ACTORS: (*Entering*) The board of directors agreed!

FIRST ACTOR AND ACTRESS: The board of directors agreed . . . hurrah for the board of directors!

(SECOND *and* THIRD ACTORS *leave.*)

FIRST ACTOR: I'd already gotten used to it. The doghouse seemed larger to me. Walking on all fours wasn't very different from walking upright. Maria and I would meet each other in the square . . . (*He goes towards her.*) You can't come into my doghouse, and since I can't come into your room . . . Until one night . . .

ACTRESS: We were walking. And suddenly I felt sick . . .

FIRST ACTOR: What's the matter with you?

ACTRESS: I feel sick.

FIRST ACTOR: How come?

ACTRESS: (*Weeping*) I think . . . that I'm going to have a baby . . .

FIRST ACTOR: And that's why you're crying?

ACTRESS: I'm afraid. . . , I'm afraid!

FIRST ACTOR: But, why?

ACTRESS: I'm afraid. . . , I'm afraid! I don't want to have a baby!

FIRST ACTOR: Why, Maria? Why?

ACTRESS: I'm afraid . . . that it will be . . . (*She whispers.*) "a dog."

(*The* FIRST ACTOR *looks at her terrified and leaves running and barking. She falls to the floor. She gets back up.*) He left . . . , he left running! Sometimes he'd stand up, and sometimes he'd run on all fours. . . .

FIRST ACTOR: It isn't true, I didn't stand up. I couldn't stand up! My back hurt me if I stood up! Bowwow! . . . Cars almost ran over me . . . People stared at me . . . (*The* SECOND *and* THIRD ACTORS *enter.*) Go away! Didn't you ever see a dog?

SECOND ACTOR: He's mad! Call a doctor! (*He leaves.*)

THIRD ACTOR: He's drunk! Call a policeman! (*He leaves.*)

ACTRESS: Later they told me that a man had pity on him and approached him kindly.

SECOND ACTOR: (*Entering*) Do you feel sick, friend? You can't remain on all fours. Do you know how many beautiful things there are to see, standing up, with your eyes turned upward? Let's see, stand up . . . I'll help you . . . Come on, stand up . . .

FIRST ACTOR: (*Beginning to stand up, when suddenly*) Bowwow . . . bowwow! . . . (*He bites the* SECOND ACTOR.) Bowwow . . . bowwow! . . . (*He leaves.*)

THIRD ACTOR: (*Entering*) Finally, when after two years without seeing him, we asked his wife, "How is he?" she answered . . .

ACTRESS: I don't know.

SECOND ACTOR: Is he all right?

ACTRESS: I don't know.

THIRD ACTOR: Is he sick?

ACTRESS: I don't know.

SECOND AND THIRD ACTORS: Where is he?

ACTRESS: In the dog pound.

THIRD ACTOR: And as we were coming here, a boxer passed by . . .

SECOND ACTOR: And they told us that he didn't know how to read, but that it didn't matter because he was a boxer.

THIRD ACTOR: And a draftee passed by . . .

ACTRESS: And a policeman passed by . . .

SECOND ACTOR: And they all passed by . . . , and they passed by . . . , and you passed by. And we thought that perhaps the story of our friend would matter to you.

ACTRESS: Because perhaps among you there may now be a woman who thinks: "Won't I have . . . , won't I have? (*She whispers.*) "A dog."

THIRD ACTOR: Or someone who's been offered the job of the night watchman's dog . . .

ACTRESS: If it isn't so, we're happy.

SECOND ACTOR: But if it's so, if there is someone among you whom others want to change into a dog, like our friend, then. . . .but well, then that . . . that's another story!

CURTAIN

After Words

1 In your journal, respond to the play. In what ways is the play fantastic? In what ways is it realistic and contemporary?

2 In a small group, discuss the man's motivation, his dilemma, and the effects of his actions.

3 In a small group, discuss the man's employers and their reasons for employing the man as they do. In role as the employers, present your reasons to the class.

4 a) What statement(s) does the playwright appear to be making? Give support from the play.

   b) Do you agree or disagree with the playwright? What examples from personal experience, daily life, and the media support your views? Present your views in a poster or a piece of writing.

5 Consider the playwright's experimental approach and its effects. What, for example, are the effects of actors speaking directly to the audience and of the "play-within-a-play" format? What alternative approaches could the playwright have used? What effect would each approach have?

6 In a small group, improvise, rehearse, and refine a sketch in which your school attempts to make an individualistic student conform to the rules. Present your sketch to the class.

The Exhibition

Scenes from the Life of John Merrick

A stage play by THOMAS GIBBONS

DURING his years at Villanova University in Pennsylvania, Thomas Gibbons read *The Elephant Man and Other Reminiscences* and began a journey. His journey led him to England, to delve into questions of appearance, identity, outcasts, objectification, humanity, and worth, and to write the following play. What intrigued Gibbons was the account by the distinguished British surgeon Frederick Treves (1853–1923) of his patient John Merrick (1860–1890), a man so distorted by neurofibromatosis that he had been exhibited as a freak—"half a man, half an elephant"—until Treves rescued him. Gibbons travelled to London where he saw John Merrick's skeleton, some of Merrick's possessions, and a pamphlet thought to be Merrick's autobiography. The first and last words in the play, and a few other passages, are direct quotations from the "autobiography." Gibbons drafted the play, titled *The Elephant Man*, for a playwriting seminar at Villanova. It was presented as a staged reading by The Philadelphia Company in 1977, and as a full-scale production in 1979. Gibbons changed the name to *The Exhibition* to avoid confusion with Bernard Pomerance's full-length play, *The Elephant Man*. A feature film, also called *The Elephant Man*, focuses on the life and times of John Merrick.

Prelude

1 We have beauty pageants and Mr. Universe contests. People spend fortunes on diets, health spas, and cosmetic surgery. Collect from the media examples of interest in physical appearance and/or write a journal entry examining why we place so much value on physical attractiveness.

2 A TV newscaster is fired for "no longer appearing attractive enough," in the words of the station's board of directors. Discuss the fairness of this situation.

The Exhibition

Characters

SIR FREDERICK TREVES: Surgeon, lecturer

THE ELEPHANT MAN: John Merrick

Scene One

Dark empty stage.

Lights come up. The ELEPHANT MAN *stands in center of stage. He wears a dark cloak-like garment extending to the floor. On his right hand is a glove; the left is bare. His head is covered by a black yachting cap from which hangs a white cloth mask with a hole for the left eye. In his left hand he carries a wooden walking stick.*

Silence.

ELEPHANT MAN: (*A recitation*) I first saw the light on the fifth of August, 1860. I was born in Lee Street, Wharf Street, Leicester. The deformity which I am now exhibiting was caused by my mother being frightened by an elephant; my mother was going along the street when a procession of animals were passing by, there was a terrible crush of people to see them, and unfortunately she was pushed under the elephant's feet, which frightened her very much: this occurring during a time of pregnancy was the cause of my deformity.

(*Lights fade. Lights come up downstage right.* TREVES *sits on a bench reading from a leatherbound journal. He is seventy years old.*)

TREVES: This is how it began. It was a November afternoon in 1884. A late hour. Pale, dwindling autumn light. (*Quietly*) I was just thirty years old, so full of confidence. (*Pause*) I happened to pass by a vacant greengrocer's, on the Whitechapel road.

(*He reads from the journal.*)

"The whole of the front of the shop, with the exception of the door, was hidden by a hanging sheet of canvas on which was the announcement that the Elephant Man was to be seen within and that the price of admission

The Exhibition

was twopence. Painted on the canvas in primitive colors was a life-size portrait of the Elephant Man. This very crude production depicted a frightful creature that could only have been possible in a nightmare. It was the figure of a man with the characteristics of an elephant."

(*He pauses, obscurely disturbed; continues*)

"The transfiguration was not far advanced. There was still more of the man than of the beast. This fact—that it was still human—was the most repellent attribute of the creature. There was nothing about it of the pitiableness of the misshapened or the deformed, nothing of the grotesqueness of the freak, but merely—(*Turns page*)—the loathsome insinuation of a man being changed into an animal. Some palm trees in the background of the picture suggested a jungle and might have led the imaginative to assume that it was in this wild that the perverted object had roamed."

(*He lowers the journal, closes his eyes.*)

The exhibition was closed. I sent a boy round to find the showman. After a while he came; reeking of liquor. "I should like to see this Elephant Man," I said. "A shilling for a private showing, sir." I gave it. We entered. Cold, damp. On a shelf, some old tins, a few shriveled potatoes. At the end of the shop was a curtain. (*Gestures*) He pulled it back . . .

(*He reads.*)

"The showman pulled back the curtain and revealed a bent figure crouching on a stool and covered by a brown blanket. In front of it, on a tripod, was a large brick heated by a Bunsen burner. Over this the creature was huddled to warm itself. It never moved when the curtain was drawn back."

(*He pauses, turns the page.*)

"Outside the sun was shining and one could hear the footsteps of the passers-by, a tune whistled by a boy and the companionable hum of traffic in the road." (*Quietly, not reading*) Innocuous sunlight. Hiding *him* all the while.

(*Pause. He reads.*)

"The showman—speaking as if to a dog—called out harshly: `Stand up!' The thing arose slowly and let the blanket that covered its head and back fall to the ground. There stood revealed the most disgusting specimen of humanity that I have ever seen."

(*He stops again. Lights come up on the* ELEPHANT MAN *upstage left.*)

"The most striking feature about him was his enormous and misshapened head." (*He shapes the deformities with precise gestures.*) "From the brow there projected a huge bony mass like a loaf, while from the back of the skull hung a bag of spongy, fungus-looking skin. On the top of the skull, a few lank hairs. The osseous growth on the forehead almost occluded one eye. From the upper jaw there projected another mass of bone. The nose was merely a lump of flesh." (*With growing agitation*) "The face was no more capable of expression than a block of gnarled wood. The right arm was of enormous size and shapeless. The hand was large and clumsy—a fin or paddle rather than a hand. From the chest hung a bag of the same repulsive flesh . . . like a dewlap suspended from the neck of a lizard—"

(*He lowers the journal, distraught.*)

ELEPHANT MAN: My deformity was not perceived much at birth, but began to develop itself when at the age of five years. I went to school like other children, until I was about eleven or twelve years of age, when the greatest misfortune of my life occurred, namely—the death of my mother . . . (*Dwindling*) Peace to her, she was a good mother to me . . .

(*He fades back into the darkness.*)

TREVES: (*Composed now, places journal on bench*) From the showman, I learnt nothing about the Elephant Man except that he was English, and that his name was John Merrick. As at the time of my discovery of the Elephant Man I was the Lecturer on Anatomy at the Medical College, I was anxious to examine him in detail and to prepare an account of his abnormalities. Therefore, I arranged for him to come to my room at the college, where I exhibited him to the Pathological Society of London. (*Pause*) After an interesting discussion the meeting was adjourned. I returned him in a cab to the place of exhibition, and assumed that I had seen the last of him. (*Pause; quietly*) The next day I found that the shop was empty. The show had been closed by the police. He had vanished, completely.

(*Silence*)

Two years passed. One day I was summoned by the police to the Liverpool Street Station. In a waiting room there, surrounded by a curious mob, I found Merrick, exhausted and starving. (*With astonishment*) He had given the police a calling card.

(*The card is in the journal. He holds it up.*)

My card. I'd given it to him at that first meeting. Two years before.

(*Lights come up on the* ELEPHANT MAN, *huddled on the floor. With his left hand he extends the card.*)

ELEPHANT MAN: (*Weakly*) The measurement round the head is thirty-six inches,

The Exhibition

there is a large substance of flesh at the back as large as a breakfast cup, while the face is such a sight that no one could describe it. The right hand measures twelve inches round the wrist and five inches round one of the fingers. The feet and legs are covered with thick lumpy skin, also the body, like that of an elephant . . .

(*Lights fade.*)

TREVES: I drove him at once to the hospital and installed him in an isolation ward in the attic. (*Pause*) I realized that a place must be found for him, and made inquiries. From the Royal Hospital for Incurables: no. From the British Home for Incurables: no. Not even if someone were to pay for him. (*Pause*) What choice did I have? It was clear that he had no place to go. I decided to keep him at the hospital. This was irregular; the hospital was not a refuge for incurables; but I would not abandon him a second time. The chairman of the committee wrote to *The Times* to appeal for funds.

(*He unfolds a faded newspaper clipping and reads.*)

"Sir—I am authorized to ask your powerful assistance in bringing to the notice of the public the following most exceptional case. There is now in a little room off one of our attic wards a man named John Merrick"—and so on and so on to the appeal. (*Reads*) "The Master of the Temple on Advent Sunday preached an eloquent sermon on the subject of our Master's answer to the question, 'Who did sin, this man or his parents, that he was born blind?' showing how one of the Creator's objects in permitting men to be born to a life of hopeless and miserable disability was that the works of God should be manifested in evoking the sympathy and kindly aid of those on whom such a heavy cross is not laid."

(*He places the clipping in the journal.*)

Our faith in the generosity of the English public was not misplaced. In a week enough money was forthcoming to maintain Merrick for life without any charge upon the hospital funds. (*Pause*) Thus the Elephant Man came to live at the London Hospital.

(*Lights come up on the* ELEPHANT MAN, *standing at center of stage. Upstage, slightly left, is a life-size poster of the* ELEPHANT MAN: *a crude exaggerated depiction, garishly colored. Hanging in front of the poster is a curtain—as* TREVES *describes it, "a red tablecloth suspended from a cord by a few rings."*

Downstage, to the left, a small table on which stands a detailed model of St. Philip's Church in London. Next to it, a candle and extinguisher.

Silence.)

ELEPHANT MAN: I've just been out walking in the garden. Alone. Treves allowed me to go. What an adventure! It's a moonless night . . . of course. Otherwise it would not have been permitted. (*Pause*) I went down to the hedge and listened to the people passing by in the street. Courting couples. (*Elegiac*) Women's laughter, their soft voices! (*Quietly*) Prostitutes from Whitechapel. I have no illusions about them. Having lived there for a time. (*Pause*) Actually . . . I remember little about that time in my life. The gaslight shining through the window. The people. When he showed me, he turned the lamps down. The only light was supplied by a single candle, flickering at my feet. To heighten the effect. (*Strident showman's voice*) Ask yourselves, ladies and gentleman: Where does he come from? (*Quietly*) Gazing at me in the mysterious light. (*Showman's voice*) You're a mystery, Merrick! (*Muses*) He said that to me quite often. A mystery. I could not speak very well then. I answered him rarely.

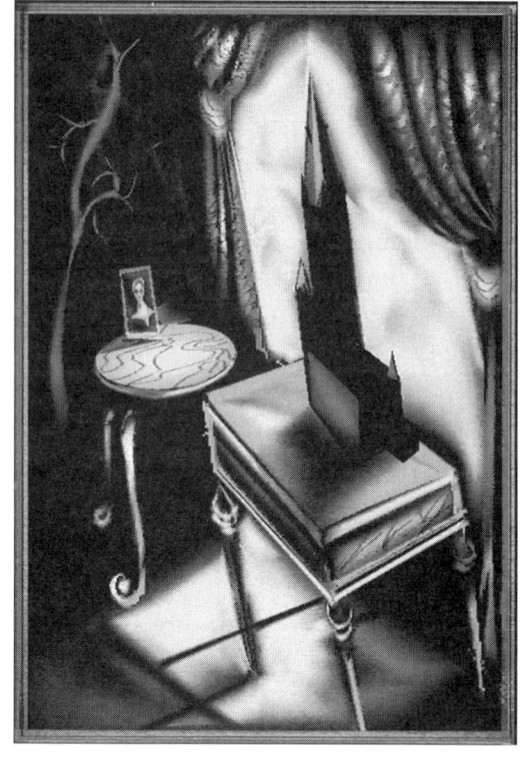

(*He lapses into silence, takes a few shuffling steps.*)

It was not what I expected. To be out in the garden, alone. Treves used to send a nurse with me. That's over now, I suppose. Not that there was anything. He never sent the same nurse. No chance for . . . attachments to develop. As if they would. No. Anything that happens, will happen only— (*Touches mask*)—within me. (*Pause*) But one needs a presence to build on. Sometimes, walking in the garden with the nurse at my side, it almost seems . . . If I forget certain facts: that this is a hospital, that she is a trained nurse, that I wear this . . . (*Touches mask*) In the end there are too many things to be forgotten.

(*Silence. Suddenly, muted churchbells pealing. He moves to the table at left, points to the model with his walking stick.*)

The Exhibition

I am not without my recreations. I built this model with my left hand alone. St. Philip's Church. I can see it from my window. (*Hesitantly*) There's a game I play . . .

(*He lights the candle, kneels behind the table. Extending the candle across the table, he slowly raises it up over the model.*)

Once I saw the sun rise like this over St. Philip's. God's fire, hanging over his house. (*Pause. Somber*) I was lying in the street. In a state of utter exhaustion. It was the end. Mud-covered, too tired to feel the indignity any longer, the humiliation. I had lost whatever humanity I possessed. No longer thought it precious, no longer cared. (*Pause*) Then the sun rose. A flame over the spire. I went in and lay down in one of the pews. It was dark. Quiet. I must have slept. A noise awakened me: two priests attending to their duties. (*His voice quickens.*) I hid in a dark alcove. Watching. Soon people began to come in. They did not see me. They knelt and prayed. I heard voices whispering somewhere. Telling of terrible deeds, terrible thoughts. The sins of man. One by one they went to their confessions. And were forgiven.

(*Silence. He extinguishes the candle. Lights come up instantly on* TREVES, *downstage right.*)

TREVES: (*Rapid, unemotional*) My life, now, soon to end, after seventy years: the essentials. Born 1853, educated in London. 1875, house surgeon at the London Hospital. Assistant surgeon four years later, full surgeon by 1884. Lecturer in Anatomy, Lecturer in Surgery until 1897. In 1898, resigned to devote full time to private practice. In 1900 appointed Surgeon Extraordinary to Queen Victoria. 1901, Knight Commander of the Victorian Order. In 1902, I saved Edward the Seventh; created a Baronet, promoted to Grand Commander of the Order. Retired in 1908. Married in 1877; by my wife Anne—two daughters; one dead. Why was he born into such pain? (*Pause. Quietly*) To never touch, or be touched. To know yourself hideous, malformed, a thing that scalds vision . . . (*Perplexed*) And yet . . . I find a beauty in that. A beauty that blinds. Am I wrong? To see beauty in him?

(*Lights fade slowly. Silence. Lights come up on the* ELEPHANT MAN.)

ELEPHANT MAN: People seem to think that I do not understand their feelings when they first see me. Their horror, their outrage. But there was a time when I first saw myself, first saw my face, and had to accept the fact that this was *me*. Of course I could see the arms, legs, the rest. And of course I touched myself. Felt myself. But touch is deceiving. And perhaps I used— (*Holds up gloved hand*)—the wrong hand. I thought I was human. I took it on faith. But I could not see the face. I always assumed the face was normal; the face at least, I thought. (*Pause*) But that ended the first time I found a mirror. I was thirteen, I believe. Placed in a workhouse to labor at some useless, forgotten task. My peculiar virginity was that I had never in my short life encountered a mirror. People always withheld them from me, or hid them in my presence. One day, though . . . *I saw.* (*Pause*) It was late. Most of the men had gone home. I remained behind for the night . . . I always waited for night to fall before venturing into the streets. I passed by the foreman's room. He was gone. The door was ajar. No one looking. I was alone. A small room: clothes, a bed, trunks. I lit a candle, began to search for the mirror I knew he must have, that everyone had but me. (*With growing agitation*) I threw clothes aside—not here, not here! I had to know. In the back, a curtain. He'll be back soon. I grabbed it—

(*He grasps curtain hanging in front of poster.*)

Draw it aside!

(*Pulls curtain aside, sees the garish, cruel, portrait. Stricken*)

Light! The mirror burst into light! All around me was light. And I saw—*I saw!* Gnarled head. Bone exploding out over the eye. The face . . . the twisted body. *My* body, *mine.* Me. All—

(*In anguish he collapses. Silence. His hands cover the mask. Long pause. Finally he lowers his hands. He draws up his legs, encircles them with his arms, places his head against his knees. Pause. Quietly*)

Treves does not allow mirrors here. It does not matter. I have seen it. It is burned in my brain. (*Pause. Bleak*) The doctors tell me my head is growing heavier and heavier. The progress of the disease. For quite a while now I have found it impossible to sleep in a normal position. It sinks into the pillow; it bends on the stalk. They tell me its weight might dislocate my neck. Instantaneous death. (*Pause*) Sometimes, at night, in bed, I think I feel the bone growing. Blossoming farther out of its proper shape. The skull becoming ever more convoluted. (*Pause. Whispers*) Must I grow more monstrous?

(*Silence. He huddles on floor. Lights fade very slowly.*
Lights come up on TREVES)

TREVES: Some notes I took, after I'd seen him, that first time; what I sensed in him at first glimpse. (*Lifts journal, reads*) "He had no past to look back upon and no future to look forward to. At the age of twenty he was a creature without hope. There was nothing in front of him but a vista of caravans creeping along a road, of rows of glaring show tents and of circles of staring eyes . . ." (*Lowers journal. Quietly, self-mocking for a moment*) That's what I delivered him from. (*Urgently*) But there was so much more that I wanted to give to him: the world in all its joy and beauty . . . I wanted him to get accustomed to his fellowmen, to become a human being himself and to be admitted to the communion of his kind. (*Pause. Very seriously*) I wanted to . . . reclaim him for the human race.

(*Silence. Slow fading of lights.*)

Scene Two

A small garden on the grounds of the London Hospital. Early 1887. Lights come up to reveal the ELEPHANT MAN *sitting on a bench, center stage. Twilight. Silence.*

TREVES: (*Calling, off*) John!

(*The* ELEPHANT MAN *looks around but does not answer.* TREVES *enters at right.*)

TREVES: Hello, John.

ELEPHANT MAN: Hello, Doctor.

TREVES: May I see your left arm, please? (*The* ELEPHANT MAN *extends his arm.* TREVES *rolls up the sleeve, examines.*) John, do you like living here at the hospital?

ELEPHANT MAN: Yes. (*Gratefully*) I am happy . . . every hour of the day.

TREVES: I'm glad. (*Examines, touches the arm clinically*) Very good. No sign of diseased tissue. Quite flawless. (*Rolls down the sleeve*) Thank you, John. (*Pause*) I have a surprise for you. You have visitors.

ELEPHANT MAN: (*Apprehensive*) Who?

TREVES: I've invited some people to meet you.

ELEPHANT MAN: Please . . . send them away.

TREVES: Now, John, they're rather eager to make your acquaintance.

ELEPHANT MAN: I would rather not see anyone.

TREVES: I think the company would do you some good. (*Pause*) You need to become accustomed to people. No one here wants to harm you.

(*Pause. The* ELEPHANT MAN *indicates the garden with his left hand.*)

ELEPHANT MAN: What do you see here, Doctor?

TREVES: (*Puzzled*) Nothing. (*Smiles*) A garden.

ELEPHANT MAN: I see . . . a circus. (*Pause*) I was told once that my mother, while bearing me . . . had something happen to her. (*Simply*) That she went to a circus and was knocked down by an elephant. (*Muses*) I see the creature, sometimes, in my dreams. Standing over her in triumph, trumpeting into the night. The image of the elephant entered her and passed into her womb. (*Intensely*) How frightened she must have been! As she lay on the ground, the lights, the noise, the hue of the circus passed through her senses and into mine. (*Pause*) My original memories are of the circus.

TREVES: (*Patiently, as if to a child*) We used to believe that was possible—to be impressed in the womb. There is a poetry to it. But we know now it is not the true explanation.

ELEPHANT MAN: It *is* very strange, for, you see, mother was so beautiful.

TREVES: (*Gently*) I'm sure she was, John.

(*Pause*)

ELEPHANT MAN: (*Hesitantly*) Doctor . . . when I am next moved, can I go to a blind asylum? (*Softly*) They would know only the sound of my voice. Strange things might happen there . . . wonderful things. (*Touches mask*) I could burn this. (*Quickly*) Or to a lighthouse? I saw a photograph of the Eddystone lighthouse once. I could stay there. John Merrick, keeper of the Eddystone lighthouse. (*Excited, pointing*) Sea captains would rejoice: There's Merrick's light! Thank God for Merrick!

TREVES: You won't be moved again, John. You have a home here. The people of London have opened their hearts to you. (*Pause; gently*) This is your home now.

(*Pause*)

ELEPHANT MAN: (*Wondering*) A home? A place of peace. (*Timidly*) Have I found that?

TREVES: (*Finds himself moved by this*) A whole new life is opening for you, my friend.

ELEPHANT MAN: (*Quiet, rapid*) In Whitechapel they came in carriages to see me. Gaslight through the window. Carriages passing back and forth outside. Rattling away across the cobblestones. They kept moving me on, never let me rest. Always carriages, trains, movement.

TREVES: (*Consoling*) That's all over now, John. Why dwell on it? Everything has changed. (*Pause*) Let me bring your visitors here.

The Exhibition

ELEPHANT MAN: Who are they?

TREVES: Friends of mine. I've told them about you. They want to be your friends.

ELEPHANT MAN: The showman was my friend.

(*Pause*)

TREVES: John, listen to me. I know what your life has been like, and I understand your feelings. You have been given nothing but hardship and cruelty. I want to show you that there is kindness, too, and pleasure. People can give you these. Later on I'll bring my wife to see you. And our little girls. Would you like that?

ELEPHANT MAN: (*Softly*) Once, I remember . . . I saw a woman with a child in her arms. How easily it rested there! (*Pause*) No child would ever come to me.

(*Pause*)

TREVES: You mustn't keep your visitors waiting. I'll bring them here.

(*He turns to go.*)

ELEPHANT MAN: (*Puts his hands to his eyes*) There is a tangible force emitted by the eyes. And I can feel it. (TREVES, *halted by this, turns back*) As I stood there in the small circle of light . . . displaying myself . . . I would register the various pressures and sort them out. Children's stares were timid and wondering. Not hard to bear. Men were different. Their eyes bored into me, brutal and hard. (*Pause*) But women's eyes were worse— oh, much the worst! Such absolute horror. (*Angrily*) Cast him out, I can't look at him, throw him out, into the trash-heap, into the night! (*Pause. Quietly*) Sometimes, when they had gone, I would gaze at my body. Amazed that I wasn't bleeding from a hundred wounds.

(*A long pause.* TREVES *is silent. The* ELEPHANT MAN *turns to him.*)

Send me to a blind asylum. Please!

TREVES: (*Gently*) John, to be accepted there . . . would mean nothing.

(*Pause*)

ELEPHANT MAN: Then bring them in, Doctor. It is not my place to deny them. I am supported on public funds.

(TREVES *hesitates, then goes out right. Silence. It is quite dark now. Quietly*)

Home. Here? I would rather it be the blind asylum. Does Treves comprehend this: This love of the deformed for the blind? (*Pause. He spreads his hands to the garden.*) This is your home. Can I believe that? (*Pause*) Now he will have them in at me. As before. But how can I say to *him*: You are diminished in my eyes. You are . . . disfigured.

(*Silence. He looks round the garden.*)

We traveled across Europe in a wagon which had painted on one side, in red letters: The Great Freak of Nature; on the other, Half a Man and Half an Elephant. When we came to a town the showman would pull up the wagon and hire a few men to erect our tent. From the inside of the wagon I would listen to them shout as they hauled on the ropes. And watch the tent rise up, again. At dusk he would set torches round the tent. The people would gather. And I sat inside, waiting for the exhibition to begin.

(*Silence. He sits without moving in the garden. Suddenly, upstage right, a door opens; a shaft of light shoots across the stage and strikes him.*)

Scene Three

November, 1889.

Darkness.

TREVES: (*Voice only*) "It was not until I came to know that Merrick was highly intelligent, that he possessed an acute sensibility, and—worse than all—a romantic imagination, that I realized the overwhelming tragedy of his life."

(*Lights come up on* TREVES *sitting on bench downstage right. The journal is open in his hands.*)

TREVES: (*In a reverie*) The sky above was the deepest blue . . . The sea within the reef was a wondrous green . . . The air was heavy with the smell of the sea . . . (*Pause*) In November of 1889, I arranged for Merrick to take a holiday in the country. He passed two weeks there in green seclusion.

(*Pause. Muses*)

I often ask myself: Was I as kind to him as I could have been? Perhaps I could have done more, something to—(*Falters*) Perhaps the kindest thing would have been to find some . . . woman, from Whitechapel, and bring her to his room one night, give her enough drink, and when she was insensible, unaware, bring him in from some dark corner and . . . let him. (*Pause*) Awful thought: to use a woman in that way. But at least he would have had some knowledge of the transactions of the flesh. Just one moment to last him for life! Did he want that? Oh, I saw his eyes when regal ladies came to visit. He was amorous, he would like to have been a lover . . . (*Pause*) Would he even have known what to do? The simple mechanics of the act? Once I *saw him weep when a woman merely shook his hand. What did touch mean to him?*

(*Pause. He lifts the journal, reads.*)

"Merrick's case attracted much attention in the papers, with the result that he has a constant succession of visitors. The Merrick whom I had found shivering behind a rag of a curtain in an empty shop was now conversant with duchesses and countesses and ladies of high degree." (*Pause; quietly*) He became the pet of the nobility.

(*Lights come up on the* ELEPHANT MAN, *seated in a chair at center stage. His cloak is new, of richer and more colorful material than the first; but around this he has wrapped a white bedsheet. In the intervening three years his head has grown considerably and is now hidden behind a larger mask. At upstage left there is a coat-stand, on which hangs a magnificent opera cape.*)

TREVES: (*Approaching him*) John. Some of your society friends are here.

ELEPHANT MAN: I will not see them.

TREVES: (*Concerned*) What's wrong? You have refused all of your visitors for the past three days.

ELEPHANT MAN: I will not see them.

TREVES: It is unhealthy to shut yourself away like this.

ELEPHANT MAN: Did you know, Doctor: on my birth certificate the space for my father's name is left blank. I've had to create myself. Manufacture a past. I'm like a character left unfinished by its author. Before he could give me my whole history he abandoned me. Or renounced his writing. Or died.

(*Pause*)

TREVES: What am I to say to your visitors? They are concerned about you.

(*The* ELEPHANT MAN *stands.*)

ELEPHANT MAN: (*With deep yearning*) To walk alone the sweet bright earth . . . with no fear. To stand with no mask in the light of the sun. In the deep country . . .

TREVES: What happened there? What happened in the country?

ELEPHANT MAN: I stood in a field and watched the sun set through the dark trees. I said to myself: I am away from them now, away from all the eyes. (*Intensely*) If I could have died in that instant! (*Quietly*) But I could not end myself like that—a hateful thing dying off in a field.

(*Pause*)

TREVES: (*Gently, hands outstretched to room*) John . . . your place in the world is here.

ELEPHANT MAN: The showman wrote a speech for me once. A spiel. To be delivered the moment I let the cloak fall. (*He lets the sheet drop to the floor.*) "I first saw the light on the fifth of August, 1860 . . ." When you brought me here I thought I'd found peace. You said: "People will grow accustomed to you." But the exhibition never ends. Their hatred grows heavier and heavier upon me.

TREVES: (*Distressed*) That's not true. No one hates you here. I took you away from the hatred.

ELEPHANT MAN: When dusk came to Whitechapel I would go to the window and look into the street. The women would stand beneath the gas lamps . . . the men drift in like dogs. And the sales would be made. All night long, the gleam of coins. (*Pause*) Once, a couple, drunk, stumbled into my shop . . . I watched from behind the curtain. Appalled.

(*Pause*)

TREVES: (*Baffled, calming*) John . . . you must forget that time. Your life has changed since then. Completely. But you must put those days behind you. You only hurt yourself. (*Pause*) I know there seems to be no purpose in your suffering.

(*Pause*)

ELEPHANT MAN: Do you remember when you first found me, Doctor? (TREVES *does not answer.*) You exhibited me to the Pathological Society of London. And then sent me back to the exhibition.

(*Pause*)

TREVES: John—

ELEPHANT MAN: (*Interrupting*) You asked me to come to your room at the College. (*Pause*) I remember how astounded I was by this invitation. This intervention. You interviewed me for an hour. I was awed. And frightened. But how kind you were, how concerned. I could not speak very well then. I made very little sense. But you listened. You smiled and nodded. And then sent me away, thinking me an imbecile.

TREVES: (*Defensive*) I realize it is no excuse, but . . . you gave me no reason to believe otherwise. (*Quickly*) I know that is harsh.

ELEPHANT MAN: The same night I was back on exhibition.

(*Pause*)

TREVES: (*Quietly*) That is the great shame of my life. That I did not see . . .

ELEPHANT MAN: (*Oblivious*) With nothing to remember you by but your name printed on a few calling cards.

The Exhibition

(*He holds up several cards.*)

TREVES: Where did you get them?

ELEPHANT MAN: I took them from your desk that day.

TREVES: I went back to the greengrocer's the following day. The police had closed it up. There was no trace of you. (*Pause*) I did go back!

ELEPHANT MAN: Doctor Frederick Treves. (*Intensely*) How I treasured the name! (TREVES *is silent.*) I thought you were my saviour. At the exhibition that night I dropped my cloak proudly. (*Rages*) The buffoons gaped at me! (*Softly*) I felt like shouting at them, joyously: I have been saved. I am saved! (*He lets one of the cards fall to the floor.*) Then the authorities closed the show down. We had to move on. This show's immoral, they said. Indecent. (*Lets a card fall*) Inhuman. (*Pause*) As if they knew what inhuman was. (*Pause*) Finally there was nowhere to go but the Continent. Then it was hard. We were foreigners, we starved. (*Lets card fall*) But I never lost my faith in you, Doctor. I was certain that Treves would come one glorious day. Out of a flaming sky. To take me away from it: the hunger, the crowds, all of it!

(*He lapses into silence, stares at the cards in his hands. After a moment he lets another fall.*)

I waited for you, Doctor. Through all the wandering, all the exhibitions. I dropped my cloak a thousand times . . . saw ten thousand women turn away in disgust. We wandered on, all over the Continent, the days ran together, little towns, strange languages. And I waited for you, Doctor. I knew that someone had been kind to me once. Had spoken to me. (*Lets a card fall*) I waited. (*Slowly*) For two years. (*Anguished*) Two years! (*Pause*) Finally, in Brussels, the showman abandoned me. I had become a burden to him. One night, as I slept, he stole the little I'd managed to save from our earnings . . . and left. When I awoke, no showman. No food, no money. Nothing left. (*He lets the last card fall and holds up his empty hands*) And still there was no Treves.

(*Silence.* TREVES *takes a few steps toward him, stops.*)

TREVES: (*Shaken, quietly*) John. Haven't I helped you? Perhaps, once, I was mistaken . . . (*He spreads his hands.*) But surely this is better than what you had. (*The* ELEPHANT MAN *regards him silently. Imploring*) John!

(*The* ELEPHANT MAN *moves to the coatstand upstage left, and drapes the opera cape around his shoulders.* TREVES *walks slowly back to the bench downstage right. A silence*)

TREVES: Merrick loved to imagine himself a dandy and a young man about town.

The Elephant Man became, in the seclusion of his chamber, the young spark, the Piccadilly exquisite. The rake, the gentleman of London. (*Pause*) He invented for himself a second life, and entertained me for hours with tales of amorous conquests, triumphs at the gambling tables, hectic revelries that lasted until dawn. The pursuits of a young aristocrat. All the while sitting furled in his opera cape, a gift from visitors. He told me of a life of pleasure, indulgence, sin. (*Quietly*) And I assisted him in this illusion. I assented.

(*The* ELEPHANT MAN *comes downstage, resplendent in his cape. On his ungloved left hand he wears several large rings. He grasps a silver walking stick.*)

ELEPHANT MAN: (*Grandly*) Good evening, Dr. Treves.

TREVES: (*Bowing*) Good evening, John.

ELEPHANT MAN: (*Extends his left hand*) I purchased a new ring this morning.

TREVES: It is very beautiful.

ELEPHANT MAN: Thank you. To adorn myself . . . is all I have left to me now. (*Pause*) I have been out walking along the river. Reliving old memories.

TREVES: (*Smiling*) Yes, that can be very pleasant.

ELEPHANT MAN: The people I've known . . . the moments I have had. I led a life of such privilege and light. The graces of civilization. (*With deep sadness*) But all that is closed to me now. For me there can be no more friendship, music . . . touch.

TREVES: (*Disturbed by the sadness in this*) Why no more, John?

(*Pause*)

ELEPHANT MAN: Something happened to me . . . a long time ago. When my life was so different. Something I have never told anyone. But I would like to tell you, Doctor.

TREVES: Yes. I will listen.

ELEPHANT MAN: I was not always like this. Not always—(*Indicates his body*)—this ruin. (*Pause*) I lived for many years in society.

TREVES: Society, yes.

ELEPHANT MAN: Yet all that time haunted by a question: Was there nothing that went deeper, to the very core of my life? Nothing but that barren journey through society? I was attracted to waste and emptiness. Loneliness fascinated me. I wanted to burn away all desire for love, all the need to touch. (*Pause*) One night I walked alone through the streets of London. I went

The Exhibition

down to the river and looked out across the water . . . at the lights of society. No voice spoke to me, no hand touched me. I felt, for the first time, the enormous beauty . . . of being apart from my own kind.

(*Pause*)

That was the beginning of the Great Experiment of Solitude. I ended all contact with others. Became, in my heart, a creature of ice. Seeking to create . . . endless loneliness. (*Pause*) I wanted to record the agony of a figure lost in an empty landscape. I knew that the figure in the landscape would be my own. That I would have to create in the midst of emptiness. Inhabit the emptiness without . . . dissolving into it.

(*Pause. He sits; no longer addressing* TREVES; *lost in a private pain.*)

I was dying in the desert of my own making but I *would not* cry for help. I made of my destruction a test of human kindness. If love existed, I would be saved. From myself, from my own silence. (*Pause*) But perhaps there exists a race of souls who never find love on this earth. The blame is not theirs. Love is not infinite. Someone must settle for solitude. (*With profound pain*) I made of my life . . . a wasteland.

(*Silence. In the darkness* TREVES *sits listening. After a moment the* ELEPHANT MAN *begins again to speak, in a new voice: rapid and flat, almost a chant.*)

One night I awoke in the grip of a strange fever. I went to the mirror and looked at my face. The skin had grown thick and rough, like the hide of a beast; it twisted into such a sight no one could describe. I raised my hand that was no longer a hand, a fin or paddle rather than a hand.

I went into the street. A storm had begun; the rain thundered down on me. I ran through the streets crying for help. The sounds from my throat were awkward and without meaning. The city was empty. All life had vanished. I stumbled down to the river and collapsed on the bank. My flesh was burning, I could feel the rending of my bones.

I dragged myself to the water and tried to drink. In a flash of lightning I saw that the river had gone dry. The city had become a famished desert of stone. I lay on my back with my mouth gaping to the rain, and I watched as my body became, finally, inhuman. Then a voice spoke to me—no, not spoke, but made itself known, like a voice in a dream: Your loneliness is a crime. You have withdrawn from humanity. The mark of your solitude has been set upon you. Take up the mask and cover your face. You are an outcast now in the eyes of men. (*Anguished*) A monster that will never find love or peace, a freak no human will ever touch! You will spend your life in a place of exhibition! Exhibition—

The Exhibition

(*He falls to the floor, convulses.* TREVES *crosses the stage, tears the cape from the* ELEPHANT MAN, *flings it away.*)

TREVES: John—what you say is not true! You are none of these things. No one is such an outcast. No one is such a monster. (*Intensely*) In every man, no matter how different—at some level, there is belonging.

ELEPHANT MAN: (*Screams*) At what level do I belong? Where can I say to men: I am like you, I am one of you?

TREVES: You are human. You have a soul, that I have seen. (*Spreads his hands*) In this place you are not strange. To *me*, not strange.

ELEPHANT MAN: (*Desperately*) Frederick! You have taken me into this hospital, into your life. Yet . . . to admit me so far . . . but no further—

TREVES: But—I have given you . . .

(*The* ELEPHANT MAN *kneels painfully before him, reaches out his left hand.*)

ELEPHANT MAN: (*Pleading*) If someone would *touch* me, I'd be human . . . for a moment. Please! The way a father does touch his son.

(*Silence, as* TREVES *comprehends what is being asked of him. The* ELEPHANT MAN *grasps his hand, brings it toward his face. With his right hand he begins to remove the mask. But at the last instant* TREVES *pulls his hand away—and immediately realizes what he has done: his failure.*)

TREVES: (*Shocked, quietly*) I cannot.

(*The* ELEPHANT MAN *lowers his mask: sinks back, turns away. Silence.* TREVES *starts to speak, says nothing.*)

ELEPHANT MAN: (*Softly*) I am sorry . . .

(*Pause*)

TREVES: (*Faltering*) John. I am . . . your friend. (*With great difficulty*) Forgive me.

(*Pause*)

ELEPHANT MAN: (*Quietly*) Give me your hand, Doctor. (*Pause.* TREVES *hesitates.*) Don't worry. Your hand.

(TREVES *extends his hand. The Elephant man begins to remove the rings from his left hand and place them in* TREVES' *hand.*)

TREVES: (*Tries to pull his hand away*) What are you doing?

ELEPHANT MAN: (*Giving him the rings.*) They gave me rings and walking sticks, diamond stickpins and pretty photographs to surround myself with. They said to me: "John, take them, you can be like us, you can be one of us." And I took them. (*He releases* TREVES' *hand.*) My last showman stole everything I owned. But I give these to you.

(*Silence.* TREVES *turns away, takes a few steps.*)

TREVES: (*To himself, an intense whisper*) Should I have turned you away that day? (*He looks at the rings in his hand. Pause. Quietly*) I think I shall go home now. It is late. Anne will worry.

ELEPHANT MAN: Yes. Go home, Doctor. Go home to your wife and children.

(*Silence:* TREVES *holds out the rings.*)

TREVES: These are not mine. Take them.

(*Silence. The* ELEPHANT MAN *does not take them.* TREVES *places them quietly on the floor next to him. Pause*)

Goodnight, John.

(*There is no answer. He hesitates, then goes out right. Silence. With his walking stick the* ELEPHANT MAN *sweeps the rings across the stage. Pause*)

ELEPHANT MAN: (*Quietly, remote, a recitation*) When I was fifteen I went into the infirmary at Leicester, where I remained for two or three years, when I had to undergo an operation on my face, having three of four ounces of flesh cut away; so thought I, I'll get my living by being exhibited about the country.

Scene Four

1923

Lights come up slowly. TREVES *sits on the bench downstage right. Also on the bench are his journal, the walking stick and mask of the* ELEPHANT MAN.

A pale cold light.

TREVES: (*Quietly*) Exhibition: exhibit . . . exhibitor. (*Pause*) Did I ever help him?

(*Silence. He stares at the ground*)

I did quite a lot of traveling after I retired. That was in 1908. (*Softly*) He had been dead a long time by then. (*Slight pause*) The first place I went to was Europe. I knew he had been there. He often took great pleasure in describing to me the scenes he remembered. A street in Paris; a tiny village somewhere; a landscape glimpsed from a moving cart . . . Fragments. Was I trying to retrace his wanderings . . . that long trail of humiliation? (*Pause*) In every city, each town or village we paused in, I wondered: Did they stop here? Was the exhibition held here? I looked into the eyes of the people. Had they been in the audience? Paid to see him, long ago? Did they remember him? I could not bring myself to ask. One night it occurred to me: What an unholy pilgrimage this had become. I had brought the exhibition with me. The exhibition was in me, in the image of him that I carried. I was the exhibition.

(*He falls silent again.*)

After that I went on, in a fever of wandering. I fled to lands he had never seen. Where the question "Was the exhibition here?" could not possibly be asked. Searching . . . (*Genuinely uncertain*) For what? All I found was a world emptied of his presence. (*Calmly*) Finally I came . . . to a place of the heart's silence, that I have never left.

(*He pauses for a moment. When he speaks his voice is tranquil, and he extends a hand as if to touch what he describes.*)

The sky above was the deepest blue, while upon the reef the surf broke in a line of white. The sea within the reef was a wondrous green . . . In the distance, where the small cliff ended, there came a beach, curved like a sickle, with palms and impenetrable trees along the rim of the strand. The air was heavy with the smell of the sea, while upon the ear there fell no sound except that of the surf on the reef.

(*Pause. His calm vanishes. He stares briefly at the ground. With self-contempt*)

No people. I just wanted to escape them. To be alone. After a lifetime of human flesh, its palsies, tumours, wounds . . . I wanted, finally, the health of earth. The calm of the tides. The silence of stones.

(*He falls into a reverie, then picks up the journal and begins to read.*)

"Some six months after Merrick's return from the country he was found dead in bed. This was in April 1890. He was lying on his back as if asleep, and had evidently died suddenly without a struggle. The method of his death was peculiar. He often said to me that he wished he could lie down to sleep . . .—(*A long silence*)—'like other people.' I think on this last night he must, with some determination, have made the experiment. The head must have fallen backwards and caused a dislocation of the neck."

(*He closes the journal, puts it aside. He takes up the mask.*)

I took his mask and walking stick from him. Without realizing, for years afterward, how much I had lost that day. (*Pause*) Did I help him? I truly believed that I could help him. (*Pause; a beginning of anguish*) Why do the failures outweigh the victories? I saved a king once. Edward the Seventh, on the eve of his coronation, fell gravely ill. I diagnosed acute appendicitis and operated on him successfully in Buckingham Palace. Beneath my hands—for me to save, to preserve—lay the embodiment of a society. Of the Empire. And I did save. His gratitude made me a Baronet. But for Merrick's pain, what operation was there? What mere operation? (*Pause*) Did I help him? Anne tries to comfort me: "Remember the thousands you have helped, have cured; have solaced when there was no cure." Yes. But I could not help *him*. Or do anything more, really, than stand guard over him in his solitude. (*Angrily*) It is not enough! (*Quietly, a realization*) I should have been . . . the keeper of his peace.

(*Ponders this. After a moment he holds up the mask.*)

Once, after he died . . . I wore his mask for a moment, secretly. Trying to see what he saw.

(*Pause. He dons the mask in silence, in a gesture oddly formal, ceremonious. He stares ahead, does not speak; a new and strange figure. After a few moments he removes the mask. He is changed, a torment deep within has been released, yet his first words are quiet.*)

His skeleton stands, now, in the college museum. In a small room it shares with a few other exhibits. (*Pause*) I stood there, in the darkness, in the silence . . . and looked at the skull. (*Carefully*) The left side is smooth and polished. But on the right the bone seems to go berserk. Becomes gnarled, twisted, creviced. Leaps outward, folds inward in intricate and useless filigree. The mouth gapes open, teeth pointing in every direction. Utterly useless. (*Pause. With great pain*) I looked into the sockets that his eyes peered from, thirty-three years ago . . . and tried to remember the intelligence imprisoned there. The mind that perceived. But all I could see was an endless stream of tears welling from that darkness. I tried to imagine words spluttering from that blasted mouth. But all I could hear was an endless shriek of agony.

(*Pause. He slips the mask over the handle of the walking stick.*)

This is the question that haunts me now: Why did people turn away when they saw him? Could it have been, truly, that he was so hideous? Or did they see in him, without realizing it, a blinding beauty? A beauty so rare and radical that it must walk cloaked and masked?

(*Pause. He closes his eyes.*)

Why was he born into such pain?

(*He stops again.*)

When he first came we knew the answer. Our appeal: "One of the Creator's objects in permitting men to be born to a life of hopeless and miserable disability was that the works of God should be manifested in evoking the sympathy and kindly aid of those on whom such a heavy cross is not laid." (*Pause*) Am *I* the manifestation of God's mercy? His love—does it touch only through human hands? (*Self-hatred*) Where is the evidence of love? That I let him inch into my life? Watched him beg, and still not give? Why—that I could not touch him, why? In my deepest self, what deformity?

(*He lifts the mask and walking stick into the air. Despairing*)

To the question of his birth: is this the only answer? For us?

(*He thrusts the walking stick into the ground. It leans at a slight angle, the mask staring out. He falls silent, exhausted, stares at the mask. Long silence. Weakly*)

It was an afternoon in late November. London autumn, cold and dull. Leaves scraped through the streets and were crushed under the wheels of carriages. I was walking down Whitechapel road, returning to the hospital. I stopped by a poster on which was the announcement that—(*Tenderly*)—the Elephant Man was to be seen within. (*Pause*) When he stood up, and dropped his cloak . . . I knew that all I had been taught, and any skills I possessed . . . were useless. (*Pause*) Something in me, now, is extinct, I will not feel it again.

(*He sits in silence; aged, dying.*)

Slow fading of lights.

Thomas Gibbons. *The Exhibition*. © Copyright, 1980, by Thomas Gibbons, © copyright, 1978, by Thomas Gibbons as an unpublished dramatic composition under the title *The Elephant Man*.

CAUTION: The reprinting of *The Exhibition* included in this volume is reprinted by permission of the author and Dramatists Play Service, Inc. The amateur performance rights in this play are controlled exclusively by Dramatists Play Service, Inc., 440 Park Avenue South, New York, NY 10016. No amateur production of the play may be given without obtaining, in advance, the written permission of the Dramatists Play Service, Inc., and paying the requisite fee. Inquiries regarding all other rights should be addressed to the author, care of Dramatists Play Service, Inc.

After Words

1. a) In your journal, respond with your feelings and thoughts about the play.

   b) In role as John Merrick, write a journal entry reflecting on your relationship with Treves.

2. Trace through the play the changing attitudes Treves has toward Merrick. What is Treves's final dilemma?

3. Comment on the dramatic impact of the following lines:

   a) I wanted to . . . reclaim him for the human race. (page 89)

   b) Cast him out, I can't look at him, throw him out, into the trash-heap, into the night! (page 91)

   c) He became the pet of the nobility. (page 93)

   d) Doctor Frederick Treves. How I treasured that name! I thought you were my saviour. (page 95)

   e) Exhibition: exhibit . . . exhibitor. Did I ever help him? (page 100)

4. With a partner, discuss how the play stresses the basic human qualities of John Merrick. Then choose one portion of the play to examine further and dramatize. Present your dramatization.

5. With a partner, roleplay John Merrick and a newspaper reporter interviewing him. Write and share the newspaper article that would result. (You might write your article in the style of a local paper or a national newsmagazine.)

6. The play suggests parallels between the showman and Dr. Treves. Explore these and other parallels within the play and parallels you see between the play and contemporary life. Present your results to the class.

7. Brainstorm a list of activities that objectify or diminish human beings. Choose one activity to debate formally. What is its supposed value? Why does it persist? Should the activity be banned?

2

Relationships

Medicine River

A radio play by THOMAS KING, based on his novel

THOMAS KING says he didn't write seriously until 1982. Since then, however, he has written acclaimed books and several adaptations to other media. King, born in 1943 to a Cherokee father and mother of Greek and German descent, spent his early years in California. While earning his Ph.D. in English literature and American Indian literature, he worked as an ambulance driver, a shoe seller, and (while in Australia for two years) a photographer and journalist. Alberta, where he taught for ten years at the University of Lethbridge, is the setting of his first novel, *Medicine River*. In it King presents with gentle humour the lives and concerns of people in a fictional town bordering a Blackfoot reserve. *Medicine River* won the Alberta Book Prize and was shortlisted for a Commonwealth Writers' Prize. King chose among the diverse tales told in his novel for adaptation as radio drama. A portion of his adaptation, which aired on CBC Radio in January 1993, is presented here.

King has also written the screenplay for the CBC movie *Medicine River*, a children's book called *A Coyote Columbus*, a collection of short stories, and the novel *Green Grass, Running Water*. After two years as Chair of the American Indian Studies department at the University of Minnesota, King returned to Canada in 1993 to work with CBC-TV.

Prelude

1 In your journal, write about 3–5 photographs—of family, friends, other special people—that mean the most to you. Explain the significance of each photograph.

2 Often in small communities it seems everyone knows a great deal about everyone else. Discuss the advantages and disadvantages of this situation.

Medicine River

Characters

WILL: Photographer, recently returned to Medicine River after many years away

HARLEN BIGBEAR: Friend of Will, Medicine River's unofficial meddler, matchmaker, gossip

EDDIE WEASELHEAD: Social director at the Medicine River Friendship Centre, friend of Will and Harlen

LOUISE HEAVYMAN: Self-employed accountant

NURSES

BERTHA MORLEY: Secretary at Friendship Centre, friend of Louise

BIG JOHN YELLOW RABBIT: Director of the Friendship Centre

CARTER HEAVYMAN | Louise's parents
DORIS HEAVYMAN |

MARTHA OLDCROW: Elder, known as Medicine River's "marriage doctor"

JOYCE BLUE HORN: Former classmate of Louise

ELVIS BLUE HORN: Joyce's husband

LIONEL JAMES: Elder, storyteller

Act One

Scene 1: Will's Studio

> SOUND/MUSIC: *The radio drama opens with traditional drumming or flute music that begins at a low volume and becomes louder. At some point, it is replaced by or shares time with the sound of the wind. The music fades and the sound of the wind takes over.*

WILL: (*Narrating*) Medicine River sat on the broad back of the prairies. It was an unpretentious community of buildings banked low against the weather that slid off the eastern face of the Rockies. Summer was hot in Medicine River and filled with grasshoppers and mosquitoes. Winter was cold and long. Then there was the wind. I generally tried to keep my mouth shut about the wind in Medicine River.

(SOUND: *A door opens. We hear a bell and then* HARLEN BIGBEAR'S *voice in the background.*)

HARLEN: Will! Will . . .

WILL: (*Narrating*) Harlen Bigbear was like the prairie wind. You never knew when Harlen was coming or when he was going to leave.

HARLEN: Will . . . Will . . .

WILL: (*Narrating*) Most times I was happy to see Harlen. Today I wasn't. I had other things to do. There were photographs in the wash and three strips of negatives that had to be printed. (*Pause*) But that didn't stop the wind from blowing and it didn't stop Harlen.

HARLEN: Will . . . Will. Where are you?

WILL: Back here, Harlen.

(SOUND: *An interior door opening and closing.*)

HARLEN: There you are, Will. (*Pause*) Say, is that a picture of you and James and your mother?

WILL: Yes, it is.

HARLEN: Looks old.

WILL: It was taken when we were living in Calgary.

HARLEN: Before your mother died?

WILL: I would think so.

HARLEN: Before you went off to Toronto and became a world famous photographer?

WILL: Before that. What's up?

HARLEN: What's your mother looking at?

WILL: What?

HARLEN: Looks kinda serious. Like she can see something important.

WILL: People just looked like that.

HARLEN: Picture looks sort of beat up, too.

WILL: (*Exasperated with* HARLEN) I'm trying to fix it. Now, what's up?

HARLEN: What?

WILL: What did you come here for?

HARLEN: Oh, yeah . . . you know Louise Heavyman, don't you?

WILL: (*Narrating*) Every year around tax time, Harlen would begin musing about the wonders of higher mathematics and the mysteries of deductions and taxable income.

HARLEN: You know, Will, they got people who get paid for figuring out ways of breaking things down into little pieces. Categories. That's what they call them.

WILL: (*Narrating*) Harlen took his tax forms to Louise Heavyman. So did I. Neither one of us could be trusted with the complexities of simple addition.

HARLEN: They got names for those categories that I can't even pronounce. You know why they do that, Will?

WILL: (*Narrating*) Before Louise opened her own tax office in Medicine River, Harlen and I took our business to Jerry Peterson. Jerry ran a finance company, but he did taxes on the side.

HARLEN: You ever read any of those brochures Jerry used to give us, Will? One of them said I should be making a thousand dollars for every year I've been alive. You remember those pens Jerry used to give us?

WILL: You mean the ones in the plastic wrappers?

HARLEN: Those are the ones.

WILL: The cheap ones that leaked after about a week?

HARLEN: You know, I really liked those pens. I told Louise she should start giving out pens.

WILL: What'd she say?

HARLEN: You know Louise.

WILL: (*Narrating*) Jerry wanted to get paid the same time he did our taxes. It wasn't good for business, he told us, and it would lower our self esteem if he gave us credit. And then he would give us a pen. Louise wanted to be paid at the same time, too. But she wasn't worried about our self esteem.

LOUISE: I've got rent to pay. I can't be spending my time chasing out to the reserve or tracking you guys down.

WILL: (*Narrating*) Harlen, who sees the good in everyone and is always trying to help, told her that he really didn't mind her not giving out pens, but now that she was a successful businesswoman, she should think about getting married.

Medicine River

HARLEN: People appreciate it when you try and help.

WILL: What'd she say to . . . marriage?

HARLEN: Said she'd think about it.

WILL: (*Narrating*) Which wasn't exactly what Louise had said. Eddie had been there when Harlen brought up the matter.

EDDIE: Should have heard her laugh, Will. Big tears in her eyes. Had to blow her nose six or seven times.

HARLEN: Louise has never been married, Will. But she's real smart. Even in boarding school she was real smart. Has a great sense of humour. Good personality, too. What do you think?

WILL: (*Narrating*) I liked Louise and I told Harlen I liked her. But that wasn't what Harlen had in mind.

HARLEN: Good-looking woman, Will. Strong hips. You know, for children. Tall, too. Always good to have a tall woman.

WILL: (*Narrating*) Harlen and I had had this particular conversation before.

HARLEN: You must be forty or so, Will. Not that you look it. You're a handsome man in your own way. Even Bertha says so. Good teeth. Good job. Good personality, too. You ever think about getting married?

WILL: (*Narrating*) And then Harlen would begin dropping hints about the way a life should be lived.

HARLEN: A man's not complete until he has a woman by his side. (*Pause*) Nothing more important than the family. (*Pause*) A son of yours would probably be a sports star of some sort. (*Pause*) Beats the hell out of your own cooking.

WILL: (*Narrating*) I guess I really didn't mind. Harlen meant well.

Scene 2

HARLEN: Seeing a man live alone is sad, Will. You get all drawn out and grey and wrinkled. Look at Sam Belly.

WILL: Harlen, Sam's over ninety.

HARLEN: And he's not married.

WILL: Harlen, Sam was married for over sixty years.

HARLEN: Course he was. Wouldn't have lived this long without a good woman. But do you think he'll live another ten years, not being married and all?

WILL: (*Narrating*) Occasionally, just to keep these conversations from being completely one-sided, I'd throw out a few statistics of my own.

WILL: You know, Harlen, I was reading an article on marriages, and it said that at least fifty percent of marriages end in divorce.

HARLEN: Hell, Will. If you could get odds like that at bingo, you'd be rich.

WILL: (*Narrating*) That was Harlen. Harlen kept up on all the gossip. Nothing happened on the reserve or in town that Harlen didn't know about.

Scene 3: Studio

SOUND: Front door opening, bell

WILL: (*Narrating*) When he stopped by the studio on Wednesday, I could see he had something big on his mind. He was smiling inside, and it was leaking out the sides of his mouth and ears.

HARLEN: Morning Will. Real nice day. You remember Louise Heavyman?

WILL: Louise Heavyman?

HARLEN: You know, the woman who did our taxes last month.

WILL: Of course I know Louise.

HARLEN: You know. I don't really mind that Louise doesn't give out pens like Jerry did.

WILL: What about Louise?

HARLEN: Those pens used to skip a lot. A couple of them leaked all over my shirt.

WILL: Harlen . . .

HARLEN: When I see Louise, I should tell her that.

WILL: Harlen!

HARLEN: What do you think, Will. You think she'll invite us to her wedding?

WILL: Who?

HARLEN: Louise.

WILL: What wedding?

HARLEN: Louise is probably getting married.

WILL: (*Narrating*) You never knew just how far Harlen's probables were from actuals, and most of the time neither did Harlen.

Medicine River

WILL: That was pretty sudden.

HARLEN: That fellow from Edmonton she's been seeing. Leroy and Floyd saw them at Casey's. Leroy says that they both sat on the same side of the table.

WILL: When's the wedding?

HARLEN: Probably pretty soon. You don't sit on the same side of the table unless it's serious.

WILL: (*Narrating*) For the next month, Harlen brought me all the new information about Louise and her boyfriend.

HARLEN: Should have seen them, Will. Walking hand in hand. Daylight, too. . . . Rita Blackplume saw them at the movies off in a corner by themselves. . . . His name is Harold. Drives a Buick. Comes down from Edmonton every weekend. Floyd saw his car in front of Louise's place all night.

WILL: (*Narrating*) After the second month or so, Louise and Harold slipped into third place behind Mary Rabbit's divorce and Elgin and Billy Turnbull's driving their father's truck off the Minor Street bridge into the river. Elgin broke his arm. Billy put his head into the windshield and broke his big toe. Louise and her boyfriend were interesting, but Harlen was intrigued by Billy's toe.

HARLEN: Can't figure how he did that, Will. Broke his toe. Can you figure that? Hit his head and broke his toe.

WILL: (*Narrating*) Billy's toe healed, and Elgin's arm was out of the cast in two months. And Louise didn't get married.

Scene 4: Phone Conversation

   SOUND: Phone ringing and **WILL** *trying to find the light*

WILL: (*Narrating*) Harlen called me at two in the morning to tell me that.

WILL: Will . . . Will. You awake?

WILL: (*Very sleepy*) Harlen . . . ?

HARLEN: Will, wake up. This is important.

   (*SOUND:* **WILL** *rolling over in bed.*)

WILL: Harlen, it's the middle of the night.

HARLEN: Will . . . Louise isn't getting married. I'll be by in ten minutes.

WILL: Harlen . . .

HARLEN: Okay, twenty minutes.

Scene 5: Apartment

> SOUND: *Water running in a sink and* WILL *brushing his teeth.*

WILL: (*Narrating*) I was in the bathroom brushing my teeth when Harlen let himself in. I knew it was important because Harlen came right to the point. Sort of.

HARLEN: Will . . . Louise and Harold broke up. Over a month ago.

WILL: That's . . . too bad.

HARLEN: It's terrible, Will. Why didn't I know about it?

WILL: Guess Louise didn't tell anyone.

HARLEN: So, what are we going to do?

WILL: Well, probably not much we can do.

HARLEN: Poor Louise. Made a mistake. Probably scared to death. Family will probably disown her. Probably lose most of her friends.

WILL: Harlen . . .

HARLEN: Most women would just fall apart, you know. You got to admire Louise. Betty says you could never tell she was on the edge of a mental breakdown.

WILL: (*Narrating*) I should have known better. I should have seen it in Harlen's eyes. But I didn't, and by the time I did, it was too late.

WILL: Harlen, I don't think Louise is going to have a nervous breakdown just because she broke up with Harold.

HARLEN: Who cares about Harold? Will, Louise is pregnant.

> (MUSIC: *Music to mark the end of the act begins.*)

WILL: Pregnant?

HARLEN: That's right, Will. And you're probably the only friend that Louise has left. (*Pause*) So, what are we going to do?

Act Two

Scene 1: Apartment

> SOUND/MUSIC: *Music begins to mark the opening of the act. In the background we can hear the sound of coffee cups and saucers clanking and the sound of pouring coffee.*

WILL: (*Narrating*) Louise was pregnant all right. Betty at the hospital had seen the tests. About two months along. Betty had told Doreen and Doreen had told Bertha, Bertha told Harlen, and Harlen told me.

HARLEN: Louise is pregnant. What are we going to do about it?

WILL: (*Narrating*) Helping was Harlen's speciality. He was like a spider on a web. Every so often, someone would come along and tear off a piece of the web or poke a hole in it, and Harlen would come scuttling along and throw out filament after filament until the damage was repaired. Bertha called it meddling. Harlen thought of it as general maintenance.

HARLEN: We got to help her, Will. Somebody's got to look after her. Be with her. Take her out, so she's not ashamed to be seen in public. You know what I mean?

WILL: Harlen, You're not suggesting I should start seeing Louise just because she's pregnant?

Harlen: No, I wasn't thinking that. Course you are single, so your wife wouldn't get upset, and you're not doing anything, anyway. And you are good friends with Louise.

WILL: I like being single.

HARLEN: You know, Will, your mother and Louise's mother used to be best of friends.

WILL: I don't want to get married.

HARLEN: Who said anything about getting married. Louise is going through a bad time. Some guy from Edmonton gets her pregnant and then runs off. All her friends and family desert her. She's afraid to be seen in public. She's your friend, Will. Couldn't hurt to help out. Take her to lunch.

WILL: I've got a lot of work to do.

HARLEN: You know what they say, Will. Lunch is the most important meal of the day.

WILL: (*Narrating*) I felt like a real ass walking into Louise's office two days later. I probably wouldn't have gone, but Harlen knew me too well. He picked me up and drove me over.

Scene 2: Outdoors

WILL: You can go now, Harlen. I can get across the street by myself.

HARLEN: I'll just wait here, Will. In case you need to ask any questions.

WILL: (*Narrating*) Louise was in and she didn't look pregnant. But she caught me looking.

Scene 3: Louise's Office

LOUISE: Yes, Will, I am pregnant. God, you guys are the biggest bunch of goats.

WILL: I didn't come here about that.

LOUISE: And Harlen didn't send you?

WILL: Harlen? No. I just thought I'd come by and say hello. See if you wanted to go . . . to go . . . to lunch.

LOUISE: The same Harlen who just happens to be parked across the street.

WILL: Really?

LOUISE: The same Harlen who has already sent over Floyd and Elwood and Jack Powless.

WILL: Jack Powless?

LOUISE: All three hundred pounds of him. They all just wanted to say hello and take me to lunch.

WILL: (*Narrating*) Sometimes you get into situations where you can do nothing but lie. It's the fear that does it, I think.

WILL: Really . . . just came by . . . lunch.

LOUISE: Thanks Will. I've already had lunch.

WILL: Ah . . . is it okay if I use your bathroom?

LOUISE: Help yourself.

WILL: I let myself out the back door and walked home. I unplugged the phone and lay on the bed. When I woke up, I felt better. I was still angry with Harlen, but I felt better. So I called Louise.

Scene 4: Phone Conversation

SOUND: Phone dialing

LOUISE: Hello.

WILL: Hi. It's Will. Listen . . . about that lunch date . . .

LOUISE: (*Pause*) Will . . .

WILL: (*Quickly*) This has nothing to do with Harlen or you being pregnant. How about tomorrow? We can go to Casey's.

LOUISE: (*Pause*) How about I pay for my own meal?

WILL: (*Nervously*) You eat that much?

Scene 5: Restaurant/Street

SOUND: Restaurant crowd noises

WILL: (*Narrating*) Casey's was crowded. The hostess jammed us into a corner, and between the lunch crowd, the music, the dishes clacking in the kitchen and the server dropping by every two minutes to ask us if everything was okay, we could hardly hear one another. We were reduced to alternately yelling across the table or just smiling and nodding. The food made me brave. On our way back to Louise's office, we passed by the Paramount Theatre. *Revenge of the Nerds* was playing.

WILL: You got plans for Saturday night?

LOUISE: This about a date?

WILL: I hear it's a good movie.

(*SOUND:* LOUISE *laughing.*)

WILL: How about it? We could see the early show and then grab some burgers at Baggies.

LOUISE: Not supposed to eat things like that. Not good for the baby.

WILL: Oh . . .

LOUISE: I better eat at home. But the movie sounds good. What say I pick you up around six-thirty?

WILL: Where am I going to eat?

(*BIZ:* LOUISE *and* WILL *laugh. Street noises fade.*)

WILL: (*Narrating*) Louise was a pretty good cook. I'm not big on vegetables, but I suppose they were better for the baby. Her car was more comfortable than my truck and it still had most of its paint. I'd been on dates where the woman used her own car. Normally, though, they always asked me if I wanted to drive.

Scene 6: Movie Theatre

LOUISE: You sure about this movie?

WILL: Well, Eddie liked it.

LOUISE: Oh . . . great.

(*SOUND: A movie starting. Crowd in background.*)

WILL: The movie was awful. But about half-way through, I realized that, while the audience was snorting and laughing, Louise was crying. She caught me looking and laughed and wiped her eyes.

Louise: It's all right, Will. It's just hormones. Watch the movie.

Will: (*Narrating*) I had a good time. So I called Louise the next week and we began to go out regular. Mostly we talked about babies.

Louise: You got to watch what you eat. You don't want to drink or smoke and you have to be careful with coffee and aspirin. Babies are sensitive.

Will: (*Narrating*) I wasn't able to avoid Harlen for long.

(*Sound: Door opening, bell.*)

Will: (*Narrating*) He came into the studio with his mouth all bent around his nose.

Scene 7: Studio

Harlen: Haven't seen you around, Will. Some of the boys been asking about you.

Will: Been busy.

Harlen: You got to get out every so often, you know. You doing anything for lunch tomorrow?

Will: No.

Harlen: How about the next day?

Will: No.

Harlen: Thursday?

Will: I'm busy Thursday.

Harlen: Business?

Will: Not exactly.

Harlen: Anyone I know?

Will: Yes.

Harlen: You know, we're friends, Will. If you have any questions, you just call, even in the middle of the night.

Will: Thanks, Harlen.

Harlen: That's what friends do. Even in the middle of the night.

Will: (*Narrating*) When I saw Louise, later, I told her about Harlen.

Louise: God, yes. Betty and Doreen and Bertha are convinced we're going to get married.

Medicine River

WILL: (*Narrating*) Louise got bigger and bigger, and I guess I began getting protective. I started opening car doors. I held her arm when we had to cross an icy street. After dinner one night, Louise took my hand and put it on her belly.

LOUISE: Here, Will, you want to feel her kick?

WILL: (*Narrating*) I was just helping, like Harlen said. I helped Louise watch what she ate. I helped her get some exercise. I even gave her a little help with some names.

Scene 8: Apartment

LOUISE: What about Wilma? I had a granny named Wilma.

WILL: Un-huh . . .

LOUISE: Jamie?

WILL: Well . . .

LOUISE: Elizabeth?

WILL: Maybe . . .

LOUISE: Sarah?

WILL: I guess . . .

LOUISE: Will, you're a big help.

WILL: (*Narrating*) We never got around to being lovers. There didn't seem to be the time for that. We were friends. Louise was good to be with, but there was a distance and Louise kept it. (*Pause*) I was dead asleep the night Louise called.

Scene 9: On Phone

LOUISE: Will, I need to go to the hospital. Don't know if I can drive myself. Do you mind?

Scene 10: Hospital

SOUND: General hospital noises.

WILL: (*Narrating*) It took the hospital a while to get Louise admitted. Every so often, she'd have to stop and bend over and take a deep breath. They finally got her into a room, and a doctor looked at her while I waited outside.

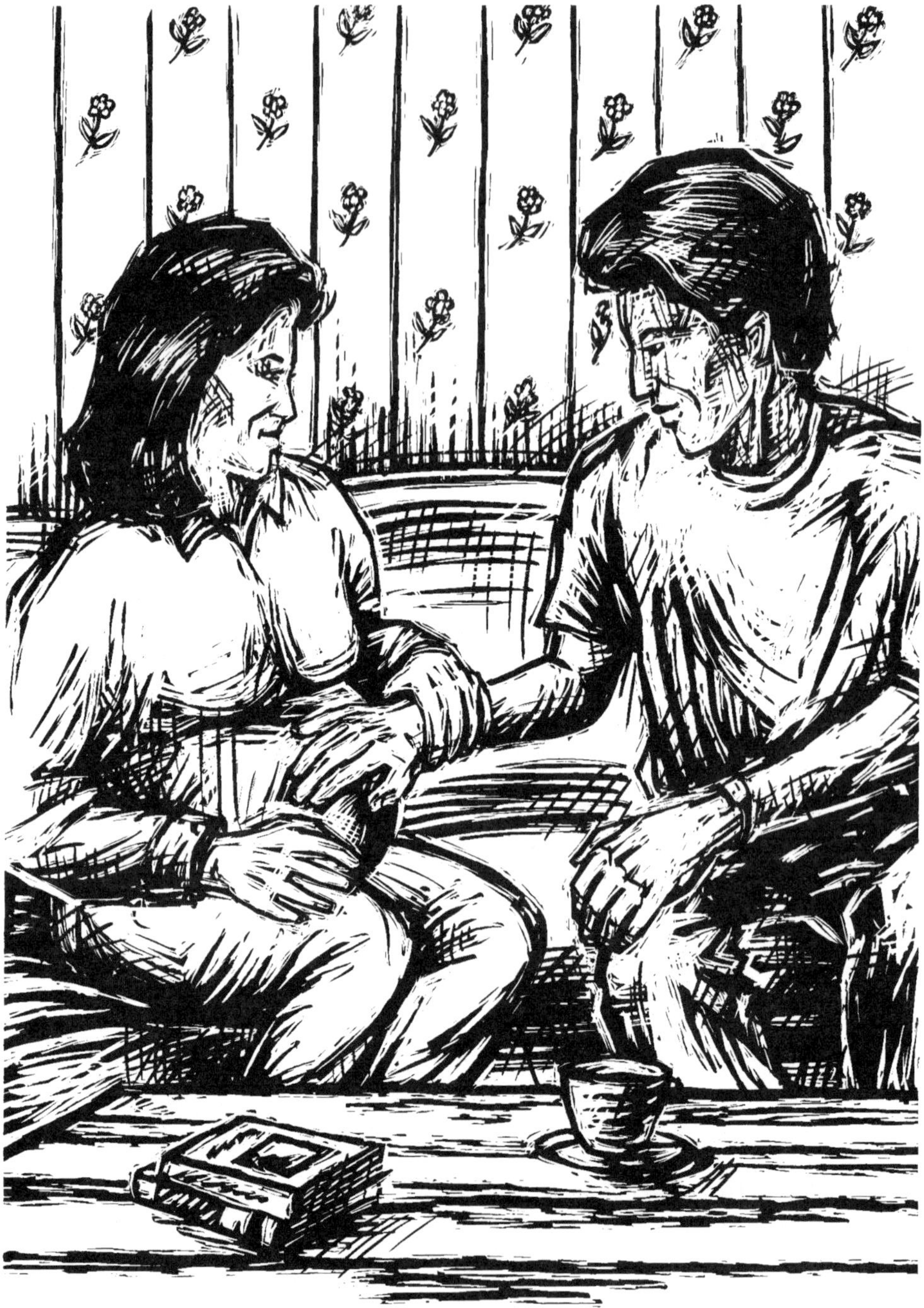

Medicine River

LOUISE: I'm only dilated four centimetres, Will. Probably won't have the baby until morning. Thanks for the ride and all the attention. I'll have them call you when she's born.

WILL: I've got nothing better to do. Don't mind waiting. Maybe it's a boy and you'll need some more help with names.

LOUISE: No sense, Will. It'll be a long wait. You've got other things to do.

WILL: Maybe I'll wait for a little while. Just in case.

LOUISE: I'll be okay.

WILL: (*Narrating*) The waiting room was small. I sat on the sofa and tried to read a magazine. After a couple of hours, I caught one of the nurses who was coming out of the maternity area.

Scene 11: Waiting Room

WILL: Ah . . . could you tell me how Louise . . . Mrs. . . . Ms. Heavyman is doing?

FIRST NURSE: What are you doing out here?

WILL: I thought I'd . . . wait.

FIRST NURSE: I'll bet your wife would love to have you with her.

WILL: Right.

FIRST NURSE: Sitting in a waiting-room is a little old-fashioned. Most men like to be there when their wives deliver. Is this your first?

WILL: Ah . . . yes.

FIRST NURSE: She's just down the hall. First door on the right.

WILL: (*Narrating*) Maternity was in the south wing of the hospital. "South Wing" was printed in large letters above the double doors. I stood in the hall for several minutes and thought about wandering down to say hello. One of the doors was slightly open, and I leaned against it and slid into the corridor, just as another nurse came out of the room.

Scene 12: Corridor

SECOND NURSE: Can I help you?

WILL: Ah . . . she's just down there . . . Louise . . . Ms. Heavyman . . . Louise . . .

SECOND NURSE: You her husband?

WILL: Sure . . . I mean, I'm her . . . in a way . . . you know . . . a friend . . .

SECOND NURSE: Friends of the family have to wait outside.

WILL: (*Narrating*) I went back to the sofa and watched the doctors and nurses move back and forth in the hall. (*Sound of voices and footsteps*) It was warm in the waiting room and I was starting to fall asleep, starting to have some pleasant thoughts about Louise and the baby and me when Harlen and Big John and Eddie and Bertha arrived.

Scene 13: Waiting Room

HARLEN: I told you he'd be here, Eddie. You owe me a beer.

WILL: What are you guys doing here?

BERTHA: How's Louise doing?

WILL: She's doing fine. Nurse said it would probably be eight or nine more hours. Maybe longer. No sense you waiting around. I'm probably going to go myself in a bit.

FIRST NURSE: There you are, Mr. Heavyman. Your wife has just gone into delivery. It shouldn't be too long, now.

HARLEN: Mr. Heavyman?

WILL: It's a mistake. Look, there's really no reason for you to stay.

EDDIE: (*Laughing*) Mr. Heavyman?

HARLEN: It's okay, Will. That's what friends are for.

WILL: (*Narrating*) So they stayed . . . Harlen, Bertha, Eddie and Big John. Every so often, I would look over my magazine to find one of them looking at me, grinning. About two hours later, another nurse came in.

Scene 14: Waiting Room, Later

THIRD NURSE: Mr. Heavyman?

EDDIE: That's him.

(BIZ: *Sound of quiet snickering*)

THIRD NURSE: Your wife just had a baby girl. We'll get her cleaned up and weighed, and you can come in the nursery and see her. Your wife had a few minor complications, but she's all right, just tired. Wait here and I'll come and get you in a few minutes.

(SOUND: *Footsteps retreating.*)

(BIZ: *There is a pause and then all the people in the room begin celebrating except* WILL.)

BIG JOHN: (*Laughing*) It's a girl, Mr. Heavyman.

EDDIE: (*Laughing*) Your wife is just fine, Mr. Heavyman.

WILL: (*Narrating*) Harlen just sat on the sofa and smiled at me. Bertha finally got up and walked over and thumped me in the chest. There were tears in her eyes.

BERTHA: You remember to treat her right.

WILL: (*Narrating*) For the next twenty minutes, I had to sit in the waiting room with four grinning idiots. I was finally saved by the nurse.

THIRD NURSE: You can see your daughter, now, Mr. Heavyman. She's a big girl. Eight pounds, seven ounces.

WILL: (*Narrating*) They made me put on a gown before they would let me hold the baby. She was wrapped up in a blanket and all you could see was her face and eyes. I thought they would be closed like puppies or kittens, but they weren't. They were open, and she was looking at me.

THIRD NURSE: I'll bet you have a name all picked out for her.

WILL: (*Narrating*) At that moment, all I could see was the big sign outside the maternity ward.

WILL: Yeah, we'll probably call her . . . South Wing.

THIRD NURSE: Is that a traditional Indian name?

WILL: No . . . actually it was just a joke. I was just joking.

THIRD NURSE: No, I think it's a beautiful name.

WILL: (*Narrating*) I sat in the nursery in a rocking chair with the baby for a long time. I would have stayed longer but the nurse came back and said that my wife was awake now and wanted to see the baby. The nurse put the baby in a bassinet and I pushed it down the hall. When I got to the waiting room, I looked in. It was empty. South Wing was still awake and looking at me. I thought about Louise and her not having anyone, how her family was angry with her, how all her friends had left. There was just me and the baby and Louise.

Scene 15: Hospital Room

HARLEN: Will . . . Will . . . There you are. Come on. What took you so long.

(SOUND: *Large crowd of people. This sound continues in the background.*)

WILL: (*Narrating*) There are times when I don't know why I bother to listen to Harlen. Louise was in 325 C. So were her mother and father, two of her brothers, all of her sisters, three of her aunts, a couple of people I didn't know, and Harlen, Eddie, Big John, and Bertha.

CARTER: Hey, Will. What are you doing here? Hey, is that my little granddaughter. Boy, is she small.

DORIS: Here, let Louise hold the baby so we can get a picture. You be quick with that camera, Carter, cause that baby needs a lot of quiet and a lot to eat. Here Will, give her to me.

CARTER: Hey, Will. You should have brought one of your cameras. (*Pause*) Say, Will. What are you doing in that gown?

WILL: (*Narrating*) Louise's father took the picture and everyone crowded around to see the baby. On the card on the bassinet, the nurse had written "South Wing Heavyman."

(SOUND: *Pause and crowd sounds fade*)

WILL: (*Narrating*) I left the hospital and thought I would just walk in the dark and look at the stars, but it turned out to be ten in the morning. The sun was up and hot. I stopped at Woodward's and bought a stuffed penguin for the baby. I went home and slept the rest of the day and then I took the penguin to the hospital that night.

Scene 16: Hospital Room

LOUISE: Will, I'm glad you came by. That was a madhouse this morning. Mom had to drag Dad away so I could get some rest.

WILL: I got this for the baby.

LOUISE: Her name is Wilma, Will.

WILL: Good looking baby.

LOUISE: Where in the world did you get the name "South Wing?"

WILL: It was supposed to be . . . sort of . . . a joke.

LOUISE: My father really liked it.

Medicine River

WILL: Wilma's better.

LOUISE: She's beautiful, isn't she. As soon as we get settled, I'll have you over for dinner. Maybe we can go to a show, too.

WILL: Sure.

LOUISE: You understand, don't you, Will?

WILL: Sure.

WILL: (*Narrating*) The nursery was bright and alive with light. Some of the babies were awake and crying. A mother sat in the rocking chair in the corner nursing her child. The plate-glass window was hard and cool, and I lay my face against it and watched South Wing sleep.

(SOUND: *Footsteps*)

WILL: (*Narrating*) The nurse at the desk smiled at me and came over to where I was standing.

Scene 17: Hall Outside Nursery

FIRST NURSE: They're lovely aren't they. This must be your first. Which one is yours?

(MUSIC: *Music begins to mark the end of the act.*)

WILL: (*Narrating*) Harlen and Eddie and Big John and Bertha were probably at the Friendship Centre. Mr. and Mrs. Heavyman were headed back to the reserve. Louise was in her room. South Wing lay in her bassinet wrapped in a pink blanket. I looked down the corridor. (*Pause*) It was clear.

WILL: That one.

Act Three

Scene 1: Studio

MUSIC: *Music begins to mark the opening of the act.*

WILL: (*Narrating*) Every so often, when I least expected it, Harlen could be blunt as a brick.

(SOUND: *Front door opening and the bell.*)

HARLEN: Morning Will.

WILL: Morning Harlen.

HARLEN: I bet Bertha a cup of coffee that you would forget.

WILL: Forget what?

HARLEN: Tomorrow's South Wing's first birthday. Have you got your daughter a present yet?

WILL: (*Narrating*) Harlen being direct always set me back a few seconds.

HARLEN: Well?

WILL: She's not my daughter, Harlen, and, no, I haven't got her a present yet. But I'm going to.

HARLEN: Bertha says that South Wing can almost say "daddy."

WILL: Bertha can talk, but South Wing can't. I'm her uncle. Just like you.

HARLEN: She's always happy to see you.

WILL: She's happy to see everyone.

HARLEN: That's close enough. You're just crabby because you almost forgot her birthday.

WILL: I didn't almost forget her birthday.

HARLEN: Bertha was afraid you'd forget.

WILL: I didn't forget.

HARLEN: Well, then, we better get moving.

WILL: (*Narrating*) There were times when conversations with Harlen would get out of control and I would lose him. We would be talking and everything would seem normal and logical and then he would just get away, vanish, and I would be standing there wondering what had happened.

HARLEN: I came to take you shopping.

WILL: What?

HARLEN: For your daughter's present.

WILL: Harlen, I have to work.

HARLEN: Stores won't be open tonight. Tomorrow's too late. If you had planned ahead, you could have got her a nice ribbon dress.

WILL: Harlen, she's only a year old.

HARLEN: You could have got it a little large. For later on.

WILL: I figured I'd get her a pair of moccasins. Friendship Centre should have some.

HARLEN: Nope. Already looked. Come on, we haven't got all day.

Scene 2: Department Store

> SOUND: *Department store noises in the background.*

WILL: (*Narrating*) We started at Eaton's. The salesclerk showed us a doll with a built-in tape-recorder and a velcro strap that went around your waist so you would never have to be without her. We looked at teddy bears at Woodward's and toy lawn mowers at Woolco. Harlen found a little red drum with white maple leaves around the sides that he thought South Wing would like.

WILL: Louise will kill me if I gave South Wing a drum.

HARLEN: I don't know. A drum's an Indian thing, you know.

WILL: (*Narrating*) It took us an hour to exhaust Medicine River.

Scene 3

HARLEN: Maybe a drum wasn't such a bad idea, Will.

WILL: It was a bad idea.

HARLEN: Maybe you should call Louise.

WILL: (*Narrating*) Louise and I hadn't gone out much since South Wing was born, but generally I would go over for dinner once or twice a week. We still joked about the mistake the nurses had made. Louise wasn't in and Harlen and I were left to our own devices.

HARLEN: You know me Will, not one to butt into other people's business, but you and Louise should probably get married.

WILL: Harlen . . .

HARLEN: I know you like being single, but everyone knows how much you love South Wing. Bertha figures you're pretty fond of Louise, too.

WILL: I like being single. Louise likes being single.

HARLEN: Maybe you two should try living together. You know, sneak up on it.

WILL: I like living alone. Louise likes living alone.

HARLEN: Okay. Then I guess we better go out to the reserve.

WILL: For what?

HARLEN: The present. I just thought of where we can get one.

WILL: Grey Horse Crafts?

HARLEN: Nope. Got another place in mind. We better take your truck, Will. We got to go out past Rolling Fish Coulee.

Scene 4: Car Interior

SOUND: A car starting and rolling down the street.

WILL: (*Narrating*) I didn't have any afternoon appointments, and Wednesdays were always slow, and we were halfway to the reserve before I figured out exactly where we were going.

WILL: (*In a friendly voice*) Harlen, who lives out past Rolling Fish Coulee?

HARLEN: Not to worry, Will. You'll see.

WILL: Wouldn't be we're going out to see Martha Oldcrow?

HARLEN: Lot's of people live out on the reserve.

(*SOUND:* HARLEN *begins humming to himself. The wind is heard rushing past the car window.*)

WILL: (*Narrating*) Which was a lie of sorts. Lots of people lived on the reserve, all right, but only Martha Oldcrow lived out past Rolling Fish Coulee, and Martha Oldcrow and South Wing's birthday present didn't seem to have much in common.

WILL: Harlen, is this about Louise and me?

WILL: (*Narrating*) Harlen had the window rolled down. He was singing to himself, which is what he does on long trips or when he's trying to ignore me.

HARLEN: Beautiful day, Will. Always nice to come back to the reserve on a beautiful day.

WILL: (*Narrating*) Martha Oldcrow was a doctor. People with problems went to see her. She was known as the "marriage doctor" because that's what she fixed best. I knew that. Harlen knew that.

WILL: What kind of present are we going to get at Martha's?

HARLEN: Look at that, Will. You can see Chief Mountain clear as can be.

(*SOUND: A car rolling down a gravel or dirt road. Sound continues under narration.*)

WILL: (*Narrating*) The road past Old Agency out to Rolling Fish Coulee was always a surprise. I'd only been on it once before. It was a standard joke on the reserve. The council didn't bother grading it like they did the other dirt and gravel roads, because no one lived out there except Martha and she didn't drive. Every year the snow and the run-off would cut new gullies through the road, and the road itself would change as the pick-ups and four-wheel drives found new ways around the cuts. Last winter, there had been a slide that took the road out about ten miles from Old Agency.

HARLEN: Slide's up ahead about two miles, Will. Better head west.

WILL: You know where we're going?

HARLEN: This is just like the explorers, Will. Head south. Those trees over there look familiar.

WILL: (*Narrating*) We headed south. We got lost. We headed north. We got lost. We headed west. We got lost.

HARLEN: Those trees over there look familiar, Will. Head east.

WILL: (*Narrating*) After an hour of wandering around on the prairies, I looked at the gas gauge and realized that we had just enough gas to get back to Standoff. But Harlen's luck held. We headed south one more time and came to the edge of a coulee and couldn't go any further.

(SOUND: *A car slowing down and stopping.*)

HARLEN: There it is, Will.

WILL: Where?

HARLEN: Down there. Best to leave the truck here. We can just walk down.

WILL: (*Narrating*) It was about a mile down to the river. Martha's cabin sat in a small meadow on the far side of the river. We were on a ridge on the other side.

Scene 5: Outdoors

WILL: Harlen, we're on the wrong side of the river. How are we supposed to get there?

HARLEN: Walk. Good exercise. River's not too deep this time of year. Should be nice and warm.

(SOUND/BIZ: *Sound of* WILL *and* HARLEN *scrambling down a cut bank.*

HARLEN's voice in the background encouraging WILL. Sound of a river in the background getting louder.)

WILL: (Narrating) Before I could think up a good reason why this was a bad idea, Harlen began scrambling down the coulee and I scrambled down behind him. The river was deeper than Harlen thought and we had to take our clothes off, tie them up in a ball, and swim across. The water was green, and murky, and freezing.

WILL: Jesus!

HARLEN: Something to tell your kids about, Will.

WILL: (Narrating) Martha Oldcrow was sitting in a white Naugahyde recliner under a cottonwood tree outside her cabin.

Scene 6: Outside Cabin

MARTHA: Oki. You boys come all this way for a swim?

HARLEN: Oki, Granny. No, we didn't come for a swim. Came to see you about a present for a little girl.

MARTHA: You get lost or something?

HARLEN: Big slide across the road. We had to come around.

MARTHA: Council fixed that two months back.

WILL: (Narrating) I looked at the river and I looked at my truck up on the ridge. And I looked at Harlen.

HARLEN: We need a present, Granny. You know Louise Heavyman's little girl, South Wing. Her first birthday's tomorrow. Wanted to get her a real nice present.

MARTHA: This one her father?

HARLEN: That's right.

WILL: (Quickly) No. I'm a friend.

MARTHA: Doesn't need a friend. Needs a father, that one.

HARLEN: This is Rose Horse Capture's boy, Will. Granny Pete's grandson.

MARTHA: Sure. I know him. Big shot photographer. No father, that one, too.

WILL: (Narrating) Martha got out of her chair and headed for the cabin. Harlen and I just stood there watching her.

MARTHA: Come on you lazy boys.

Medicine River

Scene 7: Cabin Interior

WILL: (*Narrating*) Martha's cabin was one big room, and it was dark and cool. There was an old stove in the middle of the floor and a bed near the south wall. You could smell the sage and the pine.

MARTHA: You the one that saw her born?

WILL: Well . . . I was there.

MARTHA: Okay, that'll do. You love her?

WILL: (*Narrating*) On the way back across the river I was going to drown Harlen.

WILL: Sure.

MARTHA: Don't sound too sure.

WILL: Ah . . . I love her.

MARTHA: Okay. How about the mother? You love her?

WILL: (*Narrating*) I was going to drown Harlen really slow. Let him up a couple of times, before I shoved his head all the way under.

MARTHA: You deaf or you thinking?

WILL: No . . . Yes . . . I like Louise.

MARTHA: Okay. Like is close enough.

(*SOUND:* A drawer opening.)

WILL: (*Narrating*) Martha went to a dresser and rummaged around in a drawer.

MARTHA: Here's what you boys want. Good present, this one.

(*SOUND/BIZ:* MARTHA *begins to shake the rattle and sing.*)

WILL: (*Narrating*) It was a small leather rattle made of willow and deer skin. It was painted yellow and blue and had several strands of horsehair tied to one side. There were stones or seeds inside. Martha shook it and sang a song.

MARTHA: (*Sings a little*) You know that song?

WILL: I . . . I don't think so.

MARTHA: Good thing you know how to swim. Young boys don't know anything these days. Anyway, you give this to your daughter and everything will be fine.

WILL: Well . . . I don't . . . I don't really have a daughter.

MARTHA: Then you have time to learn the song. Here you try it.

(*BIZ:* WILL *tries to sing the song.*)

MARTHA: Stop, stop. You hear that big thump. That's one of them elks falling over dead.

(*BIZ:* WILL *tries to sing the song again.*)

MARTHA: You keep singing like that and you'll freeze up the river.

Scene 8: In the River

WILL: (*Narrating*) The river was still cold as hell. It cut into me and my legs began to cramp, but when we got to the middle, I reached out with my free hand and shoved Harlen's head underwater. He came up spitting cold, green, river water.

HARLEN: Damn, Will. Why'd you do that?

Scene 9: South Wing's Birthday Party

SOUND: Crowd noises. Party noises.

WILL: (*Narrating*) Everybody came to the party the next day. South Wing was in her high chair with ice cream all over face and her dress and the chair. Louise had some in her hair.

WILL: You've got ice cream in your hair.

LOUISE: And you don't. Here's the spoon. You feed her. Everybody gets a turn.

WILL (*Narrating*) I put the present with the others and sat down next to South Wing, who gave me a big smile and opened her mouth. The first spoonful of ice cream wound up on her nose. The second wound up on the floor. We lit the candle and sang "Happy Birthday" and Louise began to open the presents.

LOUISE: This one is from Grandpa and Grandma . . . And this one is from Auntie Sue . . . And this one is from Auntie Bertha . . . And this one is . . . this one . . .

WILL: (*Narrating*) When Louise opened the rattle, she began to blush and stammer.

LOUISE: This one . . . is . . . from Uncle Will.

CARTER: Hey, looks like you got my little granddaughter one of Granny Oldcrow's rattles. Real hard to come by, those. Looks just like the one you got her, Louise.

WILL: (*Narrating*) Louise looked at me, shook her head, and reached into her apron pocket and pulled out a rattle. It looked just like the one Martha had given me.

LOUISE: Bertha took me shopping. Harlen take you shopping?

WILL: (*Narrating*) I hung around until everyone had left. South Wing hadn't made it through the cake before Louise had to put her down.

Scene 10: Louise's House, Later

LOUISE: You want some tea, Will?

WILL: Sure.

LOUISE: Granny Oldcrow talk to you?

WILL: She did.

LOUISE: I suppose they mean well.

WILL: I tried to drown Harlen.

(*BIZ:* LOUISE *laughs.*)

WILL: (*Narrating*) Louise laughed and I laughed and then she leaned over the table and kissed me.

LOUISE: That old woman is dangerous. You know what she does for a living.

WILL: Ah . . . yeah . . . sort of . . .

WILL: (*Narrating*) Louise stayed there, leaning over the table, close to me. And then she kissed me again.

LOUISE: Maybe I'll make us something to eat. You want something to eat?

WILL: Sure.

LOUISE: (*Softly*) You can stay, too. (*Pause*) If you want.

(*SOUND/MUSIC: Sound of a baby fussing—not really crying. Music begins to mark the end of the act.*)

WILL: (*Narrating*) In the middle of the night, South Wing woke up and started to cry. She was standing in her crib. One of the rattles was on the floor. I picked it up and shook it, and she smiled and reached out. I took her out of her crib. Her diaper was wet, so I changed it. She didn't make a sound. She lay there playing with the rattle, watching, and it reminded me of the morning she was born. Later, I put her back in the crib, but I stayed in the room until it got light and tried to remember the song.

Act Four

Scene 1: Studio

MUSIC: Music begins to mark the opening of the act.

WILL: (*Narrating*) Harlen Bigbear had a great many interests. He liked basketball. He liked cars. He liked golf. He liked fishing. He was a fair carpenter and a decent hockey player. He collected these interests the way some people collect stamps, and though they never seemed to last very long, the knowledge accumulated in Harlen's brain like brown grocery bags in a closet. Harlen's latest interest was . . . photography. For the last month, every time Harlen stopped by, I'd have to explain another aspect of taking pictures, or I would have to explain how a certain part of the camera worked.

HARLEN: What's that?

WILL: That's the shutter release, Harlen.

HARLEN: Right. What's this?

WILL: It's the ring that sets your f-stops. It controls things like light and depth of field.

HARLEN: Right. And this?

WILL: That sets your shutter speed.

HARLEN: What's this little button?

WILL: That's the time delay button.

HARLEN: Those guys think of everything.

WILL: I don't use it much.

HARLEN: What does it do?

WILL: Well, let's say you wanted a picture of yourself and the basketball team. You'd put the camera on a tripod and set the delay, like this. Then you would push the button right here, and you'd have about ten seconds before the camera actually took the picture.

HARLEN: So I could be in the picture, too.

WILL: If you moved fast enough. I don't use it much.

HARLEN: Damn. Those guys think of everything.

WILL: (*Narrating*) Near the end of June, Harlen decided that I should run a photography special.

Medicine River

HARLEN: Run a family-portrait special. Something like that will bring in a lot of people from the reserve. Family is an important thing.

WILL: (*Narrating*) So I ran a special. Business had been slow, and a small profit was better than no profit. So for the last two weeks in June, you could get a family portrait for twenty dollars. You got one eight by ten, two five by sevens, four three by fives, and eight wallet size photographs. It was a great deal.

Scene 2: Phone Conversation

SOUND: Phone rings.

WILL: (*Narrating*) Joyce Blue Horn was the first one to call.

JOYCE: Does that special mean all the family?

WILL: Yes, it does.

JOYCE: I got a big family.

WILL: Doesn't matter. Just bring everybody in, and I'll take the picture.

JOYCE: We got to drive in from the reserve. Saturday okay?

WILL: Sure. Let's make it late Saturday morning.

JOYCE: That's fine. Going to be real good to get a picture of the family.

WILL: (*Narrating*) When Harlen stopped by the studio, I told him about Joyce Blue Horn and Harlen, who knew about these things, gave me the family history.

Scene 3: Studio

HARLEN: Joyce is Mary Rabbit's daughter. She married Elvis Blue Horn. They got eleven kids.

WILL: (*Narrating*) Joyce, according to Harlen, was a minor celebrity on the reserve, but not because of the size of her family.

HARLEN: There were the three girls first, triplets: Frances, Deborah and Jennifer. Then you had two sets of twins: Fred and Fay, and George and Andy. Robert was the only single, and he was followed by another set of twins: Christian and Benjamin. How many is that?

WILL: Ten, I think.

HARLEN: Okay. Then there was Elizabeth and Samuel, but Samuel died. You keeping track of everyone?

WILL: I'm trying.

HARLEN: She say she was bringing the entire family?

WILL: I can handle eleven people.

HARLEN: Don't forget Joyce and Elvis.

WILL: Thirteen is no problem, either.

WILL: (*Narrating*) Harlen smiled and walked around the studio looking at the walls. He began to laugh, soft, low clucks like he was sitting on half-a-dozen eggs.

WILL: Something wrong?

HARLEN: Will, when Joyce Blue Horn said family, she wasn't just talking about her and Elvis and the kids, you know.

WILL: Her parents alive?

HARLEN: Elvis' mom and dad, too.

WILL: No problem.

HARLEN: Elvis has nine brothers and four sisters.

WILL: Come on, Harlen . . .

HARLEN: And Joyce . . . Joyce has seven sisters and five brothers.

WILL: Look, the photo special is for the immediate family.

HARLEN: Oh, then we're only talking about fifty people or so.

WILL: (*Narrating*) Harlen liked to exaggerate. I knew that. And there was no way I could get fifty people in the studio for a photograph, so I guess I didn't really think that fifty people would show up. Friday night I took Louise out to dinner. I waited until we had finished the soup.

Scene 4: Restaurant

WILL: You know Joyce Blue Horn, don't you?

LOUISE: Went to school with her.

WILL: She's coming by the studio tomorrow. You know, that special I'm running.

LOUISE: The family portrait?

WILL: That's the one.

LOUISE: You got room in the studio for everybody?

WILL: Studio will handle . . . twenty easy.

WILL: (*Narrating*) Louise shook her head, reached across and patted my hand, and then she began to laugh.

WILL: I know she has a large family.

(BIZ: *Sound of* LOUISE *trying to control her laughter.*)

LOUISE: (*Stops laughing*) Eat your dinner, Will. (*Begins laughing again*)

WILL: (*Narrating*) Saturday morning, I got in early and began moving everything out of the studio, so I'd have enough room. At ten o'clock, Harlen arrived.

Scene 5: Studio

(SOUND: *The front door opening, bell.*)

HARLEN: Morning, Will. Joyce here yet?

WILL: Not yet.

HARLEN: Thought I'd come by and watch.

WILL: (*Narrating*) Louise and South Wing arrived at eleven.

LOUISE: I haven't seen Joyce and the kids for a couple of months. South Wing and Elizabeth were born three weeks apart. You mind if we watch?

WILL: (*Narrating*) Joyce Blue Horn and her kids arrived at eleven-thirty. Elvis was right behind them with a large cardboard box that said "Huggies" on the side.

ELVIS: Where do you want this, Will?

WILL: What is it?

ELVIS: Lunch.

(SOUND/BIZ: *Crowd noises.*)

WILL: (*Narrating*) By noon, not counting Harlen and Louise and South Wing, there were thirty-eight people in the studio. Harlen knew everyone and, as people came in, he'd say hello and introduce them to me.

HARLEN: Will, this is Charlotte, Joyce's sister, and her husband Mel . . . This is Elvis' brother Rodney, and that's Ann and Sonny and Jimmy . . . Clare Blue Horn, Will. Her husband Bender used to play for the team. You remember Bender . . . This is Cindy and Betty and Katie and John and . . .

WILL: (*Narrating*) Well, I did make an attempt at remembering some of the names. And I tried to keep count. By twelve-thirty, there were in the vicinity of fifty-four people—adults and kids—in my studio. The kids were everywhere, in the bathroom, in the studio itself, in the kitchen. The adults stood around in groups, talking. Someone had opened the cardboard box and Joyce was passing around sandwiches and potato chips. Louise waved at me from behind a wall of people.

LOUISE: Will, why don't we take everybody down to the river? Should be nice down there. Wind's not bad. We can get some more food and soda, and you can take the pictures of Joyce and Elvis and the kids near that little beach with the big cottonwoods.

WILL: Horsehead Coulee?

LOUISE: Sure. Have a picnic, do some swimming, too. You could get a good picture of everyone.

WILL: (*Narrating*) There were probably lots of reasons why it wasn't a good idea to try to take a family portrait down by the river, but before I could think of any, Louise was over talking to Joyce, and Joyce was talking to Elvis, and Elvis was talking to his sisters . . .

ELVIS: That's a great idea, Will. I'll call the rest of the folks.

Scene 6: Outdoors, by the River

SOUND: River and birds and outdoor noises.

WILL: (*Narrating*) Spring and early summer are the prettiest seasons on the prairies, especially down in the coulees around the river. By the time we bounced our way down the dirt road to Horsehead Coulee, Elvis and his brothers were already setting up some makeshift tables, and Joyce and her sisters were spreading out the food. The river was lower than I had expected, green and murky, slow-moving and shallow, occasionally dropping into deep, warm holes.

ELVIS: Maybe we'll feed the grandparents first. Let them get settled in. Kids'll just as soon swim, anyway. Maybe you could take the pictures a little later, Will. That okay?

WILL: Sure.

WILL: (*Narrating*) I found Louise and South Wing and me a flat place down by the river. The sun was warm. Louise snuggled down against my shoulder.

LOUISE: This is nice, Will.

WILL: (*Narrating*) I was just getting settled, feeling warm, thinking about a nap, when I felt the sun disappear, and there was Harlen.

HARLEN: Will, get up. You're supposed to be working. Don't want to lose your good reputation by going to sleep where everyone can see you. Come on. People have been asking about you.

WILL: (*Narrating*) Harlen took me over to a group of elders who were sitting in lawn chairs, watching the kids in the river. I knew Lionel James and Martha Oldcrow. Harlen stood up straight and put his hand on my shoulder. Then he pushed me forward.

HARLEN: This is Rose Horse Capture's boy, Will.

MARTHA: Sure, I know him. He's the big shot photographer.

HARLEN: That's him.

MARTHA: The one who ran off to Toronto.

HARLEN: What a memory!

MARTHA: Your mother always said you'd come home.

HARLEN: How about that, Will.

MARTHA: And here you are.

LIONEL: Real nice day, Will. You were raised in Calgary, so maybe you don't know everybody. Maybe you should greet everyone so you know the people.

WILL: (*Narrating*) Lionel took me around and introduced me to the elders. He shook hands with an old woman and said something to her in Blackfoot. She looked at me and smiled and began to laugh to herself.

LIONEL: This is Eddie's granny. She knew your mother. She's happy to see you're alive and getting enough to eat. Her oldest boy died last year in a car accident. She wants you to get her a sandwich.

WILL: Sure. What kind does she like?

LIONEL: Maybe something soft. Peanut butter and jelly would be good.

WILL: (*Narrating*) Harlen caught up to me as I was getting a sandwich from the table.

HARLEN: You and Lionel talking to Eddie's granny?

WILL: She wanted a sandwich.

HARLEN: She likes root beer, too.

WILL: (*Narrating*) I took the sandwich and the root beer back to Eddie's granny. Lionel and the old woman were laughing quietly. Lionel had tears in his eyes.

LIONEL: Her boy was a real good storyteller. Always had a funny story to tell. He travelled all over the place and always came back with a good story.

Sometimes we'd laugh so hard, it would hurt, and we would have to lie down. We were remembering one of his stories just now.

WILL: I don't think I knew him.

LIONEL: Granny says you remind her of him. She says maybe she should adopt you. That boy of hers always had a good story.

WILL: I'm sorry about her boy.

LIONEL: Old women get like that, you know.

WILL: Sure.

LIONEL: Always worrying about the kids who don't have mothers.

WILL: Sure.

LIONEL: Fathers are important, too. That Louise is a handsome woman. That little girl of hers is real smart.

WILL: That's true.

LIONEL: People should think about these things more often.

WILL: You're right.

LIONEL: I guess that's what you're doing.

WILL: What?

LIONEL: Thinking about those things.

WILL: (*Narrating*) Elvis and Joyce began herding the kids out of the river and over to the tables. They came wiggling along like a twist of eels all wrapped around each other. Harlen came over. He had a sandwich in one hand, a soda in the other, and another soda in his pocket. He handed me the half-empty can.

HARLEN: This one's for you, Will. Been saving it.

WILL: Yeah . . . thanks.

HARLEN: How's the sun doing? You watching the sun? Don't want to forget about that portrait.

WILL: It's okay, Harlen. Lots of time.

HARLEN: You going to be able to get everyone in?

WILL: Sure. Put Joyce and Elvis off to one side and line the kids up.

HARLEN: What about the grandparents?

WILL: Well, we could set up a few lawn chairs in front.

HARLEN: We got enough chairs?

WILL: (*Slightly exasperated with* **HARLEN**) It's just the two sets of grandparents.

JOYCE: Will . . . Will. As soon as the kids get fed, we can take the picture.

WILL: Whenever. How many you figure we'll have in the picture?

JOYCE: Are there too many?

WILL: No . . . just wanted to know. You know, give me a chance to figure who should go where. Out here, I could take a picture of everyone.

JOYCE: Okay. That'll be real good.

WILL: So, how many you figure?

JOYCE: Everyone.

WILL: (*Narrating*) And Joyce walked back to where the kids were eating, leaving me with Harlen.

HARLEN: Boy, that'll be some picture.

WILL: Everyone?

HARLEN: You said you could do it, Will. Everybody's depending on you. You're the boss.

WILL: (*Narrating*) Harlen went running off to tell everyone and I was left standing trying to figure out how I had gotten myself into this situation. The kids finished eating and Harlen and Joyce and Elvis moved everyone over to the river.

WILL: Okay. We better get started. Let's put the elders in front.

HARLEN: You're the boss, Will.

WILL: Let the little kids sit on the sand. The bigger kids can stand around the grandparents, and we'll put most of the adults at the back.

WILL: (*Narrating*) Harlen ran around like a confused sheepdog trying to coax and lead and push everyone into place.

HARLEN: How's that, Will?

WILL: That's great. Okay, time to take some pictures.

JOYCE: What about you, Will?

ELVIS: That's right.

WILL: Something wrong?

JOYCE: Should have you in the picture, too.

WILL: Well, someone has to take the picture.

WILL: (*Narrating*) Through the lens, I could see Harlen bubbling out of the crowd.

HARLEN: Hey, Will. That's right. You can be in the picture, too. You can use that button thing. You know, set the button and run on over.

WILL: That's okay, Harlen.

LIONEL: Best you be in the picture, too

WILL: (*Narrating*) As soon as Harlen explained, in detail, just what a time-delay device was, everyone insisted that I had to be in the picture, too. Louise and Eddie's granny made a place for me in the middle.

HARLEN: Come on, Will. Push the button and run on over.

WILL: (*Narrating*) The first shots were easy. I set the timer and ran across the sand and sat down next to Louise and South Wing and Eddie's granny. But with a large group like that, you can't take chances. Someone may have closed their eyes just as the picture was taken. Or one of the kids could have turned their back. Or someone might have gotten lost behind someone else.

HARLEN: Come on, Will. Run.

WILL: (*Narrating*) Then, too, the group refused to stay in place. After every picture, the kids wandered off among their parents and relatives and friends, and the adults floated back and forth, no one holding their positions. Only the grandparents remained in place as the ocean of relations flowed around them.

HARLEN: Run, Will, run!

WILL: (*Narrating*) I took twenty-four pictures. And each time I had to set the camera, hit the shutter-delay button and run like hell. After the fourteenth or fifteenth picture, I tried to stay behind the camera, but Harlen wouldn't hear of it.

HARLEN: Come on, Will. This one's going to be the good one.

WILL: (*Narrating*) The pictures turned out good. There were four or five where nearly everyone was facing the camera and smiling. Harlen was in the studio when the photos came off the dryer.

Scene 7: Studio

HARLEN: These are good, Will. Joyce is going to be real pleased.

WILL: Yeah. We got lucky.

HARLEN: Hey, is this that old picture you were working on, the one of you and James and your mother?

WILL: That's it.

HARLEN: Looks a lot better.

WILL: I fixed it up and made a new negative. Thought I'd send a copy to James.

HARLEN: Real different. You and James look like someone sprayed you up and down with starch.

WILL: That's the way they used to take pictures.

HARLEN: Nobody smiling, huh?

WILL: I guess.

HARLEN: Wonder what your mother was thinking about.

WILL: Who knows.

HARLEN: You know, Will. This is the first family portrait Joyce Blue Horn has ever had. She told me that. Probably get a lot of new business once word gets around what a good photographer you are.

WILL: Don't know if I can run that fast again.

HARLEN: (*Laughing*) Well, Eddie's granny was impressed. Said you ran like the old-time men, fast, no noise.

WILL: Eddie's granny must be deaf.

HARLEN: Said you reminded her of her boy.

(MUSIC: *Music begins to mark the end of the radio play.*)

WILL: (*Narrating*) I worked late that night, got the portraits packaged and ready to mail. When I got home, I tacked the picture of Mom and James and me up on the kitchen wall. Right next to it, I stuck the picture of all of us down at the river. I was smiling in that picture, and you couldn't see the sweat. Louise and South Wing were sitting next to me, smiling. Eddie's granny was in her lawn chair looking right at the camera, with that same flat expression that my mother had, as though she could see something farther on and out of sight.

End of radio play.

After Words

1. In your journal, respond to the radio play. Focus on the characters and their relationships.
2. Contrast Will and Harlen. For what effects has the author created these characters?
3. From Louise's point of view, recall the events of the play in a series of diary entries, a monologue, or a conversation with Bertha.
4. In a small group, examine the final act. How are the concerns of the previous acts brought together and resolved? Individually, focus on one concern to examine. Share and discuss your ideas. Present your conclusions to the class.
5. Choose one portion of the play you found humorous. Examine and explain how the author has created the humour.
6. Extend the play with one of the following activities:
    a) Brainstorm other "meddling" in which Harlen will try to involve Will. Choose one situation to script as a radio play. Rehearse; then audio tape.
    b) Develop a scene in which Harlen and Will reverse roles. Refine, rehearse, and present your scene.
    c) Write a sequel in which Will and Louise explain to South Wing, now much older, how she got her name. Rehearse and present the scene.
    d) Consider Will's future. How might significant moments in his life be represented in photographs? Describe and/or sketch these images.
    e) Write a tale an elder would tell of a relationship involving Will.
    f) In a way you choose, explore another relationship (family, community, or romantic) in the play.

A Marriage Proposal

A stage play by ANTON CHEKHOV, translated by
Theodore Hoffman

ANTON CHEKHOV (1860–1904) is considered one of Russia's, and the world's, foremost dramatists. He started writing comic articles for magazines to pay his way through medical school and continued writing after graduation. Through his consultations with patients and all that they revealed about themselves, his sympathetic interest in the human condition deepened. Chekhov died in Badenweiler, Germany after a long battle with tuberculosis. His longer plays such as *Three Sisters* and *The Cherry Orchard* are still staged today, and his work continues to influence actors and writers. The following short play, a comedy of manners, recreates a time in which some marriages were arranged to consolidate estates and fortunes rather than for love.

Prelude

1. In your journal, write your thoughts on marriage. Consider your wishes for your future; then consider current, past, and future reasons people marry.

2. At their extremes, neighbours can be the best of friends or the worst of enemies. What makes the difference? What examples are there in today's world of good and bad neighbours?

A Marriage Proposal

Characters

> STEPAN STEPANOVITCH CHUBUKOV: An elderly gentleman who owns an estate in nineteenth-century Russia
>
> IVAN VASSILEVITCH LOMOV: A neighbouring landowner, a neurotic bachelor
>
> NATALIA STEPANOVNA: Chubukov's daughter, unmarried and wishing to marry

> *Chubukov's mansion: the living room.*
>
> LOMOV *enters, formerly dressed in evening jacket, white gloves, top hat. He is nervous from the start.*

CHUBUKOV: (*Rising*) Well, look who's here! Ivan Vassilevitch! (*Shakes his hand warmly*) What a surprise, old man! How are you?

LOMOV: Oh, not too bad. And you?

CHUBUKOV: Oh, we manage, we manage. Do sit down, please. You know, you've been neglecting your neighbours, my dear fellow. It's been ages. Say, why the formal dress? Tails, gloves, and so forth. Where's the funeral, my boy? Where are you headed?

LOMOV: Oh, nowhere. I mean, here; just to see you, my dear Stepan Stepanovitch.

CHUBUKOV: Then why the full dress, old boy? It's not New Year's, and so forth.

LOMOV: Well, you see, it's like this. I have come here, my dear Stepan Stepanovitch, to bother you with a request. More than once, or twice, or more than that, it has been my privilege to apply to you for assistance in things, and you've always, well, responded. I mean, well, you have. Yes. Excuse me, I'm getting all mixed up. May I have a glass of water, my dear Stepan Stepanovitch? (*Drinks*)

CHUBUKOV: (*Aside*) Wants to borrow some money. Not a chance! (*Aloud*) What can I do for you, my dear friend?

LOMOV: Well, you see, my dear Stepanitch . . . Excuse me, I mean Stepan my Dearovitch . . . No, I mean, I get all confused, as you can see. To make a long story short, you're the only one who can help me. Of course, I don't deserve it, and there's no reason why I should expect you to, and all that.

CHUBUKOV: Stop beating around the bush! Out with it!

LOMOV: In just a minute. I mean, now, right now. The truth is, I have come to ask the hand . . . I mean, your daughter, Natalia Stepanovna, I, I want to marry her!

CHUBUKOV: (*Overjoyed*) Great heavens! Ivan Vassilevitch! Say it again!

LOMOV: I have come humbly to ask for the hand . . .

CHUBUKOV: (*Interrupting*) You're a prince! I'm overwhelmed, delighted, and so forth. Yes, indeed, and all that! (*Hugs and kisses* LOMOV) This is just what I've been hoping for. It's my fondest dream come true. (*Sheds a tear*) And, you know, I've always looked upon you, my boy, as if you were my own son. May God grant to both of you His Mercy and His Love, and so forth. Oh, I have been wishing for this . . . But why am I being so idiotic? It's just that I'm off my rocker with joy, my boy! Completely off my rocker! Oh, with all my soul I'm . . . I'll go get Natalia, and so forth.

LOMOV: (*Deeply moved*) Dear Stepan Stepanovitch, do you think she'll agree?

CHUBUKOV: Why, of course, old friend. Great heavens! As if she wouldn't! Why she's crazy for you! Good God! Like a love-sick cat, and so forth. Be right back. (*Leaves*)

LOMOV: God, it's cold. I'm gooseflesh all over, as if I had to take a test. But the main thing is, to make up my mind, and keep it that way. I mean, if I take time out to think, or if I hesitate, or talk about it, or have ideals, or wait for real love, well, I'll just never get married! Brrrr, it's cold! Natalia Stepanovna is an excellent housekeeper. She's not too bad looking. She's had a good education. What more could I ask! Nothing. I'm so nervous, my ears are buzzing. (*Drinks*) Besides, I've just got to get married. I'm thirty-five already. It's sort of a critical age. I've got to settle down and lead a regular life. I mean, I'm always getting palpitations, and I'm nervous, and I get upset so easy. Look, my lips are quivering, and my eyebrow's twitching. The worst thing is the night. Sleeping. I get into bed, doze off, and, suddenly, something inside me jumps. First my head snaps, and then my shoulder blade, and I roll out of bed like a lunatic and try to walk it off. Then I try to go back to sleep, but, as soon as I do, something jumps again! Twenty times a night, sometimes . . .

(NATALIA STEPANOVNA *enters*.)

NATALIA: Oh, it's only you. All Papa said was: "Go inside, there's a merchant come to collect his goods." How do you do, Ivan Vassilevitch?

LOMOV: How do you do, dear Natalia Stepanovna?

NATALIA: Excuse my apron, and not being dressed. We're shelling peas. You haven't been around lately. Oh, do sit down. (*They do.*) Would you like some lunch?

LOMOV: No thanks, I had some.

NATALIA: Well, then smoke if you want. (*He doesn't.*) The weather's nice today . . . but yesterday, it was so wet the workmen couldn't get a thing done. Have you got much hay in? I felt so greedy I had a whole field done, but now I'm not sure I was right. With the rain it could rot, couldn't it? I should have waited. But why are you so dressed up? Is there a dance or something? Of course, I must say you look splendid, but . . . Well, tell me, why are you so dressed up?

LOMOV: (*Excited*) Well, you see, my dear Natalia Stepanovna, the truth is, I made up my mind to ask you to . . . well, to, listen to me. Of course, it'll probably surprise you and even maybe make you angry, but . . . (*Aside*) God, it's cold in here!

NATALIA: Why, what do you mean? (*A pause*) Well?

LOMOV: I'll try to get it over with. I mean, you know, my dear Natalia Stepanovna that I've known, since childhood, even, known, and had the privilege of knowing, your family. My late aunt, and her husband, who, as you know, left me my estate, they always had the greatest respect for your father, and your late mother. The Lomovs and the Chubukovs have always been very friendly, you might even say affectionate. And, of course, you know, our land borders on each other's. My Oxen Meadows touch your birch grove . . .

NATALIA: I hate to interrupt you, my dear Ivan Vassilevitch, but you said: "my Oxen Meadows." Do you really think they're yours?

LOMOV: Why of course they're mine.

NATALIA: What do you mean? The Oxen Meadows are ours, not yours!

LOMOV: Oh, no, my dear Natalia Stepanovna, they're mine.

NATALIA: Well, this is the first I've heard about it! Where did you get that idea?

LOMOV: Where? Why, I mean the Oxen Meadows that are wedged between your birches and the marsh.

NATALIA: Yes, of course, they're ours.

LOMOV: Oh, no, you're wrong, my dear Natalia Stepanovna, they're mine.

A Marriage Proposal

NATALIA: Now, come, Ivan Vassilevitch! How long have they been yours?

LOMOV: How long? Why, as long as I can remember!

NATALIA: Well, really, you can't expect me to believe that!

LOMOV: But, you can see for yourself in the deed, my dear Natalia Stepanovna. Of course, there was once a dispute about them, but everyone knows they're mine now. There's nothing to argue about. There was a time when my aunt's grandmother let your father's grandfather's peasants use the land, but they were supposed to bake bricks for her in return. Naturally, after a few years they began to act as if they owned it, but the real truth is . . .

NATALIA: That has nothing to do with the case! Both my grandfather and my great-grandfather said that their land went as far as the marsh, which means that the Meadows are ours! There's nothing whatever to argue about. It's foolish.

LOMOV: But I can show you the deed, Natalia Stepanovna.

NATALIA: You're just making fun of me . . . Great Heavens! Here we have the land for hundreds of years, and suddenly you try to tell us it isn't ours. What's wrong with you, Ivan Vassilevitch! Those meadows aren't even fifteen acres, and they're not worth three hundred rubles, but I just can't stand unfairness! I just can't stand unfairness!

LOMOV: But, you must listen to me. Your father's grandfather's peasants, as I've already tried to tell you, they were supposed to bake bricks for my aunt's grandmother. And my aunt's grandmother, why, she wanted to be nice to them . . .

NATALIA: It's just nonsense, this whole business about aunts and grandfathers, and grandmothers. The Meadows are ours! That's all there is to it!

LOMOV: They're mine!

NATALIA: Ours! You can go on talking for two days, and you can put on fifteen evening coats and twenty pairs of gloves, but I tell you they're ours, ours, ours!

LOMOV: Natalia Stepanovna, I don't want the Meadows! I'm just acting on principle. If you want, I'll give them to you.

NATALIA: I'll give them to *you*! Because they're ours! And that's all there is to it! And if I may say so, your behaviour, my dear Ivan Vassilevitch, is very strange. Until now, we've always considered you a good neighbour, even a friend. After all, last year we lent you our threshing machine, even though it meant putting off our own threshing until November. And here you are treating us like a pack of gypsies. Giving me my own land, indeed! Really!

Why that's not being a good neighbour. It's sheer impudence, that's what it is . . .

LOMOV: Oh, so you think I'm just a land-grabber? My dear lady, I've never grabbed anybody's land in my whole life, and no-one's going to accuse me of doing it now! (*Quickly walks over to the pitcher and drinks some more water*) The Oxen Meadows are mine!

NATALIA: That's a lie. They're ours!

LOMOV: Mine!

NATALIA: A lie! I'll prove it. I'll send my mowers out there today!

LOMOV: What?

NATALIA: My mowers will mow it today!

LOMOV: I'll kick them out!

NATALIA: You just dare!

LOMOV: (*Clutching his heart*) The Oxen Meadows are mine! Do you understand? Mine!

NATALIA: Please don't shout! You can shout all you want in your own house, but here I must ask you to control yourself.

LOMOV: If my heart wasn't palpitating the way it is, if my insides weren't jumping like mad, I wouldn't talk to you so calmly. (*Yelling*) The Oxen Meadows are mine!

NATALIA: Ours!

LOMOV: Mine!

NATALIA: Ours!

LOMOV: Mine!

(*Enter* CHUBUKOV)

CHUBUKOV: What's going on? Why all the shouting?

NATALIA: Papa, will you please inform this gentleman who owns the Oxen Meadows, he or we?

CHUBUKOV: (*To* LOMOV) Why, they're ours, old fellow.

LOMOV: But how can they be yours, my dear Stepan Stepanovitch? Be fair. Perhaps my aunt's grandmother did let your grandfather's peasants work the land, and maybe they did get so used to it that they acted as if it was their own, but . . .

CHUBUKOV: Oh, no, no . . . my dear boy. You forget something. The reason the peasants didn't pay your aunt's grandmother, and so forth, was that the

A Marriage Proposal

land was disputed, even then. Since then it's been settled. Why, everyone knows it's ours.

LOMOV: I can prove it's mine.

CHUBUKOV: You can't prove a thing, old boy.

LOMOV: Yes I can!

CHUBUKOV: My dear lad, why yell like that? Yelling doesn't prove a thing. Look, I'm not after anything of yours, just as I don't intend to give up anything of mine. Why should I? Besides, if you're going to keep arguing about it, I'd just as soon give the land to the peasants, so there!

LOMOV: There nothing! Where do you get the right to give away someone else's property?

CHUBUKOV: I certainly ought to know if I have the right or not. And you had better realize it, because, my dear young man, I am not used to being spoken to in that tone of voice, and so forth. Besides which, my dear young man, I am twice as old as you are, and I ask you to speak to me without getting yourself into such a tizzy, and so forth!

LOMOV: Do you think I'm a fool? First you call my property yours, and then you expect me to keep calm and polite! Good neighbours don't act like that, my dear Stepan Stepanovitch. You're no neighbour, you're a land grabber!

CHUBUKOV: What was that? What did you say?

NATALIA: Papa, send the mowers out to the meadows at once!

CHUBUKOV: What did you say, sir?

NATALIA: The Oxen Meadows are ours, and we'll never give them up, never, never, never, never!

LOMOV: We'll see about that. I'll go to court. I'll show you!

CHUBUKOV: Go to court? Well, go to court, and so forth! I know you, just waiting for a chance to go to court, and so forth. You pettifogging shyster, you! All of your family is like that. The whole bunch of them!

LOMOV: You leave my family out of this! The Lomovs have always been honourable, upstanding people, and not a one of them was ever tried for embezzlement, like your grandfather was.

CHUBUKOV: The Lomovs are a pack of lunatics, the whole bunch of them!

NATALIA: The whole bunch!

CHUBUKOV: Your grandfather was a drunkard, and what about your other aunt, the one who ran away with the architect? And so forth.

NATALIA: And so forth!

LOMOV: Your mother was a hunch back! (*Clutches at his heart*) Oh, I've got a stitch in my side . . . My head's whirling . . . Help! Water!

CHUBUKOV: Your father was a rum-soaked gambler.

NATALIA: And your aunt was queen of the scandalmongers!

LOMOV: My left foot's paralyzed. You're a plotter . . . Oh, my heart. It's an open secret that in the last elections you brib . . . I'm seeing stars! Where's my hat?

NATALIA: It's a low, mean, spiteful . . .

CHUBUKOV: And you're a two-faced, malicious schemer!

LOMOV: Here's my hat . . . Oh, my heart . . . Where's the door? How do I get out of here? . . . Oh, I think I'm going to die . . . My foot's numb. (*Goes*)

CHUBUKOV (*Following him*) And don't you ever set foot in my house again!

NATALIA: Go to court, indeed! We'll see about that!

(LOMOV *staggers out.*)

CHUBUKOV: The devil with him! (*Gets a drink, walks back and forth excited.*)

NATALIA: What a rascal! How can you trust your neighbours after an incident like that?

CHUBUKOV: The villain! The scarecrow!

NATALIA: He's a monster! First he tries to steal our land, and then he has the nerve to yell at you.

CHUBUKOV: Yes, and that turnip, that stupid rooster, has the gall to make a proposal. Some proposal!

NATALIA: What proposal?

CHUBUKOV: Why, he came to propose to you.

NATALIA: To propose? To me? Why didn't you tell me before?

CHUBUKOV: So he gets all dressed up in his formal clothes. That stuffed sausage, that dried up cabbage!

NATALIA: To propose to me? Ohhhh! (*Falls into a chair and starts wailing*) Bring him back! Back! Go get him! Bring him back! Ohhhh!

CHUBUKOV: Bring who back?

NATALIA: Hurry up, hurry up! I'm sick. Get him! (*Complete hysterics*)

CHUBUKOV: What for? (*To her*) What's the matter with you? (*Clutches his head*) Oh, what a fool I am! I'll shoot myself! I'll hang myself! I ruined her chances!

NATALIA: I'm dying. Get him!

CHUBUKOV: All right, all right, right away! Only don't yell! (*He runs out.*)

NATALIA: What are they doing to me? Get him! Bring him back! Bring him back!

(*A pause.* CHUBUKOV *runs in.*)

CHUBUKOV: He's coming, and so forth, the snake. Oof! You talk to him. I'm not in the mood.

NATALIA: (*Wailing*) Bring him back! Bring him back!

CHUBUKOV: (*Yelling*) I told you, he's coming! Oh Lord, what agony to be the father of a grown-up daughter. I'll cut my throat some day, I swear I will. (*To her*) We cursed him, we insulted him, abused him, kicked him out, and now . . . because you, you . . .

NATALIA: Me? It was all your fault!

CHUBUKOV: My fault? What do you mean my fau . . . ? (LOMOV *appears in the doorway.*) Talk to him yourself! (*Goes out.* LOMOV *enters, exhausted.*)

LOMOV: What palpitations! My heart! And my foot's absolutely asleep. Something keeps giving me a stitch in the side . . .

NATALIA: You must forgive us, Ivan Vassilevitch. We all got too excited. I remember now. The Oxen Meadows are yours.

LOMOV: My heart's beating something awful. My Meadows. My eyebrows, they're both twitching!

NATALIA: Yes, the Meadows are all yours, yes, yours. Do sit down. (*They sit.*) We were wrong, of course.

LOMOV: I argued on principle. My land isn't worth so much to me, but the principle . . .

NATALIA: Oh, yes, of course, the principle, that's what counts. But let's change the subject.

LOMOV: Besides, I have evidence. You see, my aunt's grandmother let your father's grandfather's peasants use the land . . .

NATALIA: Yes, yes, yes, but forget all that. (*Aside*) I wish I knew how to get him going. (*Aloud*) Are you going to start hunting soon?

LOMOV: After the harvest I'll try for grouse. But oh, my dear Natalia Stepanovna, have you heard about the bad luck I've had? You know my dog, Guess? He's gone lame.

NATALIA: What a pity. Why?

LOMOV: I don't know. He must have twisted his leg, or got in a fight, or something. (*Sighs*) My best dog, to say nothing of the cost. I paid Mironov 125 rubles for him.

NATALIA: That was too high, Ivan Vassilevitch.

LOMOV: I think it was quite cheap. He's a first class dog.

NATALIA: Why Papa only paid 85 rubles for Squeezer, and he's much better than Guess.

LOMOV: Squeezer better than Guess! What an idea! (*Laughs*) Squeezer better than Guess!

NATALIA: Of course he's better. He may still be too young but on points and pedigree, he's a better dog even than any Volchanetsky owns.

LOMOV: Excuse me, Natalia Stepanovna, but you're forgetting he's overshot, and overshot dogs are bad hunters.

NATALIA: Oh, so he's overshot, is he? Well, this is the first time I've heard about it.

LOMOV: Believe me, his lower jaw is shorter than his upper.

NATALIA: You've measured them?

LOMOV: Yes. He's all right for pointing, but if you want him to retrieve . . .

NATALIA: In the first place, our Squeezer is a thoroughbred, the son of Harness and Chisel, while your mutt doesn't even have a pedigree. He's as old and worn out as a pedlar's horse.

LOMOV: He may be old, but I wouldn't take five Squeezers for him. How can you argue? Guess is a dog, Squeezer's a laugh. Anyone you can name has a dog like Squeezer hanging around somewhere. They're under every bush. If he only cost twenty-five rubles you got cheated.

NATALIA: The devil is in you today, Ivan Vassilevitch! You want to contradict everything. First you pretend the Oxen Meadows are yours, and now you say Guess is better than Squeezer. People should say what they really mean, and you know Squeezer is a hundred times better than Guess. Why say he isn't?

LOMOV: So, you think I'm a fool or a blind man, Natalia Stepanovna! Once and for all, Squeezer is overshot!

NATALIA: He is not!

LOMOV: He is so!

NATALIA: He is not!

A Marriage Proposal

LOMOV: Why shout, my dear lady?

NATALIA: Why talk such nonsense? It's terrible. Your Guess is old enough to be buried, and you compare him with Squeezer!

LOMOV: I'm sorry, I can't go on. My heart . . . it's palpitating!

NATALIA: I've always noticed that the hunters who argue most don't know a thing.

LOMOV: Please! Be quiet a moment. My heart's falling apart . . . (*Shouts*) Shut up!

NATALIA: I'm not going to shut up until you admit that Squeezer's a hundred times better than Guess.

LOMOV: A hundred times worse! His head . . . My eyes . . . shoulder . . .

NATALIA: Guess is half-dead already!

LOMOV: (*Weeping*) Shut up! My heart's exploding!

NATALIA: I won't shut up!

(CHUBUKOV *comes in.*)

CHUBUKOV: What's the trouble now?

NATALIA: Papa, will you please tell us which is the better dog, his Guess or our Squeezer?

LOMOV: Stepan Stepanovitch, I implore you to tell me just one thing; Is your Squeezer overshot or not? Yes or no?

CHUBUKOV: Well what if he is? He's still the best dog in the neighbourhood, and so forth.

LOMOV: Oh, but isn't my dog, Guess, better? Really?

CHUBUKOV: Don't get yourself so fraught up, old man. Of course, your dog has his good points—thorough-bred, firm on his feet, well sprung ribs, and so forth. But, my dear fellow, you've got to admit he has two defects; he's old and he's short in the muzzle.

LOMOV: Short in the muzzle? Oh, my heart! Let's look at the facts! On the Marusinsky hunt my dog ran neck and neck with the Count's, while Squeezer was a mile behind them . . .

CHUBUKOV: That's because the Count's groom hit him with a whip.

LOMOV: And he was right, too! We were fox hunting; what was your dog chasing sheep for?

CHUBUKOV: That's a lie! Look, I'm going to lose my temper . . . (*Controlling himself*) my dear friend, so let's stop arguing, for that reason alone. You're only arguing because we're all jealous of somebody else's dog. Who can

A Marriage Proposal

help it? As soon as you realize some dog is better than yours, in this case our dog, you start in with this and that, and the next thing you know—pure jealousy! I remember the whole business.

LOMOV: I remember too!

CHUBUKOV: (*Mimicking*) "I remember too!" What do you remember?

LOMOV: My heart . . . my foot's asleep . . . I can't . . .

NATALIA: (*Mimicking*) "My heart . . . my foot's asleep." What kind of a hunter are you? You should be hunting cockroaches in the kitchen, not foxes. "My heart!"

CHUBUKOV: Yes, what kind of a hunter are you anyway? You should be sitting at home with your palpitations, not tracking down animals. You don't hunt anyhow. You just go out to argue with people and interfere with their dogs, and so forth. For God's sake, let's change the subject before I lose my temper. Anyway, you're just not a hunter.

LOMOV: But you, you're a hunter? Ha! You only go hunting to get in good with the count, and to plot, and intrigue, and scheme . . . Oh, my heart! You're a schemer, that's what!

CHUBUKOV: What's that? Me a schemer? (*Shouting*) Shut up!

LOMOV: A schemer!

CHUBUKOV: You infant! You puppy!

LOMOV: You old rat! You hypocrite!

CHUBUKOV: You shut up, or I'll shoot you down like a partridge! You idiot!

LOMOV: Everyone knows that—oh, my heart—that your wife used to beat you . . . Oh, my feet . . . my head . . . I'm seeing stars . . . I'm going to faint! (*He drops into an armchair.*) Quick, a doctor! (*Faints*)

CHUBUKOV: (*Going on, oblivious*) Baby! Weakling! Idiot! I'm getting sick. (*Drinks water*) Me! I'm sick!

NATALIA: What kind of a hunter are you? You can't even sit on a horse! (*To her father*) Papa, what's the matter with him? Look, papa! (*Screaming*) Ivan Vassilevitch! He's dead.

CHUBUKOV: I'm choking, I can't breathe . . . Give me air.

NATALIA: He's dead! (*Pulling* LOMOV's *sleeve*) Ivan Vassilevitch! Ivan Vassilevitch! What have you done to me? He's dead! (*She falls into an armchair. Screaming hysterically*) A doctor! A doctor! A doctor!

CHUBUKOV: Ohhhh . . . What's the matter? What happened?

NATALIA: (*Wailing*) He's dead! He's dead!

CHUBUKOV: Who's dead? (*Looks at* LOMOV) My God, he is! Quick! Water! A doctor! (*Puts glass to* LOMOV's *lips*) Here, drink this! Can't drink it—he must be dead, and so forth . . . Oh what a miserable life! Why don't I shoot myself! I should have cut my throat long ago! What am I waiting for? Give me a knife! Give me a pistol! (LOMOV *stirs.*) Look, he's coming to. Here, drink some water. That's it.

LOMOV: I'm seeing stars . . . misty . . . Where am I?

CHUBUKOV: Just you hurry up and get married, and then the devil with you! She accepts. (*Puts* LOMOV's *hand in* NATALIA's) She accepts and so forth! I give you my blessing, and so forth! Only leave me in peace!

LOMOV: (*Getting up*) Huh? What? Who?

CHUBUKOV: She accepts! Well? Kiss her, damn you!

NATALIA: He's alive! Yes, yes, I accept.

CHUBUKOV: Kiss each other!

LOMOV: Huh? Kiss? Kiss who? (*They kiss.*) That's nice. I mean, excuse me, what happened? Oh, now I get it . . . my heart . . . those stars . . . I'm very happy, Natalia Stepanovna. (*Kisses her hand*) My foot's asleep.

NATALIA: I . . . I'm happy too.

CHUBUKOV: What a load off my shoulders! Whew!

NATALIA: Well, now maybe you'll admit that Squeezer is better than Guess?

LOMOV: Worse!

NATALIA: Better!

CHUBUKOV: What a way to enter matrimonial bliss! Let's have some champagne!

LOMOV: He's worse!

NATALIA: Better! Better, better, better, better!

CHUBUKOV: (*Trying to shout her down*) Champagne! Bring some champagne! Champagne! Champagne!

CURTAIN

A Marriage Proposal

After Words

1 In your journal, respond to the play. What chances do Lomov and Natalia have for a happy marriage?

2 Chekhov presents Lomov as nervous, sickly, and a hypochondriac. Why? What would be the effect on the play if he were the opposite?

3 Assume the role of Natalia or Lomov. Write a letter to a confidant outlining your concerns and asking for advice.

4 How is the play a comedy of manners? What behaviour and preoccupations does Chekhov comment upon?

5 What TV shows and films have you seen that are examples of farce or comedy of manners? Choose one to compare to this play.

6 In a small group, choose one of the following; then present your dramatization to the class.

   a) Rehearse and refine a dramatization of the play.

   b) Write a follow-up scene in which Natalia and Lomov celebrate their tenth anniversary.

   c) Write a contemporary version of the play in a Canadian setting.

On the King's Birthday

A stage play by Hilda Mary Hooke

Over two hundred years ago, Upper Canada's first lieutenant-governor, John Graves Simcoe, laid the groundwork for many institutions, traditions, and communities in what is now Ontario. His private secretary was Thomas Talbot, a young army lieutenant from the Anglo-Irish aristocracy. Talbot was recalled to England for active service against Napoleon but later gave up his army career to return to Canada where he supervised colonization along the Lake Erie shore until his death in 1853. A scenic driving route in the area is named The Talbot Trail in his memory.

Hilda Mary Hooke was devoted to Canadian history. For *One Act Plays from Canadian History*—published in 1942, when many Canadians were fighting in World War II—she drew on documented incidents and tales told in letters, diaries, and oral history to write of past Canadians. One of her subjects was the controversial figure of Thomas Talbot. Hooke wrote in her foreword: "These plays are only a tiny thread in the big crazy-quilt of Canada's history and legend. But I hope there will be more of them, and by other writers, until the whole brilliant patchwork is hung out for all to see."

Prelude

1 Set in 1793 in what is now Ontario, this play involves a romance. Briefly write what you know about Ontario in that period and what you expect of the play.

2 According to some traditions, men were supposed to fight duels, sometimes to the death, if a "lady's honour was slighted"—for example, if rude remarks were made about her. Discuss the assumptions behind this custom.

On the King's Birthday

Characters

LIEUTENANT THOMAS TALBOT: Handsome soldier in his early twenties, attached to Governor Simcoe's staff at Newark

SUSANNE JOHNSON: Beautiful daughter of Molly Brant and the late Sir William Johnson, Superintendent of Indian Affairs in the Colony of New York, and niece of Chief Joseph Brant

MAJOR LITTLEHALES: Military secretary to Governor Simcoe

PRINCE EDWARD (later Duke of Kent): Third son of George III of England

LIEUTENANT GRAY
CHARLES GODDARD } Members of the Governor's staff

SOPHIA RUSSELL

CHARLOTTE JARVIS

JOHN GRAVES SIMCOE: First Governor of Upper Canada

MRS. SIMCOE

Scene

A room at Navy Hall, Governor Simcoe's residence at Newark (later called Niagara-on-the-Lake), on the King's Birthday, June 4th, 1793.

It is the 4th of June, 1793, the birthday of King George the Third. A small room off the big ballroom at Navy Hall; there are entrances from the ballroom down left and right, and a door at the back leading to an inner room. A long settle runs along one side of the room; there is a table at the rear, with wine and glasses on it; candles are burning in tall candlesticks. All the furnishings are very plain.

The Governor's Ball is in progress; gay voices, laughter and music drift in from the adjoining rooms. Presently laughing voices are heard near at hand, and LIEUTENANT TALBOT *whirls in with* MISS SUSANNE JOHNSON. *They are dancing a gavotte, and after a few more steps and turns* MISS SUSANNE *breaks away and sinks breathless on the settle.*

SUSANNE: O, indeed, Mr. Talbot, you must have mercy on me! My feet are fair mazed, for I vow they scarce touched the floor in that last sally! Do you always twist and turn your partners so?

TALBOT: When I have such as you to dance with, how can I help it? Why, you're nought but a piece of thistledown—I take you by the hand, and pff! you're gone on the wind, and I needs must follow.

SUSANNE: (*Plying her fan and laughing*) Blame me if you will, sir, but for sure 'twas a mad dance.

TALBOT: (*Drawing up a chair*) But you liked it, didn't you?

SUSANNE: Did I not! At our quiet home we don't often have the opportunity of stretching our toes so blithely. My sister Mary and I sometimes walk a minuet, with little Anne playing the harpsichord for us; but, pish! to dance with a girl is no great amusement. They cannot even turn you under their arm gracefully, and poor Mary forgets to bow, and sinks in a curtsey when she should be supporting me in the low bend I've learnt so painstakingly!

TALBOT: (*Abruptly*) Susanne. Do you feel that you know me well?

SUSANNE: (*A little startled*) Why—that's a strange question.

TALBOT: I mean—better than just a casual dancing-partner? Do you think of me any differently than you do of George Gray, for instance of Fitzgerald, or— or His Royal Highness?

SUSANNE: (*With a gleam of mischief*) I shouldn't dream of thinking in any but the most respectful and distant way of His Royal Highness.

TALBOT: Yet he pursues you intolerably. I am almost mad with jealousy sometimes; and you seem to favour him so. By St. Patrick, when you were dancing just now and he was bending his face down to yours, and you smiling up at him—I could have struck him to the floor.

SUSANNE: Mr. Talbot! I think you forget of whom you speak.

TALBOT: Even if he be the King's son, need he ogle you so?

SUSANNE: (*Laughing*) Oh, indeed, you exaggerate; the Prince is most respectful. And, to make very bold, what might *you* be doing at this moment, sir?

TALBOT: I know—I'm a hot-headed fool. I've nothing against Edward; he's a good friend of mine. But, in truth, Susanne, I am not quite answerable these days.

SUSANNE: What do you mean, sir?

TALBOT: Susanne . . . I've never thought much about women, until I met you. Do you remember that day last February, when we stopped at your uncle's house on our way to Detroit? You were away visiting . . . I can see you now, coming down the trail with your sister, your hair streaming out from your fur cap, and a scarlet blanket like a king's mantle round your shoulders. I thought you were some spirit of the Canadian woods, coming through the snow to greet me.

SUSANNE: You and Mr. Gray were riding . . . and you got off your horse and came to meet me, and you said, "Hail to the Queen of the Snows!" and kissed my hand.

TALBOT: It was snowing a little, and there were white flakes on your cheek and hair—you brushed them away, and said, "Hail, brave soldier of the Queen!" My heart turned completely over, and, believe me, Tom Talbot has never been his own man since.

SUSANNE: (*A little shyly*) You flatter me, sir.

TALBOT: I mean it. Please, Susanne, look at me.

(*He takes her hands in his, and after a moment she lifts her head and looks at him with a clear, gentle gaze.*)

TALBOT: Susanne, you know I love you dearly, don't you?

SUSANNE: I—I have not known it, sir.

TALBOT: But you must have guessed. Girls know these things . . . Have you thought what you would say to me when the moment came, Susanne?

SUSANNE: (*Gently withdrawing her hand*) Mr. Talbot, you are embarrassing me a little. I—I don't quite know what to say to you.

TALBOT: (*Kneeling beside her*) Susanne, dearest!

SUSANNE: No—please wait a moment. Sit beside me.

(*He obeys reluctantly. After a moment* SUSANNE *goes on seriously.*) There are some things that I must say to you. I hoped that I need not . . . perhaps I should have thought more carefully, known sooner . . . but you were so gay and happy, and you liked to be with me—as I with you—Please, let me finish. Until this last year, when my uncle's work brought him in contact with the social life at Newark and Quebec, my sister and I have lived very quietly, at home on the Grand River. That is why I was unprepared for—anything like this. I ask your forgiveness.

TALBOT: Forgiveness! For stealing my heart, do you mean? I can well do that, for I would rather you had it than keep it myself. Susanne . . . to think that I came all the way from Ireland to find you! If I had not come!

SUSANNE: (*Seriously*) If you hadn't come, Tom, perhaps it would have been much better.

TALBOT: Susanne! turn your face—so—there are tears in your eyes! What is it, darling! Have I startled you? It's my stupid Irish tongue that has talked too fast . . .

SUSANNE: (*Stopping him gently*) Tom. I am going to be very frank with you. Is this—a little play for you—or are you going to ask me to be your wife?

TALBOT: Susanne!

SUSANNE: Please don't be angry; I didn't mean to hurt you. But I must know.

TALBOT: Darling, I am the most colossal fool and blunderer that ever stepped from Irish soil. I can never do the simplest thing in the right way. Susanne, dearest, I want you to be my wife, and never to be parted from you again.

SUSANNE: (*After a moment*) Thank you, Tom. (*She rises and walks away a few paces. Then she turns, composed and quiet.*) Now I will try to answer you.

TALBOT: (*Going to her*) Susanne . . .

SUSANNE: Will you listen to me for a few minutes, Tom, and not say anything at all?

TALBOT: I will do whatever you ask me.

SUSANNE: I'll be as quick as I can. Sit down, Tom. (*They sit, together.*) You know, don't you, who my mother is?

TALBOT: I know that she is Chief Brant's sister, and a very beautiful and charming lady.

SUSANNE: She is the daughter of a Mohawk chieftain, and a full-blooded Indian. My father was an Irishman like yourself. They were very happy together, but even then there were difficulties. Molly Brant—"Brown Lady Johnson" they used to call her—wasn't always acceptable to the great ladies who came visiting from Albany and New York! In those days my father was an important man in the State of New York. Since we came to Canada, two of my sisters have married English gentlemen. They have not been happy; the husbands have suffered in their work, and the wives in their homes . . . Oh, Tom! I have vowed, ever since I could understand such things, that no man should ever ruin his career because of me. Now do you understand?

TALBOT: Are you trying to tell me you won't marry because of your Indian blood?

SUSANNE: Yes. I am telling you that.

TALBOT: But, my dear, I knew all about that long before I met you. Chief Brant is an ally of the Governor's, and a magnificent man—why, it means nothing to me. You said yourself that your father and mother were happy together.

SUSANNE: That was long ago. Things are different now—more civilized; people regard these matters in another light.

TALBOT: But you and your sisters are honoured wherever you go.

SUSANNE: By you, perhaps, Tom, and by people like you. But there are others.

TALBOT: You're sensitive, darling; you imagine these things. By Heaven, if any so much as raised an eyebrow in my presence . . .

(MAJOR LITTLEHALES *enters briskly from the door at the rear; smart, efficient, the typical military secretary.*)

LITTLEHALES: Lieutenant Talbot, I ask your pardon. A message from His Excellency.

TALBOT: (*Rising*) What is it, sir?

LITTLEHALES: His Excellency desires me to tell you that he wishes you to proceed to Philadelphia early in the morning, to await despatches from Europe.

TALBOT: Europe! Is there news, then?

LITTLEHALES: There are rumours. You will wait on His Excellency later in the evening to receive detailed instructions.

TALBOT: Thank you, sir. I shall be ready. (LITTLEHALES *clicks his heels, bows to* SUSANNE, *and goes out smartly.*) Despatches from Europe!

SUSANNE: What is it, Tom? Is it something serious?

TALBOT: (*Going to her, taking her hands*) If it is what I anticipate, it may be serious for me. It may take me back to England.

SUSANNE: England?

TALBOT: The Governor has heard news. France and England have been clutching at each other's throats for a long time; in the end there is bound to be war. When there is, I shall be ordered to rejoin my regiment. So you see I have not spoken too soon after all, Susanne. If I go back I must either take you with me or know that you are my affianced bride.

SUSANNE: (*Distressed*) Tom . . .

(*Loud voices are heard; a flushed, noisy group bursts into the room*—PRINCE EDWARD, LIEUTENANT GRAY, CHARLES GODDARD, *and two giggling young ladies*, MISS SOPHIA RUSSELL *and* MISS CHARLOTTE JARVIS. *They have all partaken freely of the Governor's good wine.* GODDARD'S *voice is raised truculently.*)

GODDARD: No, b' Gad, can't fool me! They're all over this accursed place . . . dozens of 'em . . . all hobnobbing and pretending to be as high as the King himself; but I know 'em!

EDWARD: (*Good-natured, baiting him*) I'll wager you couldn't pick 'em in a crowd, Charles. They're powerful good-looking, some of 'em.

GODDARD: Pick 'em? I'd pick 'em out of five thousand—or ten thousand, if you like.

EDWARD: Done! I'll lay my grey mare against your King Charles spaniel that you couldn't put a finger on one of 'em at this ball.

GRAY: That's fair; he's but newly come and don't know our girls. I'm a witness to the bargain, Charles; are you on?

GODDARD: Certainly I'm on, never refused a sporting offer. My li'l spaniel against your grey mare . . . and I'll have her, too, Teddy, and I'll give Sophy a new necklace into the bargain.

CHARLOTTE: Me, too, Charley?

GODDARD: You too. Isn't this the King's birthday? No one'll say Charley Goddard isn't a good sport, and generous too. Lead on, gen'l'men! On to the kill!

CHARLOTTE: (*Laughing*) You'll show 'em up, won't you, Charley?

GODDARD: Show 'em up? I'll turn 'em all out, that's what I'll do—shamin' all our pretty gals with their yellow faces and rollin' eyes . . . too bad! eh, my pretty? (*Chucking* SOPHIA *under the chin*)

SOPHIA: You wouldn't see us put down, would you, Charley?

GRAY: Don't forget we're stickin' up for you, too, Sophy—me and His Highness here . . .

GODDARD: That's right! Teddy ain't used to this sort of thing . . . court life in England's pure, ain't it, Teddy?

(*They all roar with laughter at this sally,* GODDARD *putting an arm round each girl to steady himself. They have paid no attention to* TALBOT *and* SUSANNE, *who have been standing in the background during this scene.*)

TALBOT: (*Drawing* SUSANNE'S *hand through his arm.*) Shall we, dance, Susanne?

(*They turn towards the ballroom, and at that moment* GODDARD *sees them.*)

GODDARD: Hi! Wait a minute! (TALBOT *pauses instinctively, turning a haughty glance on* GODDARD). Lieutenant Talbot, isn't it? . . . Just a moment, Lieutenant!

(*Crossing to them unsteadily, he stops in front of* SUSANNE *and peers into her face.*)

TALBOT: (*Sharply*) Mr. Goddard, you're drunk. Have the goodness to step out of the way.

GODDARD: (*Bursting into loud laughter*) By all that's lucky! Teddy, you won't have far to go to lose your wager!

(*Catching* SUSANNE'S *hand, he twists her neatly from* TALBOT'S *arm and swings her to the centre of the room.*)

On the King's Birthday

GODDARD: Ladies and gen'l'men—here's one of your pretty squaws!

(*Things happen swiftly. Before* EDWARD, *who realizes that events have taken an awkward turn, can intervene,* TALBOT *strikes* GODDARD *in the face with such force that he staggers, trips over a chair and crashes to the floor.* TALBOT *whips out his sword and stands over him.*)

TALBOT: Get up, you miserable hound . . . or by Heaven I'll murder you where you lie!

EDWARD: (*Seizing his arm*) Tom—not here! Control yourself!

TALBOT: Let him get up! (GRAY *drags* GODDARD *to his feet.*)

GODDARD: (*Thickly*) You'll pay for that blow, Lieutenant Talbot.

TALBOT: You'll pay for every word your filthy mouth has uttered . . . you snivelling little white-feathered cur . . .

GODDARD: (*Drawing his sword*) 'S blood . . . you accursed Irishman . . .

(CHARLOTTE *shrieks. As the swords clash the door at the rear is thrown open and* GOVERNOR SIMCOE *stands on the threshold.*)

SIMCOE: What is all this about?

(*The two young men lower their swords.* SIMCOE *comes into the room.*)

SIMCOE: A brawl in my house? Lieutenant Talbot, I had suspected you of better manners. Put up your swords.

(*They obey,* TALBOT *still smouldering with rage.* GODDARD *turns on his heel and goes out without a word.*)

I am surprised to find your Highness here.

EDWARD: I ask your Excellency's pardon. Indeed the affair happened so suddenly—we were having a little joke, and our friends here took offence—

SIMCOE: They have been taking more than offence, I judge, and too freely at that. Lieutenant Gray, have the goodness to escort the ladies to the ballroom. (*To* EDWARD) Your Highness, I'll have a word with you.

TALBOT: Sir—I am sorry if I have broken good manners. Believe me, it was to avenge a worse breach that I—

SIMCOE: Later, sir. Wait here till I return.

(TALBOT *bows.* GRAY *offers his arm to* SOPHIA *and* CHARLOTTE, *now frightened and subdued; they go out to the ballroom.* SIMCOE *and* EDWARD *go out at rear.* SUSANNE *has sunk into a chair, her face hidden in her hands.* TALBOT *goes to her and gently draws down her fingers.*)

TALBOT: Susanne . . .

SUSANNE: (*Looking up, slowly*) Now do you understand?

TALBOT: Forget that low cur. Could I have got the point of my sword at his throat sooner, I had choked him before he hurt you so.

SUSANNE: He was no worse than others.

TALBOT: Others? You mean this has happened before?

SUSANNE: Yes, and will again. It is inevitable. Even if they say nothing, it's in their eyes, their voices. Tom, my dear, go away. Forget what has happened; go back to your own country, and be a great soldier. I shall hear of you sometimes, perhaps; and I shall be so proud, remembering that once you asked me to be your wife.

TALBOT: (*Violently*) You don't know what you're saying. My life is here, with you. You can't crush the joy out of existence for a fad, a fancy, a few lies from a drunken lout—

SUSANNE: (*Gravely*) They were not lies.

TALBOT: Lies or truth, it's nothing to me. Let people clack as much as they like—why need we listen? Susanne, I care nothing for this soldier's life. We'll go away from here, you and I; I'll resign my commission, we'll seek out a home for ourselves . . . I know the place! I saw it last spring when we sailed along the shores of Lake Erie. We'll build ourselves a nest there, high on those wind-swept cliffs, up above the clatter of the world . . . a place to love and dream in . . . you and I, Susanne!

(SUSANNE *returns his eager gaze sorrowfully. Slowly she shakes her head.*)

TALBOT: Susanne—!

(*From the doorway at the rear the* GOVERNOR'S *voice is heard as he enters with* PRINCE EDWARD. TALBOT *rises reluctantly.*)

SIMCOE: That is settled, then. You will return at once to Quebec, and hold everything in readiness. As soon as I have word I will send to you.

EDWARD: I will be ready, sir. (*He bows and goes out to the ballroom.*)

SIMCOE: Lieutenant Talbot, you will proceed to Philadelphia tomorrow morning. Your orders will await you; when they are despatched, you will return to Quebec to rejoin your regiment.

TALBOT: Yes, sir . . .

SIMCOE: That's all.

(TALBOT, *dismissed, bows and turns towards the door.* MRS. SIMCOE, *a capable and vivacious lady, sails in.*)

MRS. SIMCOE: Oh, Mr. Talbot! just the man I wanted—is my husband here? (*Seeing* SIMCOE) John! here you are, talking business, I warrant, and forgetting your guests. They are just beginning a minuet; dance with Miss Johnson, and Mr. Talbot shall partner me. This is just the place for a minuet; there's such a crowd outside one can scarce breathe. (*The music is heard in the ballroom.*) There! We are just in time.

SIMCOE: (*Gallantly*) If Miss Susanne will honour me—

TALBOT: (*In a low, urgent tone*) Susanne, I implore you—

SUSANNE: (*In a clear voice, crossing to* SIMCOE'S *side*) Indeed, I shall be enchanted, sir. One does not walk a minuet with the Governor every day!

(*One or two other couples have drifted in, and the dance begins.* TALBOT *stands motionless, stricken by the finality of* SUSANNE'S *action.*)

MRS. SIMCOE: (*Sweetly*) Well, Mr. Talbot! Are you not going to ask me to dance?

(*With an effort* TALBOT *pulls himself together; bows low. They move into the dance.*)

THE CURTAIN FALLS SLOWLY.

After Words

1 In your journal, respond to the play. Consider Susanne's rejection of Talbot's proposal. Do you think she made the right decision?

2 In a group, discuss whether Talbot was right to strike and threaten Goddard. What other course of action could he have taken?

3 What functions do the following characters serve in the play: Prince Edward, Governor Simcoe, Mrs. Simcoe?

4 With a partner, write either a script for an up-to-date version of the final conversation between Talbot and Susanne OR a sequel set twenty years later in which Talbot and Susanne meet again and discuss their younger days. Refine your script; then present your scene to the class in a dramatic reading or a dramatization.

5 Discuss how prejudice plays an important role in this play. Then consider what has changed and what has not in the two hundred years since.

6 Is a writer justified in glamorizing characters and/or embellishing events from history (e.g., by inventing detail)? Explain your opinion and give support, perhaps from current events, T.V., films, or novels.

To Set Our House in Order

A teleplay by ANNE WHEELER,
based on the short story by Margaret Laurence

MARGARET LAURENCE was one of Canada's most accomplished authors. Born in Neepawa, Manitoba, in 1926, she modelled her famous imaginative setting, Manawaka, on her hometown. The Manawaka cycle—which includes *The Stone Angel, A Jest of God, A Bird in the House, The Fire-Dwellers,* and *The Diviners*—is a landmark in Canadian writing. "To Set Our House in Order" is one of the connected short stories from *A Bird in the House,* Laurence's most personal fiction, inspired by events that led to her becoming a writer. She also gave her time to young authors and to the cause of world peace. Laurence died in 1987 in Lakefield, Ontario.

Anne Wheeler, born in 1946, also on the prairies, is one of Canada's foremost film-makers, with many documentaries and feature films to her credit, including *Bye, Bye Blues, The Diviners* (from Margaret Laurence's novel) and *Cowboys Don't Cry*. Brock University in Ontario recognized her contribution to Canadian film by awarding her an honorary doctorate in 1993.

In 1984, Wheeler had the task of adapting to film "To Set Our House in Order," specifically a 24-minute made-for-TV production. Although she wanted to collaborate with Laurence in doing this adaptation, Wheeler says that the author was not interested in doing screenwriting herself and put a "terrifying trust" in her to maintain the integrity of the original story. Wheeler describes the process of adaptation as follows: "After re-reading all of her Manawaka work many times and becoming intimate with the characters who weave in and out of these stories, I sat down to write the screenplay. Much of it is directly drawn from the prose, but the ending posed the greatest challenge. Laurence does not tell the reader what to think. She provokes us to explore ourselves. She provides no conclusion, but offers insight."

Anne Wheeler and Margaret Laurence never actually met but did talk a number of times about common experiences after Laurence phoned Wheeler to congratulate her on the following adaptation.

Prelude

1 In your journal, write about your family—the members, relationships, history, and so on. Recall one change that has had a significant effect on the family (e.g., a move, a birth, a death).

2 Family members occasionally come into conflict. What are some typical areas of conflict? How are the conflicts resolved?

To Set Our House in Order

Characters

    EWEN MACLEOD: A doctor, in his late 30s or early 40s

    BETH MACLEOD: Ewen's wife, in her 30s, pregnant, a nurse

    VANESSA MACLEOD: Beth and Ewen's daughter, age 10 at the time, but, in voice over/narration, an adult

    MRS. MACLEOD: Vanessa's grandmother, Ewen's mother, a widow

    DOCTOR: Beth's doctor, Ewen's colleague in town

    EDNA CONNOR: Beth's younger sister, in her 20s; lives with and keeps house for their parents

Scene 1: Exterior; Farmyard, Circa 1936; Early Day

It is early winter. The ground is dusted with snow.

A man, woman, and small girl get into a car loaded down with boxes, suitcases and a sleigh tied to its roof. It is leaving the farmyard; the house is boarded up . . . the place looks deserted.

Scene 1A: Ext. Road, Continued

As the car carries on down the road, a town can be seen in the distance.

    HEAD TITLE AND CREDITS

Scene 2: Ext. MacLeod House; Same Day

    SUBTITLE: "Manitoba, 1935"

The large old house, once proud and carefully landscaped, is now rundown and over-grown. A pregnant woman, BETH, carrying suitcases, awkwardly climbs the porch stairs. Outside, in the front driveway, VANESSA MACLEOD (age ten) is watching her father, EWEN, unload her sleigh from the top of the car.

EWEN: There you go . . . take it around to the back.

(VANESSA *takes her sleigh around to the side of the house.*)

VANESSA: (*Adult V.O.*) We moved into town, to live with Grandma MacLeod when the Depression got bad and she could no longer afford a housekeeper . . . My father had grown up in this house . . . and had not wanted to move back . . . why I didn't know . . . but I sensed that it had something to do with the unfriendly nature of the place.

(*Her mother,* BETH, *looking very tired and very pregnant, comes out of the house, presumably to get another load.*)

(EWEN *takes down a very heavy box from the roof of the car.*)

BETH: I don't know where to put anything . . . .

EWEN: (*A little irritated*) Where's Mother?

BETH: In her room, I presume . . . having a nap . . .

EWEN: I'm sorry Beth . . . I know it's not going to be easy.

BETH: (*Reassuring*) No . . . it's not . . . but we'll make the best of it, eh?

(EWEN *is grateful for her easy-going attitude. He pulls her close and they are hugging when* VANESSA *surprises them.*)

VANESSA: (*A little suspicious*) What's the matter?

EWEN: Nothing . . . (*He and* BETH *share a smile.*) Except that your Mother's working too hard again . . .

(*He takes down two small suitcases from the roof of the car.*)

EWEN: (*Handing them to* VANESSA) Here . . . can you handle these?

VANESSA: Of course!

(*The suitcases are obviously heavy for the girl, but she manages to carry them towards the house.* BETH *goes to pick up another load.*)

EWEN: Don't Beth . . . those are full of books . . . I'll bring them in . . . Why don't you take a break . . .

BETH: I'm fine . . . really . . .

Scene 3: Interior, House; Stairway

It is a dark, gloomy, heavily decorated place cluttered with lots of wooden furniture, knick-knacks and stern-looking portraits.

VANESSA: (*Adult V.O.*) To me, the house seemed full of unseen spirits . . . which belonged to every person, young or old, who had ever lived here and had died . . . like my Grandfather MacLeod, who had lived just long enough to see me born, they said . . . and my Uncle Roderick, who had been killed in the war . . . I felt that I was being continually watched and assessed . . . and that nothing I did went unnoticed.

(VANESSA *is struggling up the stairs making quite a commotion with her wide-load.*)

Scene 3A: Roderick's Bedroom; Continued

She enters the first room at the top of the stairs and hoists her suitcases onto the bed. The room is a masculine one with a gun rack, model cars, pictures of sportsmen decorating the walls and a large high bed with a heavy wooden headboard.

A distinct commanding voice turns VANESSA *around to see her grandmother,* MRS. MACLEOD, *standing in the doorway, tidying up her hair. She is a small erect woman of about 65/70 years.*

MRS. MACLEOD: What are you doing in here?

(VANESSA *is confused . . . has she really done something awful?*)

VANESSA: Papa said . . . that this would be my room . . .

MRS. MACLEOD: Well he's wrong . . . he had no right to assume such a thing . . . he knows that it's Roderick's room. . . . It's not to be disturbed.

(*She ushers the girl out as she speaks.* VANESSA *is perplexed but does as she is told.*)

MRS. MACLEOD: I want you to take your things to the little room . . . next to your parents . . .

(*As they leave,* MRS. MACLEOD *purposely shuts the door.*)

Scene 4: The Living Room; Late Day

This is an ornate room cluttered with figurines and small objects. Several Victorian chairs, worn with age, circle an elaborate Chinese carpet. One corner of the room serves as a Library, and it is there that a stack of unpacked boxes has been placed.

VANESSA, *with her* PARENTS *and* GRANDMOTHER, *is about to have tea.* BETH *is pouring, serving* VANESSA *last. The girl handles the cup nervously and is obviously terrified of spilling it.*

BETH: Why don't you take it into the kitchen, honey?

EWEN: She's fine Beth . . .

(*He gives* VANESSA *a reassuring smile . . . she smiles an ever so tiny reply.*)

BETH: (*Glancing at* MRS. MACLEOD) I'm only thinking of the rug . . .

EWEN: (*Flaring unexpectedly*) This is her home, God Damn it!

MRS. MACLEOD: No need for blasphemy, Ewen.

EWEN: I'm sorry Mother . . . I'm tired I guess.

(VANESSA *looks to her* PARENTS *for further instructions. After a moment of complete stillness, she gets up carefully and leaves the room.* BETH *and* EWEN *exchange a helpless look.*)

FADE TO BLACK

Scene 5: Front Yard; Early Morning

VANESSA *is sweeping the snow off the front porch; she's inappropriately dressed in a good dress and coat.* EWEN *comes out of the house carrying a black doctor's bag. He is dressed in a World War I uniform, and a coat, worn open.*

EWEN: I have to go over to the hospital first . . . but I'll see you later, eh?

(*He winks. She smiles back and stops to watch him go. They are still friends.*)

Scene 6: In Front of the War Memorial/Graveyard; Mid-Day

VANESSA, *her* MOTHER, *and* GRANDMOTHER *stand on the side of the road with several others.* MRS. MACLEOD *looks particularly morose and erect and is dressed completely in black, holding a bouquet. The sound of a marching band, terribly out of tune, can be heard and everyone is looking in its direction.* EDNA, *a bright eyed, cheerful person, comes up behind the threesome.*

EDNA: (*To* BETH) Hi Sis. How are you feeling . . . nearly settled?

(BETH *nods to both questions without speaking, conscious of her mother-in-law beside her who is clearly annoyed by* EDNA'S *presence, and continues to stand rigidly at attention.*)

EDNA: Can you come for dinner Sunday . . . Mom and Dad want to see you.

BETH: (*Trying to keep it short*) Can't . . .

MRS. MACLEOD: (*Harshly*) Shh! Quiet.

(EDNA *rolls her eyes.* VANESSA *sees the expression and smiles at her aunt.*)

EDNA: (*Whispered*) Hi kiddo.

VANESSA: (*Friendly*) Hi Auntie Edna . . . You look nice . . .

(MRS. MACLEOD *scowls at* VANESSA.)

(*By now the band, playing its dirge-like march, has stopped in front of them.* EWEN, *wearing an ill-fitting uniform, stands behind the band with the rest of the veterans.*

The band plays "Lord God of Hosts, be with us yet, lest we forget, lest we forget." The townspeople sing along with the notable exception of MRS. MACLEOD *who stares straight ahead seemingly at* EWEN *for a moment, and then moves to place her flowers on the War Memorial.* VANESSA'S *voice can be heard distinctly . . . she is singing wholeheartedly.*)

Scene 7: Vanessa's Room; Late Night

VANESSA, *dressed in a long nightie, sits on the floor by the hot-air return. Light shines through from her parents' room into hers via the opening. She can hear their voices by putting her ear close to the metal grate.*

BETH: (*V.O., sounding exhausted*) What a day . . . I'm glad that's over . . . (*Pause . . . sigh*) Your mother had me read your letter to her again today . . . before we left . . .

EWEN: (*V.O.*) God . . . when will it end?

(VANESSA *is feeling disturbed and somewhat guilty about hearing her parents' private conversation. She bites her nails absentmindedly.*)

Scene 8: Parents' Bedroom; Continued

BETH *is in bed. She understands (she thinks) what her husband goes through in relationship to his mother. She knows that she doesn't like it.*

BETH: (*A little defensive*) I can't refuse her! . . .

EWEN: (*Edgy and getting loud*) I realize that! But you know how I feel about it! I wish she'd never shown it to you in the first place . . . It's history . . . God Damn it . . . it happened almost twenty years ago.

BETH: Ewen, she'll hear you . . .

(EWEN *sits down heavily on the bed. His energy spent.*)

Scene 9: Vanessa's Bedroom; Continued

VANESSA *can't clearly hear them speak in these hushed tones.* EWEN *says something about Roderick . . . but it is almost inaudible.* ("I wonder if Roderick would've wanted all this . . .") *The lights go out.*

Scene 10: Vanessa's Bedroom; Later that Night

It's a night of unidentified sounds. VANESSA *lies awake in her bed. She hears something and sits up. It sounds like footsteps . . . and crying. She gets up, goes to her door and opens it. She can hear more clearly now . . . her* MOTHER *is moaning quietly, in anguish, and her* FATHER *is downstairs speaking on the phone.*

EWEN: (*V.O.*) Hello—Paul? It's Beth. The waters have broken and the fetal position doesn't seem right. I'm afraid it's the same situation as last time . . . Jesus, I wish she were stronger.

Scene 10A: Upstairs Hallway; Continued

VANESSA *walks down the hallway, past her Grandmother's room, to the top of the stairs where she can see her* FATHER *in his pyjamas, looking frantic, pacing back and forth with the receiver in his hand.*

EWEN: I'm fine . . . Yes, that would be best . . . as soon as you can . . . Thank-you.

(*Rushing back upstairs, past* VANESSA, *he comes face to face with his* MOTHER, *who stands erect in her black quilted dressing gown.*)

MRS. MACLEOD: What is it, Ewen?

EWEN: It's all right, Mother, Beth is having . . . a little trouble. I'm taking her to the hospital. You can go back to bed . . .

Mrs. Macleod: I did tell you, did I not, that you should have had a girl to help her with the move. She should have rested more . . .

Ewen: (*Losing control*) I couldn't afford it . . . if you thought she should've had more rest, why didn't *you* ever . . . oh, God, I'm out of my mind . . . just go back to bed, Mother.

(Mrs. Macleod *doesn't like to be spoken to like this but* Ewen *gives her no chance to respond. He goes back to his wife, and* Mrs. Macleod *turns back into her room, leaving* Vanessa *unnoticed in the hallway.*)

Scene 11: Yard ext. from Vanessa's Point of View on the Landing; Night

A car drives up and stops in the drive-way. A man gets out and hurries to the house, leaving on the car's lights and motor.

Scene 12: Vanessa on the Landing; Night

The doorbell rings and Ewen, *half-dressed, comes running out of the bedroom and down the stairs past* Vanessa. *She takes this opportunity to go in to her Mother.*

Scene 13: Parents' bedroom; night

Vanessa *rushes in and looks at her* Mother *who looks dishevelled and in pain. She manages a little smile for* Vanessa *who rushes to bury her head in her Mother's lap.*

Vanessa: Mommy? . . .

Beth: It's all right honey . . . our baby is just coming a little early, that's all . . . Grandma will be here to take care of you . . .

Vanessa: Grandma! But she doesn't even know how to cook.

Beth: Of course she can! She can cook as well as anyone . . . when she has to . . . it's just that she's never *had* to very much . . . don't worry . . . she'll keep everything in order and then some.

(Ewen *and the other* Doctor *come in and* Beth *whispers to* Vanessa . . .)

Beth: Be a good girl, eh? . . . (Vanessa *nods her assent.*) Go on now . . . get some sleep.

(**Vanessa** *leaves, hesitating at the door for a moment.*)

Ewen: (*To the other* **Doctor**) I'll get her things ready.

Scene 14: Kitchen; Morning

> **Ewen**, *who looks particularly weary, is just finishing breakfast. He is hurrying to get away and clear his own dishes.* **Vanessa** *sits long-faced in front of a full plate of food.*

Vanessa: But why can't *you* be her doctor? You're the best . . .

Ewen: Doctors never attend members of their own family. They care too much and if something goes wrong . . .

> (**Ewen** *regrets having said this . . . and tries to force a reassuring smile. He holds her head tenderly in his hands.*)

Ewen: She is going to be fine. Nessa, honestly . . .

> (**Vanessa** *isn't convinced, but before she can say anything,* **Mrs. Macleod** *comes in, looking ready for the annual Strawberry Tea.* **Ewen** *stiffens noticeably upon her entrance.*)

Mrs. Macleod: Ewen, you are encouraging the child to give way . . . Vanessa . . . big girls don't make a fuss . . . Come now, finish your breakfast. (*Dismissing* **Ewen**) I'll see to everything, Ewen . . .

Ewen: (*Trying to reassure* **Vanessa**) I'll phone you from the hospital . . .

> (*He gives* **Vanessa** *a sweet kiss on the forehead, and his mother a polite peck on the cheek and leaves.* **Vanessa** *sits and unenthusiastically takes a bite of her food.* **Mrs. Macleod** *sits down across from her.*)

Mrs. Macleod: You can go out to play after you eat . . . it's not so cold . . .

> (**Vanessa** *doesn't want to go out and play.*)

Scene 15: Int. House Attic; Morning

> *The attic looks cave-like, full of drab oil paintings stacked upon the rafters, trunks full of outmoded clothing, old photograph albums, rejected furniture . . . An old victrola scratches out a war-time tune.*

> **Vanessa**, *looking dishevelled and dirty, sits with her arms around her knees, rocking . . . waiting . . . looking.*

To Set Our House in Order   181

VANESSA: (*Adult V.O.*) Superstition . . . I felt that if I left the house for even a few hours . . . that some disaster would overtake my mother . . . I did not mention this feeling to Grandmother, of course . . . she did not believe in the existence of fear . . . or, if she did, she never let on . . .

Scene 16: Upstairs Hallway; Noon

> VANESSA *emerges from the attic looking rather guilty. She walks down the hall under the gaze of the hanging portraits.*
>
> *As she passes her Grandmother's room, she notices that the door is open. She stops.*

VANESSA: Grandma?

> (*No answer.*)

Scene 16A: Mrs. MacLeod's Bedroom; Continued

> *She steps inside. It is a room, fit for a Queen, with a large four-poster bed.* VANESSA *is drawn to the dresser with its clutter of bottles and silver-framed pictures. There is a wedding picture (Mr. and Mrs. MacLeod's) and several pictures of a serious looking young man. One is signed:*
>
> "To Mother, much love, Roderick."
>
> *Leaning up against a photo of two bright young men, dressed in uniform . . . Ewen and Roderick . . . is an envelope . . . addressed to Mrs. MacLeod . . . sender . . . Sgt. Ewen MacLeod.*
>
> VANESSA *picks it up and looks at it closely. She pulls out the letter and reads:*
>
> "Dearest Mother . . . This is a most difficult letter for me to write. Roderick died today, fighting for King and country. He was a brave and gallant soldier to the end. We can only be thankful that he died quickly and painlessly . . . and that his was a life sacrificed for . . ."
>
> *The stillness of the room is suddenly broken by the sound of* MRS. MACLEOD*'s voice.*
>
> "Vanessa"
>
> (VANESSA *quickly replaces the letter to its resting place.*)

Scene 17: Outside on the Front Porch; Mid-Day

MRS. MACLEOD: Vanessa. . . . .Vanessa. . . . .

> (*There is no sign of the girl. She goes back into the house.*)

Scene 18: Front Hallway; Mid-Day

> VANESSA, *in disarray, has just made it to the bottom of the stairs when they meet.*

MRS. MACLEOD: (*Distastefully*) My word, Vanessa, what have you been doing? . . . go up and get washed for lunch . . .

> (VANESSA *turns to go back upstairs.*)

MRS. MACLEOD: Your father phoned.

> (VANESSA *is surprised and disappointed. She had expected to speak to him if he called.*)

VANESSA: He did? How is she?

MRS. MACLEOD: Curiosity killed the cat . . .

VANESSA: Is the baby born?

MRS. MACLEOD: I can't understand your parents telling you all these things at your age . . . No, the baby is not born yet . . . and your mother's just the same.

VANESSA: (*Pleadingly*) Will she be all right?

MRS. MACLEOD: If I said definitely yes, Vanessa, that would be a lie, and the MacLeods *never* tell lies . . . What happens is God's will. The Lord giveth, and the Lord taketh away.

> (VANESSA *is crushed. It's as though she's been told that her Mother is dying. She turns again to go upstairs, hiding her emotions from her Grandmother. Before she even takes a step however,* MRS. MACLEOD *stops her, placing a hand on her shoulder.*)

MRS. MACLEOD: When your Uncle Roderick got killed . . . I thought I would die . . . but I didn't die, Vanessa . . . life goes on.

> (VANESSA, *feeling overwhelmed by the moment, turns and runs up the stairs. The old woman sighs and turns for the kitchen.*)

Scene 19: Kitchen; Lunch Time, Later

> Mrs. Macleod *is trimming the crusts off of some sandwiches she has made for the two of them. She is chatting animatedly . . . seemingly trying to cheer* Vanessa *up.*

Mrs. Macleod: When I married your Grandfather MacLeod, he said to me, "Eleanor, don't think because we're going to the prairies, that I expect you to live roughly. You are used to a proper house and you shall have one . . . Before we'd been in Manawaka three years, he'd had this house built. Now *he* was a good doctor. Had many more patients than either of the others . . .

> (*She arranges the little sandwiches on two crystal plates, which are placed on a sterling silver tray.*)

We had full-time help . . . When the boys were your age . . . never less than twelve guests for dinner parties . . . and when I served Tea—there would be twenty or thirty ladies . . . Half a dozen different kinds of cake . . . No one seems to bother these days . . . too lazy I suppose.

Vanessa: Too broke. That's what Dad says.

Mrs. Macleod: I can't bear slang, Vanessa . . . If you mean "hard-up", why don't you say so.

> (*She picks up the tray and leaves.* Vanessa *follows, carrying the pickles and the salt and pepper.*)

Scene 20: Dining Room, Continued

> Mrs. Macleod *carefully sets the table for two.*

Mrs. Macleod: It's mainly a question of management . . . my house was always in good order . . . no unexpected expenses . . . no running out of preserves before the winter was out.

> (*They both sit down and prepare to eat, methodically taking the napkins, unfolding them and placing them on their laps.*)

Mrs. Macleod: Do you know what my Father used to say?

Vanessa: No . . .

Mrs. Macleod: God loves order . . . remember that, Vanessa . . . God loves order He wants each one of us to set our house in order.

> (Vanessa *immediately piles her plate full of pickles and sandwiches.*)

MRS. MACLEOD: I was a MacInnes before I got married . . . a very ancient clan . . . (*Using a Scottish accent*) "The lairds of Morven and the constables of Kinlochaline Castle . . . " (*Suddenly remembering*) Did you finish that book I gave you for your birthday?

(VANESSA *is caught with her mouth full. She swallows, immediately.*)

VANESSA: (*Not convincingly*) Yes . . . it was a swell book, Grandma . . . It said that the MacInnes motto is "Pleasure Arises from Work."

(*Thank God she remembered that!*)

MRS. MACLEOD: (*Proudly*) Yes, and an excellent motto it is, too. One to bear in mind.

(VANESSA *is relieved to have pleased her Grandmother. She relaxes a little.*)

MRS. MACLEOD: I hope Ewen will be pleased.

VANESSA: At what?

MRS. MACLEOD: (*Very pleased with herself*) I hired a girl for the housework. She starts tomorrow.

Scene 21: Kitchen; Late Evening

The room is quite messy . . . the lunch dishes haven't been done and the preparations for dinner are underway. MRS. MACLEOD *peels carrots,* VANESSA *is doing dishes and* EWEN *is cleaning a chicken.*

EWEN: I'm sorry Mother, but you'll have to unhire her.

MRS. MACLEOD: It seems distinctly odd that you, a doctor, cannot afford any help.

EWEN: (*Exasperated*) Mother . . . I have no money to pay anyone . . . my patients pay me with chickens . . . eggs . . . milk . . .

(MRS. MACLEOD'S *silence demands a solution.*)

EWEN: Look, I don't know what's happening with Beth . . . If the baby doesn't come tomorrow . . . Can't we . . . let the house go for now . . . What does it matter?

MRS. MACLEOD: (*Distinctly*) I have never lived in a messy house, Ewen.

EWEN: Oh, Lord . . . I'll phone Edna . . . though Heaven knows she's got enough to do with her own parents . . .

MRS. MACLEOD: I don't fancy having Edna Connor in to help.

EWEN: Why not! She's Beth's sister isn't she?

MRS. MACLEOD: (*Staying in control*) There is no need to raise your voice to me, Ewen. She's a poor influence on Vanessa . . . She's uncouth.

VANESSA: (*Almost without thinking*) She is not! Papa . . .

EWEN: Vanessa . . . (stay out of this)

(VANESSA *obeys the command though she is confused and hurt by her father's attitude. Why isn't he defending Edna?!*)

EWEN: (*Diplomatic, manipulative*) She'll only be here for a few hours . . . You can stay in your room.

MRS. MACLEOD: I certainly will . . . (*She straightens her necklace and leaves.*)

(EWEN *looks exhausted and gets up to wash his hands. He looks at* VANESSA *who is silently working away at the sink. Silence. He has clearly disappointed her.*)

Scene 22: Downstairs Hallway; Morning

EDNA, *energetically, is pulling a carpet sweeper, a floor polisher and other cleaning aids out of the kitchen closet. She hands a duster to* VANESSA.

EDNA: (*With humor*) Where's her royal highness, kiddo?

VANESSA: (*Smirking*) In her room . . . reading a catalogue.

EDNA: (*Sarcastic*) Good glory . . . Heaven knows what she'll order this time!

VANESSA: When I took up her coffee . . . she was looking at the lace handkerchiefs.

EDNA: Well, at least she believes we Irish are good for two things . . . making linen . . . and manual labor.

Scene 22A: Living Room; Continued

They move into the living room and start to clean.

VANESSA: Did you know that her family used to live in castles.

EDNA: Castles my foot . . . She was born in Ontario, just like your Grandfather Connor . . . and her father was a horse doctor . . .

(*She laughs at the reality of it all.*)

EDNA: I suppose she also told you that "the MacLeods never lie," eh? Hah! That's a joke.

(VANESSA *isn't sure how to take this information. It bewilders her and makes her feel even more vulnerable. She stands holding the feather duster limply.*)

VANESSA: Aunt Edna . . . what about Mother . . . is she going to be all right?

(EDNA *stops. She realizes that she has been insensitive to the girl's mood.*)

EDNA: Ah girlie . . . She's getting the best of care . . . Honestly . . . (EDNA *puts her arms around her niece.*) It's tough for you, eh? You can't even go an' see her.

VANESSA: I'm scared.

EDNA: Oh Nessa . . . I'm scared too.

Scene 23: Downstairs Hallway; Night

It is quiet, except for the clock in the hallway, and dark except for a soft light from the living room and a bright shaft coming from the kitchen. VANESSA *makes her way quietly down the stairway, through the hallway and goes to the kitchen.*

Scene 24: Kitchen; Night Continued

EWEN *has made some hot milk and is pouring himself a cup. When he sees* VANESSA *he registers her worry and welcomes her company.*

EWEN: Want some hot milk?

(VANESSA *is relieved that her father is not angry with her being up.*)

VANESSA: Yes . . . please.

(*She comes in and sits down on a stool near him and watches him.*)

VANESSA: Papa . . . what's a caesarean?

EWEN: It's an operation, honey . . . to take the baby out . . . It's not so serious . . . they do it a lot nowadays when things aren't quite right . . .

VANESSA: What's not right?

EWEN: The baby has got itself a little twisted, and . . .

VANESSA: Will it be born dead . . . like last time?

EWEN: I hope not. Your mother won't be able to have another after this one . . . She'd like you to have a sister or a brother . . .

VANESSA: (*Angry*) As far as I am concerned . . . she shouldn't have bothered . . .

    (EWEN *smiles to break the tension.*)

EWEN: Don't feel that way . . . (*Motioning to leave*) Shall we?

Scene 25: Living Room; Night Continued

> EWEN *has unpacked several boxes of books which are now in stacks, on the end tables and floor. He sits down amongst them, in a big chair beside the bookshelf.* VANESSA *finds her place near him on a hassock.*

EWEN: How are you getting along with your Grandmother?

VANESSA: Fine, I guess . . . Why did you let her say that about Aunt Edna?

EWEN: Well, I didn't want to upset her, Nessa . . . It will take her a while to get used to us living here . . . we must be as nice as we can to her.

VANESSA: Why can't she be nice to us for a change?

EWEN: Vanessa . . . she's had troubles which you really don't know about . . . life hasn't been what she hoped it would be . . . she always wanted to be a lady . . . and for a while it seemed as though she was one . . .

VANESSA: She told me that Grandpa MacLeod made a lot of money in his day.

EWEN: Well, he wasn't a millionaire . . . but he did quite well . . . That's not what I remember most about him though . . .

    (*He pulls a book from the shelf and opens it.*)

EWEN: See this . . . It's a Greek play . . . Called *Antigone*. He was the only person in Manawaka who could read these (*Indicating the shelves of volumes*) in Greek . . . no one else had even read them in English! (*He gives the book to* VANESSA *and takes another for himself.*) He must've been a lonely man . . .

    He would have liked to have been a classical scholar . . . he told me once . . . but his father was a doctor . . . so that's what he was.

VANESSA: Can you read this?

    (EWEN *laughs softly at the suggestion.*)

EWEN: No . . . no . . . I was never an intellectual . . . Rod was always much brighter than I in school . . . maybe he would have learned how, had he lived . . .

    No . . . I wanted to join the Merchant Marine . . . and travel.

VANESSA: Why didn't you then?

EWEN: Oh well . . . I was just a prairie kid who had never seen the sea . . . wouldn't have made much of a sailor . . . probably would have been seasick . . . (*Ending the conversation*) You go up to bed now . . . Try not to worry . . . I won't be here when you get up but I'll call as soon as the operation is over.

VANESSA: Promise?

EWEN: Promise.

(VANESSA *leaves her father with a kiss and climbs the stairs into the dark.* EWEN *is left sitting, looking rather lonely.*)

VANESSA: (*Adult V.O.*) There had been a sadness in my father's voice that night that I had never heard before . . . I wish I could have said something . . . to make him feel better . . . but I didn't know where to begin . . . or how . . .

Scene 26: Living Room; Day

A series of exotic pictures from all over the world flip through our vision. VANESSA *is poring through her Father's books and has them scattered all over the room. Most of them are picture books;* National Geographic, *travel guides and photo essays. She is enthralled with one and is lying on the floor with it spread before her. The ticking of the grandfather clock counts the time.*

VANESSA: (*Adult V.O.*) The next day, I refused to move far from the phone . . . I had never before examined my father's books, but now at a loss for something to do, I took them out one by one and read snatches here and there . . . It dawned on me that most of his books were of the same kind . . . full of exotic pictures from all over the world. I felt as though I had discovered my father's secret world . . . his place of hiding . . . his dream of what could have been . . .

(MRS. MACLEOD *comes in from the kitchen.*)

MRS. MACLEOD: What on earth! Look at this mess! Put it all away now, Vanessa. Do you hear?

VANESSA: Yes, Grandma.

(MRS. MACLEOD *proceeds up stairs and* VANESSA *begins her task.*)

(*Suddenly the telephone rings and she scrabbles to her feet to answer it. She stops momentarily before picking it up . . . almost too frightened to hear the news.*)

VANESSA: (*Answering the phone*) Hello . . . ?

To Set Our House in Order 189

EWEN: (*V.O.*) Nessa. It's me . . .

VANESSA: Papa . . . ?

EWEN: (*V.O.*) Everything's all right . . . we've got a fine healthy boy and he's kicking!

VANESSA: And Mom?

EWEN: (*V.O.*) She's pretty weak . . . but she's going to be just fine . . .

(VANESSA *sighs with relief.*)

EWEN: (*V.O.*) I'll be home soon . . . you tell Grandma for me, all right?

VANESSA: (*Tenderly*) Yes Papa . . . bye bye.

(VANESSA *sits down, holding the receiver and leans back.*)

Scene 27: Dining Room; Late Evening

The table is stacked with picture albums that have been brought down from the attic. VANESSA *and* MRS. MACLEOD *are huddled around* EWEN *who is flipping through the pages.*

EWEN: There I am, eh Mother? Oh yes . . . that's exactly what he looks like!

VANESSA: (*Teasing*) Is that you! (*The baby is crying its eyes out.*)

EWEN: Uh hum . . . sweet wasn't I? Is this all there is, Mother . . . I thought we had more . . .

MRS. MACLEOD: (*Ignoring the question*) What are you going to call this child, Ewen?

EWEN: (*Still jovial, teasing*) Oh I don't know . . . Hank, Cecil, Fauntleroy . . .

(VANESSA *can't help but laugh at her Father's silliness.*)

EWEN: What do you think, Vanessa . . .

(VANESSA *is about to answer . . .*)

MRS. MACLEOD: (*Without waiting a beat*) Ewen . . . I would like you to call him Roderick.

(*The good time has turned cold.*)

EWEN: I'd rather not.

MRS. MACLEOD: (*Quiet, but resolute*) I think you should. There is absolutely no reason against it.

(VANESSA *watches her* FATHER *hoping that he will stand firm. She wants to speak but is silenced by her Father's look.*)

EWEN: Don't you think that Beth should decide?

MRS. MACLEOD: Beth will agree if you insist.

(*The truth of that statement penetrates* EWEN's *argument.*)

MRS. MACLEOD: (*Shaky*) It would mean a great deal to me . . . Ewen.

(*Suddenly* EWEN *throws back his head and laughs.*)

EWEN: Roderick the Black! That's what you'll call him, eh Mother! Remember? As though he were a character out of Sir Walter Scott and not just an ordinary kid . . .

(EWEN *stops. His expression changes to one of deep regret.*)

EWEN: Oh God Mother . . . I am sorry . . . I had no right to say that.

MRS. MACLEOD: I accept your apology, Ewen. (*And fingering her beads, she leaves.* VANESSA's *expression asks "why?" but* EWEN *avoids the question by choosing another album.*)

EWEN: Here's the one I was looking for . . .

Scene 28: Ewen and Beth's Bedroom; Day

The baby is home. BETH *has just finished nursing him in bed and is buttoning up her nightgown.* EDNA *has the baby at the foot of the bed and is changing him.*

VANESSA: (*Adult V.O.*) My mother had to stay in bed for several weeks after she came home with the baby . . . Aunt Edna came in to help every day and when she had finished the housework, she would go in, close the door, and they would talk.

(BETH *is pouring the coffee which sits on a tray beside her bed.*)

EDNA: (*She puts the baby in a rocker or cradle.*) There you go . . . wee Roddy . . .

(BETH *smiles at her good-natured sister and offers her a cup of coffee.*)

EDNA: Did you mind . . . calling him Roderick?

Scene 29: Vanessa's Bedroom; Continued

VANESSA *is sitting by the air exchange grate where she can hear the conversation . . . and see some of the action.*

BETH: Oh it's not the name I mind . . . it's that Ewen felt he had to . . . Did you know that Rod was blind in one eye?

EDNA: Sure I knew . . . so what?

BETH: It was Ewen's air-rifle that did it . . .

EDNA: Oh Lord . . .

Scene 30: Beth and Ewen's Bedroom; Continued

BETH: It was an accident of course . . . they were just kids . . .

EDNA: But she blamed Ewen . . . and now he's made it up to her.

BETH: No, it's more than that . . . I shouldn't be telling you all this . . . (*She wants to.*) Remember . . . I told you that Ewen wrote to his Mother about Roderick's heroic death.

Scene 31: Vanessa's Bedroom; Continued

Unnoticed by VANESSA, EWEN *has come quietly to her doorway and has stopped to listen. He opens the door which has been slightly ajar. She sees him. He comes in, closing the door behind him.*

BETH: (*V.O.*) In fact Ewen didn't even see Roderick get hit; he doesn't know how it happened . . . he had tried to look out for him . . . because of his eye . . .

(EWEN *comes to the foot of her bed and stands awhile before sitting on the bed near her . . . he can now hear what she is hearing.*)

BETH: (*V.O.*) They were in Somme, France . . . ⸍it was night and it was chaotic. Ewen had lost Roderick . . . and was frantically searching for him . . . he found him . . . lying in the mud, alone, frightened . . . and in terrible pain . . . He was dying . . . and there was nothing Ewen could do for him.

(*The sound from the other room fades out as we hear* EDNA *comfort her sister. "Oh Bethie . . . that's enough . . . let's not talk about it anymore . . . I've got to go soon." etc.*)

(EWEN *begins to speak. It's as though he's saying it for the first time . . . reliving his private thoughts.*)

EWEN: I stayed with him all night . . . I felt so helpless . . . so angry that this boy, my little brother, should die like this . . . That's when I decided to come back here . . . to Manawaka . . . and become a doctor . . .

But nothing was the same . . . my Mother had changed so much. She just couldn't accept his death . . . and I can understand that . . . now that I have children of my own . . .

You would have liked him I think . . .

VANESSA: How old was he?

EWEN: Eighteen . . . "The Lord giveth and the Lord taketh away."

(*He shakes his head . . . in disbelief?*)

I still miss him . . . we were good friends . . .

VANESSA: Oh Papa . . . don't cry . . .

(*She gets up and goes to him. They sit, arms around each other, saying nothing more. Slowly the sound of the band from Scene 6—the Remembrance Day Ceremony—can be heard.*)

VANESSA: (*Adult V.O.*) As we sat there, I began to wonder— what kind of God is in charge of this world . . . how is it decided what happens and doesn't happen to a person? Or is it decided?

Scene 32: Ext. Remembrance Day Ceremony

The band slowly files past **MRS. MACLEOD** *and comes to a halt. The old lady walks up to the memorial, stops to pray and then places a bouquet of flowers on the statue.* **EWEN** *and* **VANESSA** *both watch the ritual in silence.*

VANESSA: (*Adult V.O.*) Grandma had said that . . . "God loves Order" . . . I felt that whatever God might love in this world, it certainly was not order.

After Words

1 In your journal, respond to the teleplay, its characters, and their conflicts.

2 In a small group, discuss each of the characters in turn. Consider, for example:

- Mrs. MacLeod's relationships with her sons, her motivations, her dreams
- Ewen's roles and relationships
- the MacLeods' impact on Beth and on Vanessa
- the effect of Edna on Vanessa

3 Comment on the dramatic impact of the following lines:

   a) To me, the house seemed full of unseen spirits . . . (page 174)

   b) Ewen, you are encouraging the child to give way . . . (page 180)

   c) *God loves order* . . . remember that, Vanessa (page 183)

   d) . . . life hasn't been what she hoped it would be . . . (page 187)

   e) I felt as though I had discovered my father's secret world . . . his place of hiding . . . his dream of what could have been (page 188)

   f) . . . it was night and it was chaotic (page 192)

4 In role as a character other than Vanessa, write a diary entry that either retells a portion of the script or provides a sequel.

5 In a group of three, roleplay the members of a casting team:

   Casting director: selects actors and negotiates contracts

   Director: works with the actors and crew to make the actual film—focuses on artistic success

   Producer: controls the whole production, including finance and budget—focuses on financial success

   Evaluate well-known, contemporary actors for two of the main roles in *To Set Our House in Order*. Consider the demands of each role and the past performances of the actors you suggest. Present and explain your final choices to the class.

6 Read the short story "To Set Our House in Order" (and perhaps, the rest of the collection *A Bird in the House*) and note how Anne Wheeler has adapted the story to film. In a small group, discuss the changes made, the possible reasons, and the effects. Present your findings to the class.

7 For a short story you have enjoyed, propose a film adaptation. What changes are needed in order to transform the written story into a film? Why? Present your ideas in one or more of the following ways:

   a) Give a synopsis of the story and your film treatment.

   b) Rewrite a segment as a screenplay.

   c) Sketch and annotate storyboards for 3-5 significant scenes.

3

Power

Compensation Will Be Paid

A stage play by GWEN PHARIS RINGWOOD

GWEN PHARIS RINGWOOD (1910–1984) was one of Canada's most prolific dramatists and a pioneer of western Canadian community theatre. *Still Stands the House*, which is included in *The Collected Plays of Gwen Pharis Ringwood*, is probably her most famous work and is still performed today. In 1913 Ringwood's family moved from Anatone, Washington to southern Alberta, where her parents hoped to farm less expensive land and to teach. Most of Ringwood's life was spent in western Canada—studying at the University of Alberta, writing and producing at the Banff School of Fine Arts, writing radio plays for Edmonton's CFRN, reviving community theatre in Williams Lake, B.C., teaching at Cariboo College, and so on. She received many awards, including the 1941 Governor General's Award for outstanding service to Canadian drama, and a theatre has been named for her—the Gwen Pharis Ringwood Civic Theatre in Williams Lake. In tones ranging from high tragedy to light comedy, Ringwood's plays focus on western Canada to explore a variety of specific and universal issues and themes. This short sketch, written in 1970, illustrates Ringwood's ability to compress great social concern into very few words.

Prelude

1 In your journal, list the issues you consider of greatest importance in the world today. For one issue, explain its importance, give examples, and note your thoughts and feelings.

2 Consider the title of the play. "Compensation" usually involves paying someone to make up for loss or damage. Note any examples of compensation you have heard of lately. Speculate on who, in this play, might be paying compensation, to whom, and for what loss.

Compensation Will Be Paid

Characters

    LINDA: Local woman

    GRANDMOTHER: Mollie, Linda's grandmother

    SHARON: Neighbour

    ANNETTE
    JANICE | Linda's children
    LENA

    ABNER: Linda's grandfather

    YOUNG MAN

    MARGOT: Neighbour

Scene

A segment of a yard in the prairie village. An old fashioned pump at a well, a clothes line, a watering trough, a bench and the front stoop of a house.

LINDA *is hanging out clothes. Her* GRANDMOTHER *sits on stoop knitting.* SHARON *comes by with shopping basket.*

SHARON: Good morning. It's a lovely morning. The sun's turned the world into a jewelry shop. Diamonds on the grass.

LINDA: There's spring in the air.

GRANDMOTHER: A silent spring, I'm thinking.

LINDA: Now Grandma, don't start that again. You're forever crying doom.

SHARON: What if she's right? They made the test this morning.

LINDA: Albert drove the sheep into the hills yesterday.

SHARON: Larry too. Everything in sixty miles had to be moved. Every animal. Every person. Larry thinks they shouldn't test that gas here. He thinks it's dangerous.

GRANDMOTHER: In the old days they fought with swords and guns. Now it's bombs and chemicals. No one's safe.

LINDA: Albert talked to those scientists. He's sure there's no chance of contamination beyond the sixty miles.

GRANDMOTHER: The wind changed an hour ago.

SHARON: She's right, Linda. The wind's in the south now.

LINDA: The government knows what's best. They don't need us to tell them.

(ANNETTE *and* JANICE *run in with a dead frog.*)

ANNETTE: Mama, look at this frog.

JANICE: This tiny green frog, it's dead, Mama.

LINDA: Then throw it away, dear. If it's dead—things have to die you know.

ANNETTE: I hate it when it's dead. Throw it away.

(JANICE *reluctantly throws frog away.* LENA *comes out of the house.*)

LENA: I feel better now, Mama. Can I go with them?

LINDA: If you're feeling better.

ANNETTE: Come on, we'll look for a live frog.

LENA: Wait for me, you kids. I'm coming.

(*She follows.* ABNER, *an old man enters.*)

ABNER: A strange thing, Mollie. (*He speaks to the* GRANDMOTHER.) A chicken is dead on her nest. I go out to feed the chickens and I find this hen. Just—dead.

LINDA: Are the others all right, Grandpa?

ABNER: They seem all right.

(*A* YOUNG MAN *in a protective suit with mask hanging around his neck enters.*)

YOUNG MAN: I beg your pardon. Could I borrow a pipe wrench?

ABNER: Sure. I'll get it. You the fellow from the testing site?

YOUNG MAN: That's right.

GRANDMOTHER: The wind changed an hour ago.

SHARON: And the children found a dead frog.

ABNER: This chicken—she is dead on her nest.

(*He goes inside for wrench.*)

SHARON: Our men are driving the stock up into the hills. You're sure there's no danger?

YOUNG MAN: Nothing to worry about. Nothing at all. As long as you keep out of that 60 mile radius.

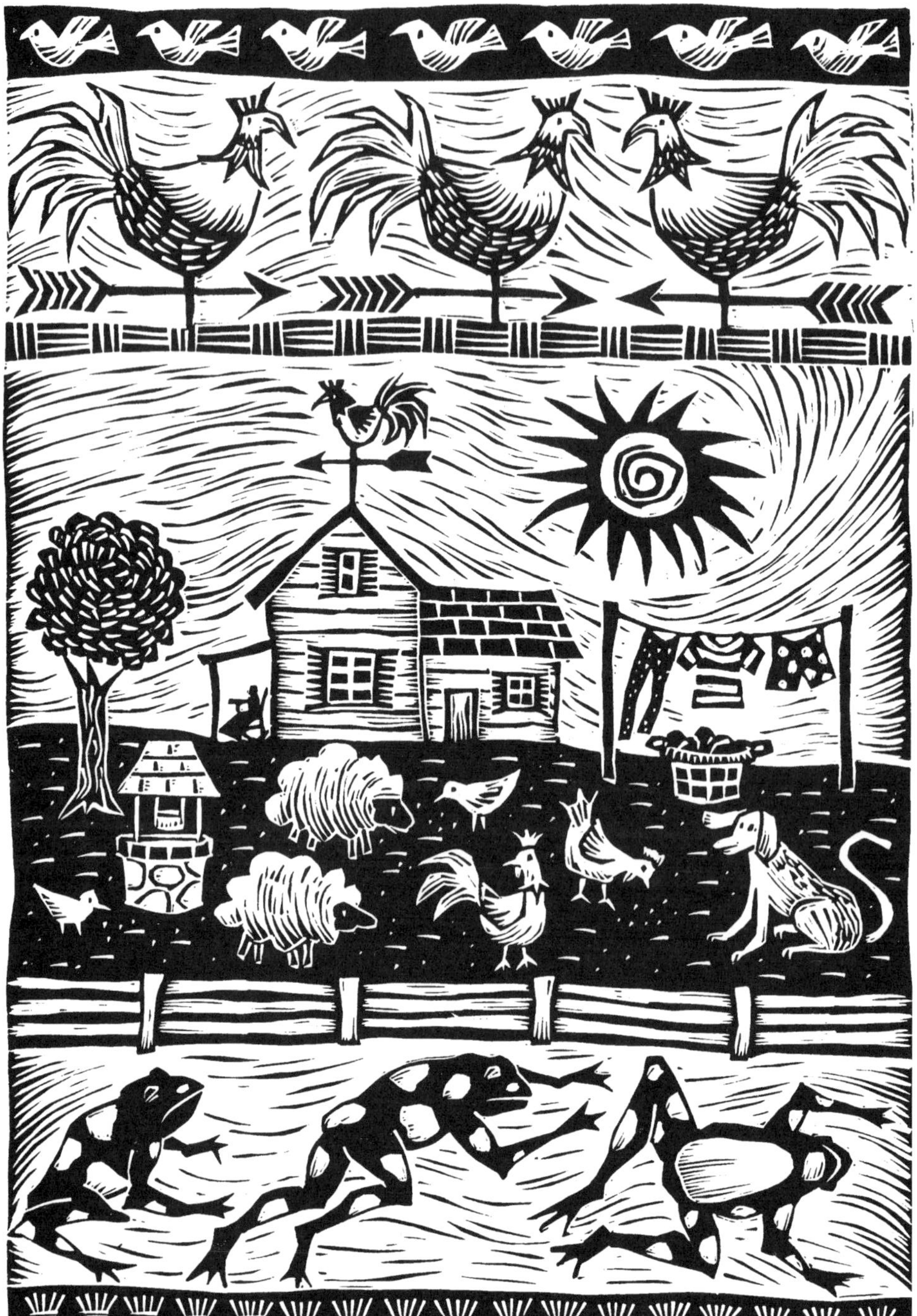

Abner: (*Returning*) There you are.

Grandmother: Tell him about the chicken, Abner. A hen nesting.

Young Man: Lady, hens die. However if by chance it had anything to do with the plant, I assure you compensation will be paid. I'll bring the wrench right back.

(*He goes out.*)

Linda: You see, he said we're safe. They know what they're doing.

Sharon: You could ask him for compensation for the hen. After all, the way they spend money they can afford it.

(**Annette**, **Janice**, *and* **Lena** *return*.)

Annette: Mama, we found two frogs.

Janice: But we let them go. We watched them hop and then we let them go.

Linda: That's good, dear.

Annette: I'm tired of hunting frogs.

Janice: So am I.

Lena: I'm tired too.

(*Children group together.*)

Annette: We can play mumblypeg.

(**Young Man** *returns with wrench*.)

Young Man: That did the trick. Thank you.

(*Gives wrench to* **Abner**.)

Abner: You figure on going down to there, to the site?

Young Man: Of course. Why?

Abner: I think I'd be nervous about going down there, if it was me.

Young Man: I've got this special suit, face mask, gloves. You know.

(**Margot** *enters*.)

Margot: Oh Linda, my puppy. My puppy's dead. Just now. While I was coming here.

Annette: We found a dead frog, Margot.

Abner: That hen was dead on her nest. I told you, Mollie, they should never put that plant here. I told you all along didn't I? Now see what's happened. Our livestock's dying. What's your plant going to do about that?

Young Man: If the plant's responsible I assure you you'll be reimbursed. Compensation will be paid.

(*There is an uproar as they all speak at once.* ANNETTE *rushes to the adults.*)

ANNETTE: Mama, Mama, Lena's sick. Lena's very sick.

LENA: Mama. Mama.

(*She dies. They turn together and look at the* YOUNG MAN *who has donned his mask.*)

YOUNG MAN: Compen—Compensation . . .

(*They freeze.*)

CURTAIN

After Words

1. In your journal, respond to the play. Note your feelings, questions, associations with real life happenings.

2. a) In a small group, identify and discuss the issues the playwright raises.

    b) Either find and present examples in the news of stories that raise one or more of the issues OR create an advertisement based on one issue.

3. In role as the Young Man, write your report to the company.

4. In a group, take on the following roles:
    - government spokesperson
    - chemical company spokesperson
    - newspaper reporter(s)
    - irate citizen(s)

    Improvise a press conference following the action of the play.

5. a) Examine the play to see how the author achieves maximum impact with minimum length.

    b) In a group, develop a skit about your community and an issue affecting it.

Frankenstein
The Man Who Became God

A stage play by ALDEN NOWLAN and WALTER LEARNING,
based on the novel by Mary Shelley

A<small>FTER</small> nights of reading ghost stories together during a rainy summer, one of a group of friends made a challenge: "We will each write a ghost story." Mary Shelley, daughter of the authors William Godwin and Mary Wollstonecraft, and her husband, the poet Percy Bysshe Shelley, had rented a Swiss villa for the summer of 1816. Another poet, Lord Byron, made the challenge, and the young Doctor John Polidori joined in. Polidori wrote *The Vampyre: A Tale*, which may be the root of all Dracula stories. Mary, who was then 19, spent days pondering and suffering false starts, then woke from a nightmare with her story in mind. *Frankenstein, or the Modern Prometheus*, as she called it, drew on two sources: discussions of contemporary science, and the Greek myth in which Prometheus steals fire from the gods and gives it to humanity. Her story, published in 1818, is considered the original science fiction novel.

From the earliest adaptation in 1823, stage and film versions of the Frankenstein story have increasingly focused on, and reinterpreted, the creature rather than creator. In 1974, two Canadians decided to return to the original for a new adaptation. Alden Nowlan, born in 1933 near Windsor, Nova Scotia, was a journalist, novelist, playwright, and award-winning poet. Beginning his writing career at age 11, Nowlan escaped bitter poverty and published 12 books before his death at age 50. Born in 1938 in Quidi Vidi, Newfoundland, Walter Learning has had a long and productive career in Canadian theatre. While artistic director at Theatre New Brunswick, he and Nowlan co-wrote three plays, which Learning then produced. Since then he has directed plays in Vancouver, Charlottetown, and Stratford, Ontario.

Prelude

1 In your journal, list 5–10 innovations of modern science and technology (e.g., genetic cloning, bioengineered food). For each, note some possible advantages and disadvantages.

2 Discuss what you know about Frankenstein—the story, the creature, various films. What other strange beings or monsters do you recall from stories or films?

Frankenstein

Characters

  ROBERT WALTON: Captain of ship bound for North Pole
  MR. WILLIAMSON: Walton's second-in-command
  VICTOR VON FRANKENSTEIN—Scientist, inventor, Baron
  SEAMEN: Three, aboard ship bound for North Pole
  HENRY CLERVAL: Victor's and Elizabeth's friend
  CONRAD: Servant at Castle Frankenstein
  FRITZ: Assistant to the Baron
  ELIZABETH LAVENZA: Victor's fiancée, Countess
  HANS
  LOUISE } Servants at Castle Frankenstein
  WILLIAM VON FRANKENSTEIN: Much younger brother of Victor
  THE CREATURE
  DE LACEY: Blind man living in countryside
  FELIX: His son, visiting from Geneva

Act One

Scene 1

The Captain's cabin on a sailing ship in the year 1840. Night. We hear a gusting wind. ROBERT WALTON *is seated centre on a stool; he holds a portable secretary with an inkwell, writing paper, and quill pens. At the right there is a door; behind him a row of windows; at the left, a cot. The cabin also contains a sideboard, on which stand a decanter of brandy and several glasses. As the lights go up,* WALTON *picks up a sheet of writing paper and begins to read aloud from it.*

WALTON: My Dearest Margaret. Yesterday our ship became locked in the ice. Although my crew consists of veteran seamen, well accustomed to the rigours of these Arctic waters, it was obvious that they were afraid, for there was ice as far as the eye could see. (WALTON *drinks a sip of brandy and continues reading.*) Then the most incredible thing happened. We saw a sled drawn by dogs pass us toward the north at a distance of about half a mile. A creature—(*He stops, takes up his pen, dips it in the inkwell, scratches out the word "creature" and substitutes the word "man."*)—a man of unnatural form sat in the sled. Being many hundreds of miles from any land. . .

(*There is a knock on the door.* MR. WILLIAMSON *enters. He wears heavy winter clothing and as he enters, he gestures in the manner of a man coming in from extreme cold.*)

WILLIAMSON: Am I interrupting anything, sir?

WALTON: Mr. Williamson, come in, man.

WILLIAMSON: I heard you talking.

WALTON: Just to my sister in London. (WALTON *rises; turns upstage; puts desk on window seat.*) I like to write her even though I'll arrive home with the letter. (*Laugh*)

WILLIAMSON: (*Crossing to Stage Right of* WALTON, *unbuttoning his jacket and removing his gloves.*) That may be longer than we think, if at all. Looks like our luck isn't about to change, Captain—the bergs are drifting toward us. The men are frightened, sir.

WALTON: Well there isn't much we can do except to wait, pray, and perhaps share a glass of brandy. (*He fills a glass and hands it to* WILLIAMSON.)

WILLIAMSON: (*Crossing to Stage Right to cot*) I had hoped we might get moving by morning. I think you should consider turning back if we get the chance.

WALTON: Turn back! Never!

WILLIAMSON: The situation could get ugly. (WALTON *laughs.*)

WALTON: Mr. Williamson, a toast. (*He raises his glass;* WILLIAMSON *follows suit.*) To the North Pole and then home! (*They drink.*) (WALTON *signals* WILLIAMSON *to sit on cot; he does.*) We're going to make Columbus look like a little boy sailing a paper boat on a lily pond. In the next century nobody will remember anything about 1840—except that it was the year when man first reached the North Pole.

WILLIAMSON: (*Amused by* WALTON'S *enthusiasm*) The crew would gladly trade your North Pole for a hold full of herring. If they have to risk their lives they'd rather do it for something they can understand.

WALTON: (*Crosses Upstage; sits on window seat*) I know that. There's not a man among them that would be aboard if I hadn't offered to pay twice as much as any other master sailing out of Archangel. But you should understand. Think of the glory!

WILLIAMSON: (*Good-humouredly*) Experience has taught me that when men go in search of glory fate usually kicks them in the arse.

WALTON: (*Laughing*) My friend, you're hopelessly practical. (WILLIAMSON *crosses Upstage, puts glass on window seat.*) Well, perhaps we'd better issue the crew a double tot of rum to raise their spirits and to lower their tempers. (*He is interrupted by cries of "Watch out, man," "Look out there," "Hold him back," from off right.*)

(VICTOR *enters followed closely by* THREE SEAMEN.)

FIRST SEAMAN: For God's sake, stop! Nobody's going to hurt you!

(WALTON *and* WILLIAMSON *turn to the door.*)

VICTOR: Help me!

(*He collapses in* WILLIAMSON'S *arms.*)

WALTON: Put him on my bunk. (WILLIAMSON *does.*) What's going on here?

FIRST SEAMAN: We took him out of the sea, sir. Floating on a cake of ice.

VICTOR: I must go on! (*Unable to resist*)

WILLIAMSON: Poor devil. His ship can't have been as lucky as ours was.

FIRST SEAMAN: He didn't come from a ship.

SECOND SEAMAN: There was a sled and five dogs beside him.

THIRD SEAMAN: All dead. Froze up, sir!

WILLIAMSON: (*Trying to calm* VICTOR *down*) Easy man! (VICTOR *faints.*)

SECOND SEAMAN: He's crazy. He was raving when we took him aboard, something about a daemon—.

WALTON: You'd rave too if you were starving and frozen. Fetch some water, as hot as you can get it, and blankets.

THIRD SEAMAN: Aye, aye, sir.

WALTON: And bring something hot to drink. (*Exit the* SEAMEN.) (WALTON *crosses to door and closes it.*)

(VICTOR *comes to, again.*)

(WALTON *crosses to* VICTOR. WILLIAMSON *gives* WALTON *a glass of brandy.*)

WALTON: (*To* VICTOR) You're going to be all right. You're among friends. We'll take care of you.

(WILLIAMSON *breaks to centre.*)

VICTOR: Please let me go, I can't stay here.

WALTON: I'm afraid you don't have any choice. There's nowhere else to go, and even if there were, you're in no condition to move.

VICTOR: I must find him and kill him, or he must kill me. (*Faints again*)

WILLIAMSON: I'm worried sir, coming on top of all the other bad luck. The crew will probably think he's a Jonah.

WALTON: They'll have to make the best of it. They've nowhere else to go, either.

WILLIAMSON: That business yesterday spooked them. First that ice, and then that bloody giant driving his dog team as if the devil himself was after him. And now this.

WALTON: Mr. Williamson, this poor soul is no threat to anyone. (*The* THREE SEAMEN *return, with a container of boiling water, blankets and broth.*) Good. Now to work. (*To* SECOND SEAMAN) You there, cut open his clothes.

SECOND SEAMAN: Me, sir? (*He crosses himself.*)

WALTON: Yes, damn it, you. (WALTON *pushes him to* VICTOR.) And if you want to ward off evil stop making those stupid gestures and wash your hands occasionally. (WALTON *crosses to the other two* SEAMEN. VICTOR *moans; all activity stops.*) There's nothing to be frightened about; you've seen frostbitten men before. Wring it out well.

(*The* FIRST *and* SECOND SEAMEN *wet and wring out a blanket. The* SECOND SEAMAN *takes out his knife and bends over* VICTOR, *and cuts open his pant legs.*)

SECOND SEAMAN: (*Seeing* VICTOR'S *frozen legs*) Jesus, Mary and Joseph—look at that! (*He turns away.*)

WILLIAMSON: I don't ever remember seeing anyone in a condition like that, sir!

(WALTON *goes over to look.*)

WALTON: My God, what's been keeping him alive!

VICTOR: Hate!

WALTON: Calm yourself, my friend.

(SECOND SEAMAN *crosses down to* FIRST *and* THIRD SEAMEN.)

SECOND SEAMAN: Mark my words, no good will come of this. It's bad luck for every man aboard ship.

WALTON: (*Grabs first blanket; quickly puts it on* VICTOR'S *legs*) That's enough of that superstitious nonsense.

VICTOR: I don't feel anything. My legs! I don't feel anything!

WALTON: (*With pity, knowing that soon* VICTOR *will experience severe pain as the life returns to his legs*) I'm afraid you'll feel more than enough in a moment, my friend. (*He places another blanket on* VICTOR'S *legs. Aside, to the* SECOND SEAMAN) Get ready to hold him down. (WALTON *puts on third blanket; the* SEAMEN *take hold of* VICTOR'S *ankles.* VICTOR *moans softly. He groans loudly and begins to struggle.* WALTON *to the* FIRST SEAMAN) Grab his shoulders. (VICTOR *cries out in agony and struggles violently; then he faints. The* SEAMEN *back away in horror and congregate by the door.*)

WILLIAMSON: He's fainted again. That's just as well.

WALTON: (*In admiration as he sits on the window seat*) Who'd have thought he had so much strength in him! By God, he's all man, is our mysterious guest.

FIRST SEAMAN: Is he going to live, Captain?

WALTON: I don't know—by rights he shouldn't be alive now.

SECOND SEAMAN: If it were up to me, I'd throw him back into the sea.

THIRD SEAMAN: Amen to that.

WALTON: (*Rises*) Stop it! Where in God's name is your humanity? (*To the* FIRST *and* THIRD SEAMEN) Take that away. We won't need it anymore.

(*The* FIRST SEAMAN *takes tub and exits with the* THIRD SEAMAN. *The* SECOND SEAMAN *starts to leave as* VICTOR *regains consciousness. Frightened and in pain,* VICTOR *is momentarily insane—literally paranoid. Screaming, he falls off the bed.*)

SECOND SEAMAN: My God, he's possessed!

WILLIAMSON: I'd advise you to keep that talk to yourself. Now get out!

WALTON: Mr. Williamson, perhaps you should stand by in case you're needed. (WILLIAMSON *and the* SECOND SEAMAN *move to door;* WALTON *moves toward* VICTOR.) I'll look after our guest. (*Exit* SEAMAN. *Extending the glass to* VICTOR) This will help. Drink. (VICTOR *dashes the glass from* WALTON'S *hand.*) There's no reason for you to be afraid of me. I only want to help you. And my brandy is quite drinkable. (*He pours a glass and takes a sip from it.*) You see, no ill effects. (*He extends the glass to* VICTOR.) Come, it will do you good. (*After a momentary hesitation,* VICTOR *allows* WALTON *to put the glass to his lips.*) That's better. You must trust me. I'm a friend. (*He fetches soup.*) Now, drink a little of this broth. (WALTON *picks up the blankets and throws them out the door.*)

VICTOR: In what direction are we bound?

WALTON: Northwards—to the pole itself.

VICTOR: Tell me, have you seen another traveller driving a dog team across the ice?

WALTON: We saw him yesterday.

VICTOR: Good. Then he will not escape me.

WALTON: For whatever reason you have suffered so, your ordeal is over. In a week or two we'll be walking the deck together. We'll have a great deal to talk about as we inch toward the pole. (WALTON *gets fur cover from cupboard.*)

VICTOR: I see that you suffer from the same affliction as myself.

WALTON: Affliction?

VICTOR: You too are cursed with an insatiable desire to accomplish that which no man has done before.

WALTON: I suppose you are right—reaching the pole has been my obsession for years. (*Puts fur on* VICTOR)

VICTOR: Beware of obsession.

WALTON: But can you imagine the benefits to mankind of such an obsession?

VICTOR: How could this wasteland benefit anyone?

WALTON: The pole is not a wasteland. It is a place where the sun shines every hour of the day. Imagine the extent and quality of the vegetation if there is eternal light! I've spent my whole life preparing myself for this voyage, and now, by God, I'm almost there. Soon we'll be standing on the roof of the world.

VICTOR: (*Sharply*) You arrogant fool! (*Apologetically*) I shouldn't have said that. You take me on board this ship, try to save my life, and I insult you before I even know your name.

WALTON: I am Robert Walton.

VICTOR: Are you the master of this ship?

WALTON: I am.

VICTOR: Forgive me. (VICTOR *extends hand; they shake.*) I am Victor von Frankenstein. (VICTOR *sits, holding* WALTON'S *hand.*) My anger came from a personal knowledge of what ambition such as ours can do. (*Desperately*) Let me give you a warning that may save your soul. Let me show you where the search for knowledge can lead. (*Lost in his own revelation*) Prometheus stole fire from the gods and gave it to mankind. I am the new Prometheus. I brought down a fire from heaven that created a new hell. Listen, and I will tell you the strangest story you have ever heard. (*A loud roll of thunder as lights fade.*)

Scene 2

The Great Hall of Castle Frankenstein. A prominent feature is the staircase leading up to VICTOR's *laboratory. As the lights go up there is a vigorous knocking off Stage Right.*

CLERVAL: (*Shouting from outside. Knock.*) Come along! Come along! (*Knock. We hear the sound of rain and thunder.*)

(CONRAD *enters S.L. and crosses to S.R. to answer.*)

FRITZ: (*Coming down the stairs*) Conrad, why aren't you with young Master William?

CONRAD: (*Stops*) He's just finishing his bath, sir. There's someone at the door. (*Knock*)

FRITZ: (*Crossing S.R.*) I'm aware of that. You shouldn't leave him alone. Get back and see him to bed. I'll answer the door. (*He hands* CONRAD *a stained cloth.*)

CONRAD: Yes, sir. (*Knock*)

FRITZ: I'm sure it's Mr. Clerval again. (FRITZ *exits S.R.*)

CLERVAL: (*Off stage*) Come along. Come along.

(CONRAD *remains left of centre trying to see who* FRITZ *is talking to. By this time the thunder is a low rumble and rain has begun to fade.*)

FRITZ: (*Off*) Mr. Clerval, I've told you time and again that the Baron cannot be disturbed.

ELIZABETH: Nonsense, Fritz. (ELIZABETH *enters pulling* FRITZ *on after her.*)

FRITZ: Countess Elizabeth! What are you doing here?

ELIZABETH: (*Laughing*) Good heavens, Fritz. You wouldn't leave us all night in the rain!

CLERVAL: (*Enters, crosses left, removes his gloves. Lightly*) Yes, Fritz, where are your manners?

FRITZ: My apologies, Countess.

(HANS *and* LOUISE *enter carrying luggage.*)

HANS: (*Dropping piece of luggage on his toes*) Ah! Ouch, Jesus!

ELIZABETH: (*To the servants*) Hans, you and Louise take the bags to the lower west suite. You know the way.

HANS and LOUISE: Yes, ma'am. (*They cross left.*)

FRITZ: (*Guardedly*) Countess, you aren't planning to stay!

CLERVAL: No, Fritz, we've just come for tea.

FRITZ: (*Crossing to the servants*) Put those down! (*Turns to* CLERVAL) Excuse me, sir, but the master is not expecting you.

CLERVAL: (*Losing control*) Damn it, man, I've been trying to deliver the Countess Elizabeth's message for weeks, but you wouldn't let me inside the door.

ELIZABETH: (*Stepping between them*) Henry! Henry! If you shouted at me like that I wouldn't let you inside the door, either.

CLERVAL: (*Somewhat calmed*) But, damn it, Elizabeth, enough is enough! How can I perform my functions as best man if I'm not allowed to see the groom?

FRITZ: (*Stubbornly*) I'm sorry, sir, but the Baron forbade me to allow anyone to interrupt him. He is coming to the conclusion of years of work.

CLERVAL: I don't give a damn about his work!

(ELIZABETH *signals the servants. They exit S.L. with bags.*)

ELIZABETH: Now, Fritz, I know you were doing exactly what the Baron asked you, but with no replies to my letters for almost three months, you must admit I have some cause for concern. If the wedding is to take place as planned we must interrupt the Baron's work—even if only for a very short time. Believe me, I have no desire to impede his progress. I know how important his work is.

FRITZ: Oh, very well. (*Exit S.L.*)

CLERVAL: Elizabeth, nothing that Victor is doing in that god-forsaken laboratory of his can justify the way he has ignored his friends, to say nothing of how he has treated you.

ELIZABETH: (*Crossing U.L. and sitting*) Henry, when will you realize the contributions the new science is making? Would you put your personal convenience ahead of a vaccine that would eliminate smallpox and benefit all mankind?

CLERVAL: My dear, mankind is a mere abstraction. I value individual men and individual women, but I don't give a damn for mankind.

(VICTOR *appears at the head of the stairs. He wears a smock and carries a pair of forceps.*)

VICTOR: (*Descending stairs*) Fritz, I need you. Come here at once. It's almost time.

ELIZABETH: (*Rises*) Hello, Victor.

VICTOR: (*Unpleasantly surprised*) Elizabeth! Henry! (*He backs away.*)

ELIZABETH: Victor, darling. What is it? (ELIZABETH *turns to* CLERVAL) Henry, see how pale he is!

CLERVAL: We've been worried about you, old friend.

VICTOR: Fritz, I told you, I don't want to be disturbed!

FRITZ: (*Enters*) I'm sorry, sir; they're planning to stay with us.

VICTOR: No. You can't stay, Elizabeth. You shouldn't have brought her here, Henry. My work has reached a critical point. I can't afford to stop now.

ELIZABETH: I made Henry bring me, Victor. Was that really so dreadful of me? After all, the wedding arrangements have to be made sometime.

VICTOR: (*Sharply*) Tomorrow, Elizabeth. (*He turns and goes upstairs.*) You can stay with Henry's parents tonight. We'll talk tomorrow. Quickly, Fritz.

ELIZABETH: Victor!

VICTOR: You must excuse me, Elizabeth, I have work to do. (*He turns and exits;* FRITZ *follows.*)

CLERVAL: (*Distastefully*) That was disgraceful.

ELIZABETH: (*Protectively*) Don't be ridiculous, Henry. You know that was not our Victor speaking. He must be under some terrible strain to act that way.

CLERVAL: I love him, too. But he's behaving like an absolute ass.

ELIZABETH: He's a scientist. He's not like other men.

CLERVAL: (*Laughing*) Not like other men; you sound like a stupid Jane Austen heroine defending the honour of her gentleman. Elizabeth, that is the most ridiculous statement I have ever heard you make.

ELIZABETH: (*Cheering*) That's much better, Henry. Anger doesn't suit you. It's the wrong colour; it doesn't match your eyes. (*Laughs*)

FRITZ: (*Comes down the stairs*) Excuse me, Countess, the Baron would like you and Mr. Clerval to wait. He has something he must finish and will join you in a few moments.

ELIZABETH: Thank you, Fritz. Would you please tell Conrad there *will* be guests for dinner.

FRITZ: Whatever you say, ma'am.

(FRITZ *exits left.*)

CLERVAL: I've known Victor ever since we were children, but there have been times lately when I've wondered if I really know him at all.

ELIZABETH: (*Enthusiastically*) We're living in a new age, Henry.

CLERVAL: (*Sighs*) For God's sake, Elizabeth.

ELIZABETH: (*Going right on*) Men like Victor are transforming the world. Thanks to science, nothing will ever be the same again.

CLERVAL: (*Crossing up to chair and sitting*) Elizabeth, please don't give me another sermon about progress and the perfectibility of man. (*With mock weariness*) I've heard it all before, and I'm no nearer to being converted.

ELIZABETH: Doesn't it make you happy to see the old superstitions withering away?

CLERVAL: I prefer the old ones. Incense smells better than coal smoke. (VICTOR *enters.*) The dragon frightens me far less than the locomotive. (VICTOR *stands beside* ELIZABETH's *chair;* CLERVAL *turns and sees him.*) Ah! Our gracious host.

VICTOR: Darling, I was very rude to you. Forgive me. (*He kisses her hand.*)

ELIZABETH: There's nothing to forgive.

CLERVAL: Oh!

VICTOR: (*Crossing to* CLERVAL, *shakes his hand*) Henry, please accept my apologies. I'm afraid I've been working too hard, although of course that's no excuse. You must stay. However, I'm afraid I can't entertain you as I would like. I'll have to spend a good deal of time in the laboratory.

CLERVAL: (*Scoldingly*) You ought to get out of that damned laboratory and into the sunshine. You look like a ghost. What I prescribe for you, Doctor Frankenstein, is a long cruise on the lake, starting right after breakfast tomorrow.

ELIZABETH: Oh yes!

VICTOR: I'd love that, Henry. But it's impossible. I have things to do that can't wait.

ELIZABETH: (*Slightly hurt*) We understand perfectly, darling. At the moment your work is more important than anything else.

CLERVAL: Speak for yourself, Elizabeth. You may understand perfectly. I don't understand at all. (*He sits.*)

VICTOR: (*Laughing*) Henry, you're the only literate man in Christendom who still insists that the sun goes around the earth.

CLERVAL: I've no curiosity about the sun. I'm content to let it (*Pause, smile*) shine on me. You know all about the sun and yet you're too busy to allow it to touch you. It seems to me that my ignorance is more profitable than your knowledge.

VICTOR: (*Earnestly*) Be serious, Henry. We've been privileged to be born at the beginning of a new phase in human history. Think about the steam engine.

CLERVAL: (*Flippant*) You think about it, my dear Victor. The thought of it huffing and puffing away makes me quite sick.

ELIZABETH: But it has made it possible for us to travel faster than human beings ever travelled before.

VICTOR: Yes!

CLERVAL: So! (*He proceeds as though speaking before a large adoring audience.*) What can we perceive travelling at thirty miles an hour. Within ten years some damn fool will invent a machine that will travel even faster—and one day people will travel so fast that if they blink when they're passing through Switzerland, they'll miss it altogether. The world will be smaller, but so will the minds of its inhabitants. The age of science will be the age of boredom. (**ELIZABETH** *and* **VICTOR** *applaud approvingly.*) Thank you!

VICTOR: (*Laughing*) It is good to see you, Henry. I need your old-fashioned nonsense to keep me from becoming too pompous.

CLERVAL: (*Honestly*) And it is good to see you, Victor. (*Rising*) But now I'll leave you two alone. I'll go and assist Conrad in choosing the wines for dinner. (*He crosses left.*)

ELIZABETH: Tonight we must have champagne.

VICTOR: Yes.

CLERVAL: Then I'll make certain that it's the very best champagne, the kind that butlers and footmen usually reserve for themselves.

(Exit CLERVAL)

(VICTOR *takes* ELIZABETH *out of her chair; they embrace and kiss.*)

VICTOR: Elizabeth, the last time I saw you, I thought I loved you as much as it was possible for one human being to love another— and yet tonight I find that I love you even more.

(*They kiss again.*)

ELIZABETH: Oh, Victor! Darling, you'll think I'm being foolish interrupting your work this way, but I'd been so worried.

VICTOR: Worried?

ELIZABETH: Worried about you, about us.

VICTOR: Oh, Elizabeth!

ELIZABETH: Now I see that nothing has changed. I need only worry about my rival, your mistress!

VICTOR: My mistress!

ELIZABETH: Science.

VICTOR: (*Laughing*) You have no rival, not even science. Oh, Elizabeth. (*They kiss.*)

ELIZABETH: (*Tentatively*) Victor, this work you're doing; is it very dangerous?

VICTOR: (*Turns away*) Everything worth doing involves an element of risk.

ELIZABETH: Can you tell me about it?

VICTOR: (*Excited*) Oh, Elizabeth! I feel as Balboa must have felt when he first looked out at the Pacific Ocean. (ELIZABETH *is just as excited as he.*) I'm like an explorer about to pass through the gates of a lost city that he's been searching for all his life. If old Professor Waldman could see me now! He used to say that the ancient teachers of science promised impossibilities and performed nothing, while the modern masters promise very little, but they indeed have performed miracles. (*Arrogantly*) Well, by God, tonight Victor Frankenstein will perform one of those miracles.

(*He turns faint and becomes unsteady on his feet.* ELIZABETH *reaches out and seats him.*)

ELIZABETH: Victor, darling, what's wrong?

VICTOR: (*Recovering*) Nothing. I'm just a little tired.

ELIZABETH: (*Maternally*) You've probably been working day and night, and half the time you've been forgetting to eat.

(*Enter* CLERVAL *and* FRITZ.)

CLERVAL: Well tonight you will eat. Fritz has done very well by us. The cook is preparing quail and salmon.

ELIZABETH: Oh!

FRITZ: Excellency, I trust that will be satisfactory.

VICTOR: That sounds very satisfactory indeed. Thank you, Fritz.

ELIZABETH: (*Crossing to* CLERVAL) Henry, I was just asking Victor about his latest experiment.

VICTOR: It has to do with electricity. (*Thunder*) Listen. The ancients called that the Hammer of Thor, but we know better. (*Thunder*) Ah! Nothing else in the universe has a power to compare with that.

CLERVAL: My dear Victor, you talk about it as if it were God.

VICTOR: In a sense it is God. It is the source of life.

CLERVAL: (*Sitting*) Now you're the one who's not being serious.

VICTOR: Yes I am! Galvani suspected as much.

ELIZABETH: Victor, I know Galvani regarded electricity as a potential source of motive power, but surely not as the source of life.

VICTOR: He did, my darling, but he did not dare tell the world. (*Crosses left*)

Galvani learned more from applying electricity to the body of a frog than from a hundred tedious Greek and Latin treatises. God, what a man he was! But come. You must see for yourselves. (*Starts them up the stairs;* FRITZ *intervenes.*)

FRITZ: (*Alarmed*) Baron, are you sure that's wise?

VICTOR: Good old Fritz. Always the cautious one. I assure you that I know exactly what I'm doing. We need have no secrets from the Countess and Mr. Clerval. (FRITZ *exits to lab.*) My dear Henry and my dearest Elizabeth, you are about to see something that you will remember for the rest of your lives. Come. (VICTOR *and* ELIZABETH *walk around ramp.* CLERVAL *holds back, then follows.*) Newton said that he felt like a child gathering pretty pebbles on the seashore. The pebbles represented what he had learned and the sea symbolized all that there was to know. I feel like a child who has dived into the ocean and come up with a pearl. (*During this speech a transition is made from the Great Hall to the laboratory. The lights on the Forestage dim and the lights on ramp U.S. and in the lab come up so we see the three of them and all the lab equipment in the background. We see* FRITZ *already busy adjusting dials and knobs. As* ELIZABETH, CLERVAL *and* VICTOR *come down the ramp S.R., the lights in the lab and Forestage come up.*)

VICTOR: Well, Fritz, let's check the instruments.

CLERVAL: (*As they enter the lab*) I feel like Ulysses entering the cave of Polyphemus.

ELIZABETH: Polyphemus, the Cyclops.

(VICTOR *takes the chairs from their Great Hall position and puts them side by side D.S.L.*)

CLERVAL: Your science is a cyclops, too, Victor. It looks at the world with only one eye. (*Crosses left*)

(*The laboratory contains at right the control console with numerous switches and dials, and a wall U.C. with curtains on it. Since this is actually using the same stage space as the Great Hall, there are still the stairs S.L. and the ramp and arch S.R.*)

ELIZABETH: (*Crosses to console*) Here is my rival. I am a little jealous of this room.

VICTOR: (*Crossing to console*) (FRITZ *adjusts dials and checks readings.*) Yes. Fine. Very good indeed.

FRITZ: The storm could present a problem. But all the connections seem to be working perfectly.

VICTOR: Yes, everything seems to be in fine shape for our little demonstration.

ELIZABETH: (*Crossing to* CLERVAL) I feel as if I were about to witness the unveiling of a new painting by Leonardo.

CLERVAL: (*Crossing to chair and sitting*) It's more like a travelling magician getting ready to perform his act in the village square.

VICTOR: Watch out, Henry.

CLERVAL: Good heavens!

FRITZ: Excuse me, Mr. Clerval.

VICTOR: (*Taking* ELIZABETH *left and seating her*) All right, Fritz, we're about to cure Mr. Clerval of his cynicism. Turn down the gas.

(*The lights dim to a low reading as* FRITZ *pulls large handle on control console.*)

VICTOR: The world has waited millions of years for what you're about to see.
(VICTOR *crosses Upstage and opens curtain on arch, revealing a silver coffin-like cabinet.*)

CLERVAL: (*To* ELIZABETH) These sleight-of-hand artists always insist that the lamps be put out. Well, Victor, I'm waiting to be impressed.

ELIZABETH: Henry, you're not fooling anyone. The truth is you know you're going to be impressed, but you're determined not to admit it.

(VICTOR *opens the cabinet. It is too dark to see what it contains. The lights go out completely so the only illumination is the red light on the control console.*)

VICTOR: Now, Fritz, the motor! (FRITZ *throws power switch and grabs the large brake lever. A low frequency power hum is heard.*) That's right, but not quite so fast. Good. Now, Henry, you doubting Thomas, watch carefully.

(*In the cabinet a small faint glow appears.*)

ELIZABETH: Oh!

VICTOR: Keep your eyes on it now. (*Very slowly the light swells and brightens; the hum continues.*) The brake, Fritz. (FRITZ *adjusts brake.*) You're not saying anything, Henry. Could it be that you don't believe your eyes?

CLERVAL: I've yet to see anything, except a glimmer of light.

(*Gradually the light becomes bright enough that we can discern that the cabinet contains a primitive electric light bulb. The hum increases in frequency and volume.*)

ELIZABETH: Light without a flame.

VICTOR: Light electric, darling. The day will come when such light illuminates every city in the world.

Frankenstein

ELIZABETH: It's almost frightening.

VICTOR: Anything new and strange is a little frightening. But this is nothing to what I can do. Perhaps, some day soon I'll show you a creation that will make this look like a child's toy. This will light houses, but I mean to light the universe. (*The light has become very bright, the hum very loud and high.*) Fritz! Quickly, the brake!

FRITZ: (*Pulling on the brake*) It's stuck! (*The light is brighter.*)

VICTOR: Don't be a fool. It can't be stuck. Here—switch off the motor.

(*The light has become blinding, the hum deafening.* FRITZ *and* VICTOR *grasp the great lever.*)

VICTOR: Pull, Fritz, pull.

FRITZ: I'm pulling as hard as I can.

CLERVAL: (*On his feet, screams*) For God's sake, look out!

(*The bulb explodes.* CLERVAL *throws himself in front of* ELIZABETH *to protect her. The hum dies away.*)

VICTOR: Elizabeth, are you all right? (*The lights come back up as* FRITZ *pushes on gas control.*)

CLERVAL: (*Turning on* VICTOR) Victor, you damned fool, you could have killed her. You could have killed us all.

ELIZABETH: (*Recovering but shaken*) I'm quite all right. It was a little startling, that's all.

VICTOR: (*Losing concern for* ELIZABETH *and turning back to his machinery*) It's never done anything like that before. But it's not a serious problem.

FRITZ: The brake is working.

VICTOR: It must have been a faulty connection.

CLERVAL: (*Crossing to ramp*) The man almost blinds us. Then he says it's not a serious problem. I'll stick with gaslight and candles, thank you. Although this damned bomb of yours might be useful as a weapon of war.

VICTOR: (*Turning back*) It was no one's fault, and no harm was done (*Crossing to* ELIZABETH), aside from ruffling your feathers a bit, Henry. Anyhow, this light is a very minor affair, compared with another experiment I have in progress.

CLERVAL: Please don't show us anything else, Victor. I've had enough of your science for one day.

VICTOR: Henry, I have no intention of showing you my other experiment. Your nerves are too delicate. You need medication. I prescribe champagne. (*They walk up the ramp.*)

(*During this speech, the former process is reversed.* FRITZ *replaces chairs in their Great Hall positions and goes back U.S. to the console to shut it down. Stage lights dim, and the Great Hall lights come up.*)

CLERVAL: Now there is a civilized remark. Champagne and an enormous dinner, and afterwards a long conversation over brandy. Elizabeth will tell us all the Geneva gossip. We will find out if it is true that the Duchess of Zelle is having an affair with her footman. I will read you my latest translations from the Sanskrit. We will discuss all the politicians of Europe and agree that we could do the job better if we had the chance. We will damn the Austrians, castigate the Prussians and excoriate the French, as befits good citizens of the Swiss Republic. (*This is spoken as they go down the stairs.*)

VICTOR: Unfortunately, I won't be able to join you for dinner.

ELIZABETH: Oh!

VICTOR: Perhaps I'll come down later for a glass of brandy. You'll understand that I have certain things to do that can't be postponed.

CLERVAL: I spoke too soon. Like all scientists—the man's a savage.

ELIZABETH: You must eat, darling.

VICTOR: Fritz will bring me something.

(*Enter* HANS, LOUISE, *running.*)

LOUISE: Is anything wrong? We heard the most dreadful noise.

HANS: Pardon, sir. She's deathly afraid of lightning.

VICTOR: It was nothing. A slight accident.

CLERVAL: The Baron dropped the Hammer of Thor on his toe.

LOUISE: Oh, that must have hurt something awful, sir.

VICTOR: Nothing is hurt except my pride, Louise.

WILLIAM: (*Off*) Victor! Victor! (*Runs on followed by* CONRAD)

ELIZABETH: William! (*He runs and hugs her.*)

WILLIAM: Elizabeth!

CLERVAL: (*Offers hand*) Comment allez-vous, William?

WILLIAM: (*Shaking hand*) Très bien, merci, et vous?

CLERVAL: Je suis très bien aussi.

WILLIAM: (*To* VICTOR) I heard a noise from your laboratory—I was afraid something had happened to you.

CLERVAL: (*Gently*) There was nothing to worry about, William—your brother was merely playing with one of his damn toys.

Frankenstein 221

ELIZABETH: Henry!

WILLIAM: Victor does not play with toys in his laboratory—his work there is very important.

VICTOR: Thank you for defending me, William. Mr. Clerval obviously lacks your understanding.

WILLIAM: When may I visit the laboratory again, Victor?

VICTOR: Soon, William, but now I'd like you to be the host for this evening. Elizabeth and Mr. Clerval are staying for dinner. Perhaps you would take them in.

WILLIAM: (*Offering arm*) Certainly, right this way. (*Leads them off right.*)

ELIZABETH: (*Stopping and turning*) Darling, won't you change your mind and join us?

VICTOR: I can't, darling, I'm sorry.

ELIZABETH: Then we'll see you in a little while.

(*Exit* FRITZ *and* ELIZABETH.)

VICTOR: (*To the servants*) Conrad, see to my guests. Tonight everyone should celebrate. It may be the most important night of my life. See that all of you have as much wine as you can drink.

CONRAD: Thank you very much, Excellency.

(*Exit* VICTOR *by way of the stairs, and* CONRAD *left.*)

HANS: (*Crossing right*) He's a strange one, the Baron.

LOUISE: Now that Countess Elizabeth is here she'll soon get him out of that laboratory. (HANS *gives a dirty laugh.*) I wonder what he does up there?

HANS: (*Nonchalantly*) One thing I know, he buys dead bodies.

LOUISE: (*Crossing to him*) No! (HANS *nods.*) And what would a man like the Baron want with a dead body?

HANS: He eats them, my girl.

LOUISE: No!

HANS: Yes! Why like as not, that's what they're serving up downstairs now.

LOUISE: No!

HANS: Yes! Roast leg of corpse . . .

LOUISE: No!

HANS: Yes, and jellied dead men's eyeballs.

LOUISE: No!

HANS: Yes!

LOUISE: (*Starting to doubt him*) Nah!

HANS: Yes! (*He mimes eating an eyeball.*)

LOUISE: No! I won't listen to any more of your nonsense. (*She goes to leave.*)

HANS: Louise, me darlin' (*She stops.*), you've heard of the grave robbers haven't ya! (*She is terrified.*) The Resurrection Men?

LOUISE: I don't know anything about any Resurrection Men, you Black Protestant, and me a virgin since I was almost fifteen (*Exits S.L.*)

HANS: (*Turns to audience*) Fifteen? Thirteen! (*Exits S.L., chuckling to himself.*)

(*As* HANS *exits, there is a transformation from the Great Hall to the lab. Lights in lab come up.* VICTOR *and* FRITZ *move the chairs from the Great Hall positions to D.S.R. and D.S.L.*)

VICTOR: (*As he moves his chair D.S.L.*) Now Fritz, to work! Hurry, man, hurry. We must catch the storm at the height of its power. (*Crossing to centre*) Oh, Fritz, I don't know how you can be so calm. Switch Gamma! (*The trap starts to go down with* VICTOR *on it.*) We've worked and waited for this moment for so long. (*Hopping off the lowering trap*) I'm tempted to skip and dance. I'd like to play leap-frog as I did when I was a child. (*He jumps over the open hole.*) I feel as if I'd drunk laudanum. (*He floats into chair D.S.L.*)

FRITZ: (*Running the trap switch*) You'd better come down to earth, then. It wouldn't do for your hands to shake. (*The trap hits the bottom; where no trap is available, use an upstage entrance.*)

VICTOR: (*Leaping out of the chair*) Table switch, Fritz. (FRITZ *throws another switch; we hear a motor sound.* VICTOR *watches the hole in the floor intently.*) Further, further, further, stop! (FRITZ *throws the switch back; the motor stops.*) A little more . . . (FRITZ *again throws the switch; again we hear the motor.*) There, stop.

(*A low rumble of thunder is heard from here to the end of the scene.*)

VICTOR: (*Moving to Upstage of the trap*) Now, Fritz, the moment has arrived. Let's not keep our friend waiting. (FRITZ *throws the switch and the trap starts up. As the trap raises, we see a table with a body on it. The body is covered with a sheet. The head faces Stage Left and is on a headrest. As the trap becomes level with the floor,* VICTOR *raises the Upstage edge of the sheet.*) Ah, you're a fine fellow. The new Adam. (*To* FRITZ) Switch Theta. (*The back wall flies out revealing the bellows and the blood machine. We hear a motor as the wall flies.* VICTOR *moves the control console D.S.R.* FRITZ *moves the bellows to D.S.L.* VICTOR *then moves the blood machine to U.S.R. of the table.*) Now we attach his umbilical cord. (*He attaches a long black hose from the blood machine to the* CREATURE'S *abdomen under the cloth.*) Like so. Switch Gamma! (*He turns on the blood machine which starts to bubble and* FRITZ *adjusts the dials on it.*) Increase temperature. Slowly, slowly, there! (*Feeling the* CREATURE'S *pulse*) Beautiful! Fritz, you can connect the table. And now for the air supply. (VICTOR *lifts up the sheet and inserts the breathing hose from the bellows into the* CREATURE'S *mouth.*) And now, Fritz . . . (*He turns the table so that the* CREATURE'S *head is Upstage.*) The brain . . . (FRITZ *gets a large jar of green liquid with the brain floating in it from behind the blood machine.*) We must give our friend the machinery for thought. (VICTOR *removes the brain from the jar and holds it high in the air, admiring it.*) The face of a handsome peasant youth and the brain of one of the wisest men in all of Switzerland. (*Inserting brain seemingly in the* CREATURE'S *head, but actually in the hollow headrest.* FRITZ *crosses up to Stage Right of the* CREATURE'S *head.* VICTOR *pulls a needle and thread out of the headrest. The following is said as* VICTOR *sews up the* CREATURE'S *scalp.* FRITZ *cuts the thread after each stitch.*) The brain won't remember anything, but it will learn very quickly. Our friend's infancy will be very brief. In a couple of months we may be arguing philosophy with him. He'll be a handsome devil too, once his hair has grown back and the scars have healed.

FRITZ: He won't be very handsome if the chemicals affect him the way they did the animals. (*They finish sewing.* FRITZ, *facing* VICTOR *across the table*) I wish I could be sure that we're doing right.

VICTOR: Life is good and death is evil. Knowledge is good and ignorance is evil. That's the only true moral code.

FRITZ: (*Crossing to console*) But perhaps the dead have a right to stay dead. Haven't you ever thought that you might be going against God?

VICTOR: (*Turning Downstage*) In this instance I am God. Switch Delta. (FRITZ *throws a switch and a large electronic apparatus with two wires hanging from it flies in directly over the head of the* CREATURE. *We hear the sound of a motor.* VICTOR *is Downstage Centre facing Upstage guiding the apparatus in.*) And now we must draw on the energy of the heavens, the source of life!

FRITZ. A little more, higher, higher, there!

VICTOR: Stop!

(FRITZ *throws the switch back and the apparatus stops with the two wires resting on the floor.* VICTOR *pulls two large half circles of silver metal out from underneath the operating table. He throws one to Upstage of the table.* VICTOR *moves to Stage Left of the table,* FRITZ *to Stage Right. They insert the first ring in slots right and left of the* CREATURE'S *abdomen.* VICTOR *picks up the second ring and they insert it in slots right and left of the* CREATURE'S *head. They then attach the wires to the metal rings.* VICTOR *puts headrest on the blood machine.*)

VICTOR: Napoleon conquered a continent, tonight Victor Frankenstein will conquer death.

(FRITZ *goes to the console and puts on the pair of goggles sitting on top.* VICTOR *goes to the bellows and gets the pair of goggles from there and puts them on.*)

VICTOR: Now, Fritz, give us power.

(FRITZ *throws the power switch and takes hold of the brake. We hear the power hum and the electronic apparatus lights up.*)

VICTOR: Now increase the temperature slowly! More. There! Now more power.

(FRITZ *moves the brake, the hum becomes louder, the light brighter. Suddenly,* FRITZ *pulls the brake back and shuts off the main power. The light on the electronic apparatus dims out, and the power hum dies.*)

VICTOR: My God, man, why did you do that?

FRITZ: (*Takes off goggles*) It's no use. I can't go through with it.

VICTOR: What do you mean, you can't go through with it!

FRITZ: (*Crosses to Stage Right chair*) It's not the same with a human being.

VICTOR: (*Crossing to the body*) This damn thing isn't a human being. I made it—out of corpses. I'm not asking you to help me commit murder, I'm asking you to help me create life.

FRITZ: I can't do it, Victor, it's too much to ask of me.

VICTOR: Damn you! (*Pulling a scalpel from his smock and crossing to left of* FRITZ) Nothing is going to stand in my way now. You'll go through with it or so help me God, I'll drive this scalpel into your heart.

FRITZ: (*Sitting, resignedly*) I'm afraid you'll just have to kill me then.

VICTOR: (*Puts scalpel on console; crosses to table.*) God. (*Crosses to* FRITZ) Oh, Fritz, I'm sorry—so sorry—my dear old friend, it would be easier for me to kill myself. Fritz, I beg of you, help me. Help me because you love me.

FRITZ: No, Victor, I can't.

VICTOR: (*Kneeling beside him*) When my father asked your father to follow him into battle, he didn't hesitate. He took up his pike and charged.

FRITZ: Excellency, I would rather fight in a hundred battles than do this thing.

VICTOR: Please, Fritz! Please!

FRITZ: Then let it be on your conscience, not on mine.

(**Fritz** *rises, crosses to console.*)

Victor: (*Excitedly*) Let's begin again. Power, Fritz. (**Fritz** *throws the power switch and grabs the brake; the electronic apparatus lights up and the power hum is heard.*)

Victor: Increase the temperature slowly. More. There.

(*The light on the apparatus gets brighter and the hum increases in volume and frequency.*)

Victor: More power. More! More!

(*During this entire sequence it is the movement of the large brake at the left of the console which controls both the brightness of the apparatus and the volume and frequency of the hum.*)

Victor: More! More! More! More!

(**Fritz** *pushes the brake to about three-quarters of its capacity and then appears as if he can go no further. They must both shout to be heard over the power hum.*)

Fritz: That's the best it will do.

Victor: (*Crossing to the console*) No it isn't.

(*He helps* **Fritz** *push the brake to its capacity. The hum becomes even louder and the frequency greater. The general stage lighting dims to one-quarter and the light from the electronic apparatus becomes much brighter. The stage is bathed in a dull red light.*)

Victor: The bellows, Fritz. It's time.

(**Fritz** *crosses left to the bellows and starts to pump slowly on* **Victor's** *cries of "IN." The* **Creature's** *chest rises and falls with each pump of the bellows. After five intakes of breath, the body on the table twitches as if it had received a massive electric shock.*)

Fritz: My God! It lives!

(**Victor** *rushes from the console to the body and listens to its chest with his ear.*)

Victor: (*Jubilantly*) Yes! The table, Fritz.

(*They tip the table up so that the* **Creature** *is standing Downstage Centre but still on the table. They remove the metal half circles from the table and* **Victor** *rips the cloth off the body, revealing a hideous face.* **Victor** *becomes engrossed in listening to the* **Creature's** *heart and pulse.* **Fritz** *recoils in horror.*)

FRITZ: But look at the face!

VICTOR: (*Not looking*) It's the chemical reaction. But he's alive, Fritz, he's alive!

FRITZ: It's horrible. Like something from the depths of hell. You'll have to kill it.

VICTOR: Don't talk like a fool, Fritz. I can't halt the experiment now.

FRITZ: You've got to do it. You haven't the right to let that hideous thing live.

(VICTOR *sees the* CREATURE *for the first time.*)

VICTOR: Oh my God!

(VICTOR *is at a loss as to what to do.*)

FRITZ: For God's sake, hurry.

(VICTOR *steps toward console, and stops.*)

VICTOR: No. I can't.

FRITZ: (*Running to console*) By God, if you won't kill it, I will.

(FRITZ *pulls brake back and shuts the console down completely. The hum dies; the blood machine stops bubbling, and the light returns to normal. There is total silence on stage.* FRITZ *picks up the scalpel from the console and crosses around to Stage Left of the table. He stops. There is no movement. The* CREATURE *shudders uncontrollably.* FRITZ *raises the scalpel to stab it and the* CREATURE'S *left arm flails and accidently knocks* FRITZ *left. The* CREATURE *steps off the table. It rips the breathing hose from its mouth and spasmodically sucks its first breath of air. It gropes at its abdomen and grasps the hose from the blood machine firmly in its two hands. With a great effort it rips the umbilical cord from its stomach, emits an horrendous wail of birth, and its eyes spring open wide in wonderment and pain. As the* CREATURE *turns and recognizes* VICTOR *as its "mother," the painful wail becomes a wordless cry for help as it reaches out for* VICTOR *imploringly.*)

VICTOR: Get back, damn you! Get back!

(*As the* CREATURE *stretches its arms to* VICTOR *for help,* FRITZ *raises himself from the floor and attacks the* CREATURE, *plunging the scalpel into its back. At the sudden shock of pain, the* CREATURE *wheels around again, smashing* FRITZ *to the floor.* VICTOR *faints. The* CREATURE, *puzzled, kneels beside* VICTOR's *body, whimpering. We then hear* CLERVAL *and* ELIZABETH *Offstage Left entering onto the ramp. When the* CREATURE *hears the voices, it crosses Up Left and hides behind the arch.*)

ELIZABETH: Something dreadful has happened.

CLERVAL: Stay here, Elizabeth, I'll go and see.

Frankenstein 227

ELIZABETH: No, I'm going with you. (*They enter the lab through the arch Stage Right.*)

CLERVAL: Oh God! (*They both rush to VICTOR's side.*)

ELIZABETH: Victor, are you all right? Victor!

(CLERVAL *hears* FRITZ *groan and rushes to his side.*)

VICTOR: Fritz warned me, but I wouldn't listen.

ELIZABETH: It was only an accident, darling. (*She helps him to his feet. The* CREATURE *peers out from behind the pillar.*)

VICTOR: The gods chained Prometheus to a rock where a vulture tore eternally at his flesh. I wonder what punishment they have in store for me?

Act Two

Scene 1

A peasant's cottage in the forest on the Frankenstein estate. Late afternoon is becoming dusk. We hear the sounds of night birds and crickets. The blind man, DE LACEY, *and his son,* FELIX, *are finishing their evening meal.*

DE LACEY: (*As he puts empty bowls on shelves*) Admit it, Felix, I make the finest stew in Switzerland.

FELIX: (*Teasingly*) Father, I've never tasted anything quite like it, that's certain.

DE LACEY: (*Laughing*) Ah, Felix, it's so good to have you here. (*He sits.*)

FELIX: I wish I could be here with you all the time. Sometimes I think I'm not cut out to be a scholar.

DE LACEY: Nonsense. You were born to be a scholar, my son. It's in your blood. What you really mean is: you think you should stay home and look after your poor old helpless father.

FELIX: (*Rises, crosses to fire*) Perhaps you could come with me to Geneva. You'd like there, Father. (FELIX *picks up pipe from mantel and packs it.*)

DE LACEY: Since my retreat to the simple life, I've been perfectly happy here, Felix. I carry a hundred books in my head, and I know the way to the village so well that I can walk there and back without ever once stumbling. That's more than most people can do. But in Geneva I'd be lost. (FELIX *gives his father the pipe. Goes back to the fire, lights taper.*)

FELIX: Still, I worry about you living here alone.

DE LACEY: I'd be hurt if you didn't. But I'll be annoyed if you worry about me too much. (FELIX *holds the taper over the pipe, lights it.*) Let's talk about more pleasant things, such as how well you're doing in your studies. (*We hear the distant sound of a horn.*) Ah! Your Uncle Philippe. He never fails me. (*He gets to his feet.*) Fetch me my horn.

(FELIX *gets the horn. He and his father go outside. They face U.S.*)

FELIX: It's getting dark.

DE LACEY: Yes, I can feel it.

(*Again we hear the horn.*)

FELIX: Father, don't answer the horn.

DE LACEY: But if I don't answer, your Uncle Philippe will think that's something's wrong.

FELIX: And what will happen if he thinks that something's wrong?

DE LACEY: He'll come over to see if I'm all right.

FELIX: Good. I'll surprise him as I surprised you last night.

DE LACEY: Oh, I don't know. You remember the boy who cried "wolf."

FELIX: He won't have time to get worried. I'll meet him at the bridge.

DE LACEY: (*Laughing*) Sometimes I think you'll never grow up. But go ahead, then. Be off with you.

FELIX: I'll be back soon.

(Exit FELIX *up ramp.* DE LACEY *enters cottage, puts the horn down and picks up his guitar.*)

DE LACEY: (*Taking up the guitar*) I wonder if I was ever that young. (*He returns to his chair.*) Well, what do you have to say for yourself, Master Guitar? (*He strums the guitar. He utters the next sentence as though repeating words that the guitar had said to him.*) Old guitars are best and so are old fathers. (*He strums the guitar again.*) Nice of you to say so, Master Guitar. (*During the playing, the* CREATURE *enters and crosses to the cottage, stops outside and listens—it enters.*)

CREATURE: You did not answer the horn.

DE LACEY: (*Rising*) Welcome, my friend.

CREATURE: I was afraid for you.

DE LACEY: And where have you been these past two days? (*Hanging guitar on wall*) I've missed you.

CREATURE: I have been searching for my maker.

DE LACEY: A man should go in search of his maker from time to time. But, come.

(*Crossing to shelves and getting bread and cheese.*) You must be hungry. Eat. There's plenty of food. My son arrived from Geneva last night.

CREATURE: (*Turning to leave*) Then I must go.

DE LACEY: There's no need for that. He'll be away for a while. He's gone down to the bridge.

CREATURE: Then I will eat of your bread.

(*It locks the door and closes the shutter, sits on the right of table and eats.*)

DE LACEY: You are welcome to anything that I have. You must know that by now.

CREATURE: Thank you, my friend.

DE LACEY: (*Sitting*) Well, we mustn't neglect your lessons. You have bread for the body. Now you must have bread for the mind. What will it be today? History? Philosophy? Literature? You've been an apt pupil. It's astonishing how much you've learned in a few short months.

CREATURE: It is as if all knowledge were asleep within me and needed only to be nudged awake.

DE LACEY: You said you'd been searching for your maker. (*The CREATURE replaces uneaten bread on shelf.*) Perhaps today's lesson should deal with religion.

CREATURE: (*Turns to DE LACEY*) "Did I request thee, Maker, from my clay to mould me man? Did I solicit thee from darkness to promote me?"

DE LACEY: You remember your Milton. Good.

CREATURE: Even Satan has his fellow devils to admire and encourage him. I am the only one of my kind.

DE LACEY: Each of us is the only one of his kind. Plato said . . .

CREATURE (*Impatiently*) You have told me what Plato said, and all the others. But their words do not comfort me. They only increase my capacity for pain.

DE LACEY: Pain is the sternest but the greatest of teachers.

CREATURE: (*Its impatience increasing*) Words. Words. Your words begin to offend me.

DE LACEY: Through words we reach out and touch each other. There is no greater power in the universe.

CREATURE: (*With a scornful laugh, crosses to DE LACEY*) I could put an end to all your words by strangling you. There would be an unanswerable argument.

DE LACEY: You would not hurt me.

CREATURE: I could tear you apart. You cannot see me but I am raising my arms. (*It does so.*) I am reaching out for your throat. (*It does so.*)

De Lacey: So!

Creature: (*Closing its fingers lightly around* De Lacey's *neck*) Feel my hands. They are strong enough to snap your neck.

De Lacey: (*Pause*) I refuse to fear you.

Creature: (*Dropping its hands*) You are right. I could not hurt you. Oh, De Lacey, you must help me. You tell me what to do. You must be my judge.

De Lacey: I cannot judge you. But come! I can listen. Sometimes that is enough.

Creature: Be grateful that you cannot see me. For I am a hideous, misshapen thing. The sight of me would make you sick.

De Lacey: That explains so much. Is there anything I could do to comfort you, my friend?

Creature: (*Taking a medallion from his pocket, gives it to* De Lacey) Take this. Do you know what it is?

De Lacey: (*Holding the medallion and fingering it*) It's a medallion. A cameo. Bearing a head; a man's head.

Creature: It is the face of my maker.

De Lacey: Your maker? I don't understand. (*He puts the medallion on the table.*)

Creature: (*Crosses left, reliving the experience*) This morning at the river I saw a child. He had fallen into the water and was crying out for help. I went into the water, took him in my arms and carried his unconscious body to the riverbank. I laid him on the ground. He was beautiful. My heart went out to him. Then as I bent over him trying to restore life to his body, I hear a shout. I looked up to see a man lift a musket to his shoulder and shoot at me.

De Lacey: But why?

Creature: It was the gamekeeper, who had failed in his duty to protect the boy. And now the villain was trying to kill me. I struck him dead.

De Lacey: God have mercy upon us.

Creature: I turned back to the child, who was beginning to revive. A thought flashed through my mind. The child is innocent. He will not find me loathsome. (Victor *and* Clerval *enter and cross to cottage.*) He will see in me only the being who had saved his life. I would take him away with me, to be my companion. I looked down at him, lovingly. His eyes opened . . .

(Clerval *knocks at the door.*)

De Lacey: Just a moment.

CLERVAL: (*From outside*) Hello! Is there anyone in there?

(DE LACEY *signals the* CREATURE *to hide in the shadows*.)

DE LACEY: I'm coming. I'm coming.

(DE LACEY *opens the door. Now it is quite dark outside.* VICTOR *and* CLERVAL *stand there. Each carries a musket.* VICTOR *obviously is exhausted*.)

CLERVAL: (*Entering*) Forgive this intrusion. I am Henry Clerval. This is my friend, Baron Frankenstein. Could we rest here for a few minutes?

DE LACEY: (*Awed*) You honour me, gentlemen. Come in, by all means. My name is De Lacey.

(*They leave their muskets by the door*.)

CLERVAL: We've been searching in the woods all day. The Baron's brother is missing. He's only a child.

DE LACEY: How terrible. Poor little fellow. How could such a thing have happened?

CLERVAL: I'm afraid we don't know. Would you mind if I lit a lamp?

DE LACEY: Of course! May I offer you something?

(CLERVAL *crosses to the fire, lights a taper and lights the lamp over the mantel*.)

VICTOR: (*Wearily seating himself at the table*) No. Nothing. Perhaps a glass of water. (DE LACEY *brings him water*.) Thank you. It's a cold, dark night for a little boy to be alone in the woods.

CLERVAL: (*Optimistically*) William is a very competent young man, Victor. Before morning we'll find him sleeping under a tree. He'll laugh when he sees us, and you'll cheerfully spank him for wandering off.

VICTOR: I wish I could believe that, Henry! Oh God, if only we had more searchers.

DE LACEY: My son and my brother could help. They know these woods very well.

CLERVAL: A marvellous idea.

DE LACEY: They should be down by the bridge.

CLERVAL: (*Crossing to the door*) Victor, what do you say that I go and enlist them while you get your second wind?

VICTOR: Good, Henry. Mr. De Lacey, thank you. (CLERVAL *takes his musket and exits.*) You are a father. I am so much older than William and I have been his father as well as his brother. If anything should happen to him . . . (*He puts his elbows on the table and his head in his hands. When he takes his hands away he sees the medallion.*) My god. (*He takes it up and looks at it as if unable to believe what he sees.*) How did that come to be here?

DE LACEY: How did what come to be here, sir?

VICTOR: (*Coming to his feet*) William's medallion. Bearing my picture.

DE LACEY: I am blind, Baron. I know nothing of the medallion.

VICTOR: (*Waves his hand in front of* DE LACEY's *sightless eyes*) This precious son of yours, would his hobby be poaching by any chance?

DE LACEY: Felix is a student. He has done you no harm. He will help you find your brother.

VICTOR: I can see how it could have happened. Your son was poaching and this morning the gamekeeper caught him at it.

DE LACEY: Felix did not kill the gamekeeper.

VICTOR: (*Seizing* DE LACEY) How did you know the gamekeeper was dead? Because your son killed him. (*He shakes* DE LACEY.) And William saw him do it. (*He shakes* DE LACEY *again and harder.*) Where is my brother?

DE LACEY: Please, Baron.

CREATURE: (*From the shadows*) Victor, your business is with me.

VICTOR: (*Releasing* DE LACEY) Who are you?

CREATURE: You know me well, Victor.

VICTOR: Why are you hiding. Come out where I can see you.

(*The* CREATURE *steps into light*)

VICTOR: My God! (*Covers his face. Turns Downstage*)

CREATURE: (*Disappointed, angry*) You call upon your maker. I hope you will be more successful than I have been in calling upon mine. Look at me!

VICTOR: I cannot. The sight of you repels me.

CREATURE: Has it never occurred to you that your creator may find you as repulsive as you find me?

VICTOR: (*Looking up*) I had almost convinced myself that you were dead. He is helpless, I told myself. He will die of hunger or exposure. As the months passed it seemed that you had never existed, except in my imagination.

CREATURE: (*Moves a step toward* VICTOR) You cast me forth, a poor helpless miserable creature tormented by hunger, thirst and cold.

VICTOR: I could not bear the burden of what I had created.

CREATURE: And what of my burden? I could distinguish no sensation but pain. I lived in a pig-sty and ate the slops which are their food. For a time I could not speak but only babble like a beast.

VICTOR: I didn't wish it so. (*Woefully*) I wanted to create something beautiful.

CREATURE: Beautiful! I was driven from your village by men with scythes and pitchforks because the sight of me so sickened them. (*It stalks* VICTOR, *who edges away*.) And yet I am made of flesh. As I ran from them, I called out to you, my creator, to help me. Help me! Help me!

VICTOR: (*Crosses right*) What could I do? What could I do? I am only a man.

CREATURE: (*Losing control*) Accursed creator! Why did you form a monster so hideous that even you turned from me in disgust? God in pity made man in His own image. But my form is a filthy imitation of yours, made more horrible by its very resemblance.

DE LACEY: (*Crossing to* CREATURE) What is all this? I don't understand.

CREATURE: (*Seats him gently*) It is not necessary that you understand, my friend. After I go, remember only that I loved you.

VICTOR: You have been staying here. Living in this cottage. That explains how you've survived.

CREATURE: I was more dead than alive the night I crawled to this good man's door. He fed me. Through him I learned to shape my thoughts into words. To ask myself: Who am I? What am I? Where did I come from? Like Adam I was apparently linked to no other creature in existence. But Adam had been guarded by the special care of his creator. I was abandoned and alone. I went in search of my maker and this morning I saw his face. (*It takes up the medallion.*)

VICTOR: The medallion. So it was you who brought it here. You damned fiend. It was you who took away my brother. And you who murdered the gamekeeper.

CREATURE: The gamekeeper tried to kill me. He failed. I tried to kill him. I succeeded. As for your brother—

VICTOR: Damn you! Tell me what have you done with him?

(VICTOR *throws himself upon the* CREATURE. *The* CREATURE *grasps* VICTOR *and holds him at arm's length as if he were a small child having a tantrum.*)

CREATURE: What would you have done were you I? Perhaps I have taken him to a cave high in the mountains. Perhaps we will go away together, to a place where you will never find us.

VICTOR: I'll kill you first!

CREATURE: (*Laughing*) It seems that your skill at taking life is no greater than your skill at creating it. (*It tosses* VICTOR *on the floor.*) Well, what now? Will you call down a thunderbolt to strike me?

(VICTOR *seizes a stick of firewood and again attacks.*)

VICTOR: Damn you!

DE LACEY: (*Rising*) Stop! In the name of God, stop!

CREATURE: (*As* VICTOR *strikes him again and again*) Harder, Victor, harder!

VICTOR: Damn you, damn you!

CREATURE: (*Grabbing* VICTOR *and throwing him to the floor*) This game bores me! (VICTOR *is slammed against the wall where his gun is, and he picks up the gun and fires at the* CREATURE *who has turned to exit. The* CREATURE *groans and turns to* VICTOR.)

DE LACEY: No! No!

(VICTOR *raises the musket to fire the second barrel.*)

CREATURE: (*To* VICTOR) Yes, you are right. It is best that I die.

DE LACEY: (*Stepping between them*) Please, I beg you. Don't . . . (*The* CREATURE *goes to move* DE LACEY *out of the way and* FELIX *comes bursting through the door. He assumes the* CREATURE *is attacking his father.*)

FELIX: Father!

DE LACEY: (*Warning*) Felix.

CREATURE: This is not your affair. (FELIX *launches himself at the* CREATURE *who picks him out of the air and throws him back against* VICTOR.) You fool! (*When* FELIX *collides with* VICTOR, *the first thing his hand falls upon is* VICTOR'S *gun.* FELIX *tries to take it from* VICTOR *who fights to keep it.*) Put down that gun. I have no desire to harm you.

DE LACEY: No! (*He lurches himself into the path of the shot just as* FELIX *wrenches the gun from* VICTOR *and fires.*)

CREATURE: (*Holding* DE LACEY *up*) Not you.

FELIX: Father! (*The* CREATURE *lets go of* DE LACEY *who falls into* FELIX'S *arms.*) Merciful God!

CREATURE: (*Enraged, it strides across the room, picks* FELIX *up by the throat, grabs* VICTOR *with the other hand and pins them both against the wall.*) I'll kill you both, you murderous fools. You deserve to die. (*It holds them both against the wall, choking them for a moment, trying to will itself to strangle them.*) I cannot! There have been enough deaths! (*It releases them and exits out the door. They both slump to the floor.*)

FELIX: *Crawls to his father's side and cradles him in his arms*) I've murdered my father.

(VICTOR *rises and goes out the door and sees* CLERVAL *walking down the ramp carrying* WILLIAM'S *body in his arms.* VICTOR *emits a wordless cry of grief and collapses on the ground.*)

Scene 2

(*In front of the curtain.*) Enter HANS *and* LOUISE. *They are laughing: a couple who have spent a pleasant and exciting afternoon together.* LOUISE *carries a picnic basket.*

LOUISE: It was a grand day for it, too. Not a cloud in the sky. (HANS *approaches*) What's the matter with you?

HANS: Is there any of that cheese left? (*He looks in the basket.*) Nothing but a crust of bread and not a drop of beer. You should have made a bigger lunch.

LOUISE: Is food all you ever think about?

HANS: I think a lot about you. (*He embraces her and kisses her.*)

LOUISE: (*Pushing him away*) Garlic!

(Enter CONRAD *from the other side of the stage. He has been working hard while* HANS *and* LOUISE *were off having fun. His sleeves are rolled up and he carries cooking utensils. He is also wearing an apron and a chef's hat.*)

CONRAD: (*Resentfully*) Well, it's about time you got back.

LOUISE: Hello, Conrad.

HANS: You should have come with us.

CONRAD: Somebody has to do the work around here. (HANS *laughs.*)

LOUISE: There was people there from every village in the valley.

HANS: Thousands of them.

LOUISE: You should have heard the trumpeters. On horseback, they was. Come all the way from Geneva.

HANS: And the drummers. Don't forget the drummers.

Frankenstein

LOUISE: They had plumes in their hats.

CONRAD: (*His resentment giving way to his curiosity*) That must have been something to see.

LOUISE: It was better than a carnival.

HANS: It cost me five kronen for two seats right down front. But it was worth it.

CONRAD: How did young master Felix take it?

LOUISE: Felix? He was pretty as a picture.

HANS: He wasn't so damned pretty when they took him down from the scaffold with his body in one basket (*Indicates an imaginary basket*) and his head in another (*Indicates the picnic basket*).

(HANS *picks up the picnic basket slowly.* LOUISE *and* CONRAD *believe he has* FELIX's *head in it. They back away.* HANS *steps towards them, the basket outstretched. He quickly opens the basket and yells.* LOUISE *and* CONRAD *scream. He tips the basket upside down and a cabbage falls out.* HANS *chuckles at his joke.* LOUISE *and* CONRAD *sigh in relief.*)

LOUISE: That executioner! I almost fainted when I first saw him standing there with that black hood over his head.

HANS: He's a good man with an axe, I'll say that for him. One blow and it was over. (*He demonstrates.*) He took the axe in his mighty hands and lifted it up and up and up and the sun glittered off the blade and it came down THWACK! (LOUISE *and* CONRAD *scream.* HANS *picks up the basket and the cabbage, takes* LOUISE *by the hand, starts to exit, turns and gives* CONRAD *the cabbage.*) It was a lovely day. A lovely day. (*He exits followed by a shocked* CONRAD.)

Scene 3

VICTOR's *bedroom. Entrance Stage Left. A large double window in the background. A dim pool of light over* VICTOR's *bed. S.R.,* ELIZABETH *and* CLERVAL, *sitting nearby. They have obviously been sitting up with* VICTOR *who starts to whimper and moan as if in a nightmare.* ELIZABETH *and* CLERVAL *move to the bed.* ELIZABETH *touches* VICTOR, *who speaks in his sleep.*

VICTOR: No . . . my . . . God, no . . . William? William?

ELIZABETH: Victor, Victor . . .

VICTOR: I didn't mean it—William, didn't (*Pushes* ELIZABETH *away*) . . . Help me!

CLERVAL: (*Grasps* VICTOR *and shakes him*) Victor, wake up! Wake up, you're dreaming.

VICTOR: (*Waking*) A dream—it was a dream, wasn't it, Elizabeth?

ELIZABETH: Yes, Victor.

VICTOR: But such a dream (*Pauses as he tries to put it together*) . . . in my laboratory . . . William, but not William. I was . . . arms . . . legs . . . cutting. My dreams accuse me.

ELIZABETH: Don't torture yourself, Victor. It was still only a dream.

VICTOR: But William does lie in the crypt below and that poor crazed Felix . . .

ELIZABETH: (*Scolding sharply*) Darling, you must stop blaming yourself.

CLERVAL: (*Softly*) It was a clear-cut case, Victor. Felix went mad. He murdered three people, one of them his own father. (CLERVAL *rises, crosses down right.*) If it was anybody's fault, it was the devil's.

ELIZABETH: (*Laughing*) You don't believe in the devil, Henry.

CLERVAL: (*Turning*) No, of course, I don't. But I doubt very much that His Satanic Majesty is disturbed by my disbelief.

VICTOR: I used to think you were talking nonsense when you said things like that, Henry. But lately . . . (*He begins to shiver violently.*) . . . I've seen the devil, Henry, I've talked with him face to face.

ELIZABETH: (*Crossing to Stage Left*) Darling, you're freezing. I'll have the servants bring some hot stones for your bed. And may I bring you a warm brandy?

VICTOR: Yes, darling. Thank you.

CLERVAL: What, no brandy for me?

ELIZABETH: Certainly not, Henry. We certainly don't want a confirmed atheist like you seeing the devil. (*Exits*)

VICTOR: (*Sitting up*) Henry, it is you who should marry Elizabeth.

CLERVAL: Don't talk nonsense, Victor.

VICTOR: You love her. You always have. And she loves you.

CLERVAL: (*Turning away*) Victor! . . .

VICTOR: I'm sick in body, sick in mind and sick in soul. For God's sake, take her away from here.

CLERVAL: (*Meaningfully*) Don't you think I would if I could?

VICTOR: If only you could, Henry, but I know you too well. Though I would suffer if she were to go, I fear more what will happen if she stays.

CLERVAL: (*Moving to the bed*) Fear—for Elizabeth? But why? What is there that could harm Elizabeth?

VICTOR: (*Uneasy*) Nothing, Henry, nothing. I'm sorry, sometimes I hardly know what I'm saying.

CLERVAL: Victor, there's something you're hiding. Something that's tearing you apart inside. I've known that ever since that night at the De Lacey cottage. Now what is it?

VICTOR: You could never understand, Henry.

CLERVAL: There is something. Tell me, Victor.

VICTOR: No! If I told you, you'd think I was out of my mind. You'd never believe me.

CLERVAL: Let me decide that.

VICTOR: (*Relenting*) Very well. You remember that night that you and Elizabeth first arrived?

CLERVAL: How could I forget it! You and your damned exploding light electric!

VICTOR: No, it's the other experiment. I told you then that electricity was the source of life. Henry, I have actually found a way to . . . (*Thumps are heard approaching the bedroom.*) Listen! Do you hear that? (*He gets his pistol box from under the pillows.*) Oh my God, where are my pistols?

CLERVAL: It's all right, Victor. It's only . . .

VICTOR: My pistols! (*He opens the box which is empty.*) They're not there.

CLERVAL: Tell me!

VICTOR: You took them away, Henry. You damned fool.

CLERVAL: Tell me.

VICTOR: (*Jumps out of bed and runs Down Right, cowering*) Oh God.

CLERVAL: Tell me.

(FRITZ, HANS *and* LOUISE *enter Stage Left with box of hot stones. The heavy container of stones has made a sound similar to the* CREATURE'S *footsteps.*)

FRITZ: Baron.

CLERVAL: Send them away, Victor. You must finish . . .

FRITZ: Mr. Clerval, the Baron should be in bed. Here, let me help you.

VICTOR: (*Leaning on* FRITZ) Fritz, I thought . . . I thought . . .

FRITZ: (*Leading* VICTOR *back to bed*) I know what you thought.

CLERVAL: For your own good, Victor, tell me.

VICTOR: (*Climbing back into bed*) Go away, Henry.

(*Exit* CLERVAL.)

(HANS *and* LOUISE *begin to wrap the hot stones in cloths and place them one by one under the quilts.*)

LOUISE: We'll soon have you as warm as a bug in a rug, sir.

HANS: That we will, Baron. You'll sleep like a baby.

FRITZ: (*To* LOUISE) See if there's anything Mr. Clerval wants before he retires. I'll finish this.

HANS and LOUISE: Yes, sir. (LOUISE *puts the remaining stones on the bed. They both exit.*)

(FRITZ *puts the last stone under the covers.*)

VICTOR: Ah, that does feel good.

FRITZ: There's nothing like a little warmth, sir.

VICTOR: Oh Fritz, how can you bear to look at me. That boy, Felix, and the old man; they wouldn't have died if it hadn't been for that damned thing I created. And the more I think about it the more I suspect it was that damned monster that killed William.

FRITZ: (*Tucking* VICTOR *in*) We can't know that for sure.

VICTOR: Can't we? I'd like to believe that it was Felix but I know better, just as you do.

FRITZ: I can sit with you tonight if you like.

VICTOR: No, that won't be necessary. (FRITZ *moves the pistol box from the bed to the chair.*) I suppose it was you who took my pistols? You needn't have. I have no intention of killing *myself*. Old friend. Thank you; it seems that all of my life I've been thanking you.

FRITZ: Good night, Excellency. Sleep well.

(FRITZ *exits. After a moment,* VICTOR *gets out of bed, goes to the window and throws open the window curtains. The balcony is empty.*)

VICTOR: Not there. I half expected to find you perched on the balcony like a carrion crow. You are near. I can feel it. (*Turning to the bed; realizing his paranoia. Although he tries to fight it, still he falls to his knees and searches under the bed. When he's satisfied nothing is there, he is filled with disgust for himself. He crosses right.*)

(*Enter* ELIZABETH.)

ELIZABETH: Victor! You'll catch your death of cold. (*Gets his robe from the chair*)

VICTOR: (*Putting on his robe*) I was restless. Thank you. I'll be all right now.

ELIZABETH: (*Holding up small poetry book*) Would you like me to read to you?

VICTOR: (*Attempting humour*) No, I don't think I could concentrate tonight. (*Turning away*) Oh, Elizabeth, my precious darling, I love you so much.

(*We see the* CREATURE *silhouetted against the window.*)

ELIZABETH: Soon we'll be in Italy, darling. The Baron and Baroness Frankenstein. We'll lie together in the sunshine and laugh. (*They kiss.*)

VICTOR: Yes, you're all the medicine I need, Elizabeth.

ELIZABETH: I must go now. In the morning we'll have breakfast together. Good night, darling. (*She exits.*)

VICTOR: Good night, my love. Good night.

(VICTOR *gets back into bed. The* CREATURE *opens the window, parts the curtains and steps into the room. Hearing it,* VICTOR *sits up.*)

CREATURE: (*With a laugh*) You do not seem surprised to see me.

VICTOR: Somehow I expected that you'd come tonight. You claimed another victim today.

CREATURE: (*Crossing to the bed*) Felix? Say rather *you* claimed another victim, or that *we* claimed another victim. You lay on your bed and whined with self-pity and let them kill him.

VICTOR: I couldn't have stopped it. They wouldn't have believed me. They'd have locked me up in a madhouse and Felix would have been killed anyway.

CREATURE: (*Laughing*) Victor, we are alone. There is no one here you need to impress. The Countess Elizabeth . . .

VICTOR: Don't speak of her. I can't bear to hear her name on your lips.

CREATURE: Victor, what a sense of delicacy you possess. (*Bowing*) I have no wish to besmirch the lady's honour. But I have seen how you look at her and how she looks at you.

VICTOR: Leave Elizabeth out of this. Call me a murderer if you like. Perhaps I am one. But Elizabeth . . .

CREATURE: (*Turning away*) Victor! You know, of course, that it was I who killed your brother.

VICTOR: (*Sinking down on the bed with a groan*) Yes, I tried to lie to myself, but in my heart I always know. But why?

CREATURE: (*Reliving it as he had in the cottage*) I had saved him from the water where he would have drowned. And when his eyes opened and he saw me, he began to scream. Ogre! he shouted at me. Monster! If you dare to hurt me, my brother Victor will punish you. My brother, Baron Frankenstein! (*It turns back to* VICTOR.) My creator who had denied me. And here was a spoiled, ungrateful puppy, whom I ought to have left in the river. (*It raises its arms.*) I took his head between my hands and crushed him, crushed him . . .

VICTOR: (*Cowering*) Please, no more. Please, have mercy on me. Tell me no more. (*Long pause*)

CREATURE: (*Calming*) I am sorry, Victor, truly sorry. I have been tortured by remorse. I am malicious because I am miserable. Why should I pity man who does not pity me? You would not even call it murder if you took my life. If one human being accepted me, I would weep in gratitude. But I will not be an abject slave! I will revenge my injuries!

VICTOR: You've already revenged yourself upon me!

CREATURE: (*Losing control*) What I have done is nothing to what I can do. (*Turning away and calming*) But I came here to reason with you, not to threaten you. (*Turns to* VICTOR) You (*Pointing*) are my creator and I have come to you with a request. (*It bows.*) I am alone and miserable. Humans will not associate with me. But one as deformed and horrible as myself would not refuse to be my companion. What I ask is moderate and reasonable. (*Crosses left to bed*) You must create a female for me.

VICTOR: (*Rises, crosses right*) No! No matter how you torture me I won't do that. Go. You have my answer.

CREATURE: You humans delight in the mating of beautiful things, but even the rat in the sewer has its mate.

VICTOR: I cannot. I will not.

CREATURE: (*Crossing to* VICTOR) Victor, my creator, make me happy. Let me feel gratitude toward you. Let me see that I excite the sympathy of some living thing. Do not deny me my request.

VICTOR: I dare not!

CREATURE: She and I would go to the farthest corner of the earth where we would threaten no living thing, not even to satisfy our hunger. My food is not that of man. The earth shall satisfy our needs and the sun will shine on us as on man.

VICTOR: (*Moved by the* CREATURE'S *appeal*) Oh God! I don't know, I don't know.

CREATURE: Victor, I begin to see compassion in your eyes. I swear to you, that my companion and I will go where no human being will ever find us. Our lives will flow quietly away. We will not be happy, but we will be harmless. And in my dying moments I will not curse my maker.

VICTOR: You swear to it. But why should I trust you? Perhaps this is some trick.

CREATURE: The love of another such as myself will remove the cause of my crimes.

VICTOR: God, help me, I will (*The* CREATURE *emits a cry of joy.*)— on your solemn oath that you will go with her to an uninhabited part of the earth and stay there forever.

CREATURE: I swear that after that I will trouble you no more.

VICTOR: It will take time.

CREATURE: I am accustomed to waiting.

VICTOR: And during that time you'll harm no one else.

CREATURE: I will harm no one else. I swear by the sun and by the blue sky of Heaven and by the fire of love that burns in my heart that if you grant my prayer, you shall never behold me again.

VICTOR: Then I agree.

(*It makes a move toward* VICTOR *as if to touch him.*)

VICTOR: Damn you, I don't want your gratitude.

CREATURE: (*Backing off*) As you wish. As you wish. As you wish!

(*Exit the* CREATURE.)

(*There is a moment's pause and then* VICTOR *kneels by his bed. The lights go down as he begins to recite the Lord's Prayer.*)

Scene 4

VICTOR'S laboratory in Castle Frankenstein. As the lights go up, FRITZ is carrying a large jar containing the brain to be inserted in the CREATURE'S bride. The electronic apparatus hangs over the operating table, the wires are tied. The new CREATURE'S body lies on the table, under a sheet, its head facing S.L. VICTOR lies asleep on a chair S.L. FRITZ goes over to wake VICTOR.

FRITZ: Baron, wake up.

VICTOR: (*Opening his eyes and stirring*) What is it? (*He sits up.*) I didn't intend to fall asleep.

FRITZ: (*Putting the brain jar on the table*) You've been working too hard, repairing the equipment.

VICTOR: (*With disgust*) Yes. It's strange, Fritz, there was a time when opening a grave troubled me no more than opening a book. But lately each time that we've done it, I've felt that I ought to beg someone to forgive me but I'm not sure who.

FRITZ: (*Turning the table so the head is Upstage*) After tonight you'll be free.

VICTOR: (*Putting on his smock, which is on the table*) I wish I could be sure of that, Fritz. At times I'm afraid that I'll be loosing more horror upon the world.

FRITZ: It's different this time. You're rectifying a wrong rather than committing one.

VICTOR: (*Taking the brain from the jar and examining it*) This was once inside the head of a beautiful peasant girl. I suppose she liked to dance and sing before . . . And when it wakes up it will be inside . . . that. (*He gestures toward the table.*) I can't be certain but I suspect there are times when the brain of the other one almost remembers who it used to be. That must be sheer hell. (*He puts the brain in a small dish on the table.*)

FRITZ: (*Moving to the table*) Perhaps this one won't be as hideous as the other. She's certainly not ugly now.

VICTOR: She'll be hideous enough by the time her heart starts to beat. And, anyway, he wants her to be ugly. He insisted upon it. Even if I knew how to overcome the chemical reaction, I couldn't allow her to be beautiful. (*VICTOR removes the scalp.*)

FRITZ: I'll see to the apparatus. (*FRITZ crosses back to the console and starts checking gauges, and adjusting dials.*)

VICTOR: It was so different the last time. Then I thought of myself as the great benefactor of mankind. Now I feel as if I had signed a pact with Satan.

FRITZ: Everything is in order here. There's not so much interference as there was the other time.

VICTOR: No, this storm is weaker than the other. (*Looking to heaven*) What! No, great crashes of thunder and lightning? Somehow it seemed so appropriate then.

FRITZ: Could the storm have damaged the other thing's brain?

VICTOR: There's nothing physically wrong with his brain. He's filled with hatred for the human race—and especially for me. He's determined to revenge himself on those who have rejected him. My God, what if this one should be more malignant than her mate!

FRITZ: He swore to take her away with him.

VICTOR: Yes, he swore, and I believed him. But what if he finds it impossible to keep his oath? What if life there is so harsh they cannot bear it? And she has taken no oath. How can I be sure that she'll keep the agreement?

FRITZ: (*Crossing to the table*) They'll have each other—only each other. They'll have no reason to go among human beings.

VICTOR: That's wishful thinking, Fritz. (*He crosses left.*) The very self-deception that I practised when I allowed myself to be bullied and cajoled into this. How in God's name can we know that they won't hate one another? What if he can't bear the sight of his own deformity reflected in her? (*Crosses right*) What if he seems as horrible to her as he does to us?

FRITZ: (*Moving to* VICTOR) Come, Victor, we've gone too far to turn back now. We'd best get on with it.

VICTOR: I won't do it. No! No! No! (VICTOR *rushes to the table, picks up the brain and tears it in half.*)

(*The* CREATURE *enters from behind the curtains in the lab arch where it has been hiding. It moans in grief and disappointment.* VICTOR *grabs a scalpel from his smock, plunges it into the heart of the body on the table.*)

CREATURE: No, No, No! (*It steps forward, in horror and disgust. It covers the head of its bride.*)

CREATURE: There was a contract between us. You have broken it. (*Pushes the table Upstage.*)

VICTOR: (*He works himself into a rage to stifle his feelings of guilt. Collapsing in the chair S.L.*) I couldn't buy my own peace at the expense of the human race.

CREATURE: You have violated your covenant with me, your creation. Victor, you do not find me one-half so sickening as I find you.

VICTOR: (*Without conviction*) I have no covenant with you. (*Rises, turns away*)

CREATURE: (*Stalking* VICTOR) I have reasoned with you and that has failed. You have sentenced me to eternal loneliness. Are you to be happy while I grovel in wretchedness?

(FRITZ *attacks the* CREATURE *with the scalpel he gets from the table. The* CREATURE *turns when it sees the look in* VICTOR'S *eyes as* VICTOR *sees* FRITZ.)

CREATURE: Slave!

(*It twists* FRITZ'S *arm around so that, in effect, he stabs himself in the chest—as bigger boys sometimes force smaller boys to punch themselves with their own fists.* FRITZ *falls dead.*)

VICTOR: (*Grief-stricken*) Fritz! Fritz! (*He cradles* FRITZ'S *head.*)

CREATURE: What was he to you? No more than any other part of the machinery. Now he is only a mess on the floor that you will order another of your slaves to clean up. (*The* CREATURE *turns to go.*)

VICTOR: You didn't have to kill him.

CREATURE: (*Stopping*) Ah, I was mistaken. His death does sadden you. Victor, your grief gives me pleasure. I wish I could stay to enjoy it. But I have plans to make and things to do. If my maker will not look after me, I will have to look after myself. (*At the foot of the ramp*) But remember—I will be with you on your wedding-night.

VICTOR: Kill me now! Why wait until then! Do you think I care if I die? Kill me! Kill me!

(*The* CREATURE *laughs as it exits.*)

Act Three

Scene 1

The courtyard of Castle Frankenstein. Night. At far left there is an arch, and the stairs leading up to the Ballroom. To the right is a wall behind which we see a coach, on the box of which sits a figure in a long cloak with a scarf around his face. Between the stairs and the coach we see HANS *and* CONRAD, *wearing hats and coats and moving briskly in an effort to warm themselves. From inside the Great Hall we hear music.*

HANS: It's cold enough to freeze the arse off a polar bear.

CONRAD: Aye, it's cold. But we won't have to wait much longer. The Baron and Baroness will be coming out any minute now.

(*The great door opens.*)

HANS: That will be them now.

(LOUISE *comes down the stairs wrapped in a shawl against the cold and carrying a bowl of hot punch.*)

CONRAD: It's nobody. Only Louise.

LOUISE: Only Louise! I've half a mind to pour this hot punch over your head.

HANS: Hot punch! Louise, me girl, you're an angel of mercy. (*He rubs her shoulders.*) I can feel the wings beginning to sprout.

LOUISE: It wasn't my idea. Mistress Elizabeth told me to bring it out to you.

HANS: (*Taking bowl*) May all her sons be soldiers that live to die of old age and may her daughters never want for a man to pleasure them. (*He drinks.*)

CONRAD: That's no proper toast. (*He takes the bowl.*) To Their Excellencies, the Baron and Baroness Frankenstein—may God bless and prosper them. (*He drinks.*)

(HANS *takes the bowl.*)

LOUISE: And what about the Coachman?

HANS: Hey—do you want a drink?

(*The* COACHMAN *grunts and waves in refusal.*)

HANS: Well, then, to your very good health. (*He drinks deeply, overturns the empty bowl and hands it to* CONRAD.) You can have the rest of it, my friend.

(VICTOR *and* CLERVAL *come down the stairs.* CLERVAL *is slightly drunk and carries a silver goblet.*)

VICTOR: Fresh air is what you need, Henry. It will blow some of the champagne bubbles out of your head.

CLERVAL: Victor, you scientists can have your balloons. I prefer to fly on the wings of the grape. (*Crosses right*)

VICTOR: (*To the servants*) My friends, thank you for all you've done tonight.

LOUISE: The Baroness made a beautiful bride, sir.

VICTOR: She did indeed, Louise. We'll be leaving soon. I suspect your mistress has need of you.

LOUISE: I'll go to her at once, sir. (*She exits up the stairs.*)

VICTOR: Hans, you know where the trunks are. Take Conrad with you and fetch them down.

(*More or less simultaneously*)

HANS: Right you are, sir.   CONRAD: Yes, sir.

(HANS, CONRAD *exit.* VICTOR *takes* CLERVAL'S *arm.*)

CLERVAL: (*By the coach*) There have been so many tragedies this year. It's time we had a season of happiness.

VICTOR: When William died I went almost insane with grief. Now, although I'm almost ashamed to admit it, whole days pass without my ever once thinking of him.

CLERVAL: (*Crossing to* VICTOR) Victor, if we humans were a little less sensitive we'd all be brutes and if we were a little more sensitive we'd all be lunatics.

VICTOR: Henry, there is something I must tell you. I have an enemy.

CLERVAL: (*Laughs*) Of course you do, we all have enemies. (*He crosses right.*)

VICTOR: No, Henry, I mean an enemy who is determined to kill me this very night.

CLERVAL: You've been challenged to a duel. Well, that's no problem. I rather enjoy duelling.

VICTOR: Henry, Henry, you don't understand at all.

CLERVAL: (*Acting out a duel*) Mind you, I wouldn't like it if there were any risk of killing or being killed. But you have a better chance of being injured by a champagne cork at ten paces than a duelling pistol at sixty.

VICTOR: Henry, let me explain.

CLERVAL: As to the sword, which I prefer, you don't kill your opponent and he doesn't kill you. One of you draws blood—usually about as much blood as when you skin your knuckles—and you bow very deeply to one another. It's great fun.

VICTOR: Henry, for God's sake, be quiet for a moment. My enemy is a monster. Cunning, treacherous and bestial. Compared with him, Caliban was an Apollo.

CLERVAL: (*Becoming serious*) How in God's name did this come about, Victor?

VICTOR: I undertook an experiment in which this (*He hesitates*) creature assisted me. Something went wrong. He was horribly disfigured.

CLERVAL: Good God.

VICTOR: He swore revenge, warning me that he would murder me on my wedding-night.

CLERVAL: Victor, this is ghastly. Of course, you've alerted the guard.

VICTOR: It's not a matter for the guard. But I have taken measures of my own. (*He pats the breast of his coat.*)

CLERVAL: Good God! But Elizabeth . . .

VICTOR: He has no cause to hate Elizabeth. But if anything should happen to me, if I should die . . . I put her under your protection.

CLERVAL: Of course, Victor. (CLERVAL *assumes his mock-flippant manner.*) And if necessary I am even prepared to protect her from you. If you do not treat her like an Empress I swear that I'll thrash you.

VICTOR: (*Throwing his arm across* CLERVAL'S *shoulders*) Dear old Henry. I can always depend on you. Now I must go and get Elizabeth. We must be on our way if we are to catch the boat to Evian.

CLERVAL: Then I think perhaps I'll walk in the garden.

VICTOR: At this time of night?

CLERVAL: You told me once that my Sanskrit and Persian poets wrote only about the sun and roses. But they wrote about the moon and roses also.

VICTOR: You'll find no roses blooming in the garden tonight.

CLERVAL: Poets prefer the roses they can't see, just as they prefer unrequited love.

VICTOR: Do they, Henry? Do you?

CLERVAL: I don't know—I certainly hope so—perhaps I'll go to the study and lie down for a moment to clear my head. Be sure to call me before you go. I will want to kiss the bride goodbye.

VICTOR: Of course, Henry. (*A pause*) And thank you.

(VICTOR *exits upstairs.*)

CLERVAL: (*Turning to the* COACHMAN) Coachman, I don't know how much of that you heard, but I do know that good servants are highly skilled in selective deafness.

COACHMAN: Yes, sir.

CLERVAL: You must drive carefully tonight. You will carry a precious burden. And you may run into danger.

COACHMAN: Danger, sir?

CLERVAL: (*He sits on the footboard of the coach*) The road through the woods is shortest, but the trees would provide cover for an attacker. (*He is saying all this as much to himself as to the* COACHMAN.) Two years ago I was attacked by a highwayman there. A grinning rogue in a plumed hat who opened my purse and handed one gold ducat back to me. So you'll not want for food or shelter when you reach an inn, he said to me. Poor rascal, I had the honour of sending him another such ducat as he lay in prison, so that he might have wine and clean linen while he waited for his meeting with the headsman. (*The next is spoken more directly to the* COACHMAN; CLERVAL *rises*.) I think you should take the longer and safer route along the river and whip the horses if anyone tries to stop you.

COACHMAN: Yes, sir.

CLERVAL: (*Turns toward the garden*) And now I'll go and commune with those invisible roses. (*He takes a few steps, pauses thoughtfully for a moment and then turns back, and again looks up at the* COACHMAN *and addresses him.*) You are not Baron Frankenstein's regular coachman, are you? (*Suspecting something*) Do you live in the village? (*The* COACHMAN, *still with his back turned, gestures* CLERVAL *away.*) I asked you a question. (*No reply*) I don't find your silence amusing. Turn around—let's look at this coachman who doesn't speak and will not show his face. (*He leaps up on the footboard and grabs the* COACHMAN'S *coat. As he does so, the* COACHMAN *swings around and* CLERVAL *looks into the face of the* CREATURE.) Holy Mother of Jesus.

(*He staggers back, drops his empty goblet. The* CREATURE *leaps down from the box.*)

CREATURE: Why could you not have gone on your way and left me to do what I had to do?

(CLERVAL *is frightened, but stands his ground.*)

CLERVAL: What is it you have to do?

CREATURE: That is no concern of yours!

CLERVAL: Anything which touches the life and happiness of a friend concerns me.

CREATURE: If you knew what Frankenstein had done you would not count him among your friends.

CLERVAL: Victor may have disfigured you but you can't . . .

CREATURE: He has injured me much more than this and he will suffer as I have suffered.

CLERVAL: Do you think you're God that you can sentence him to death?

CREATURE: I will punish him beyond the pain of death.

CLERVAL: (*It dawns*) Not Elizabeth—(CREATURE *laughs.*) No, not that—I won't let you do that. (*Jumps at the* CREATURE; *the* CREATURE *knocks him down. The* CREATURE *then walks to* CLERVAL, *picks him up and throttles him.*)

CREATURE: What is the use of talking to you, human! (CLERVAL *dies*.) You despised me, but what were you? An aristocratic fop who scribbled verses while others slaved that you might sleep between silk sheets. (*The* CREATURE *lifts* CLERVAL's *body and places it inside the coach; then seats itself on the driver's box as before.*)

(*After a moment's pause,* HANS *and* CONRAD *come down the stairs.* HANS *carries a satchel while* CONRAD *staggers under the weight of a trunk.*)

CONRAD: This is another of your dirty tricks.

HANS: Rank has its privileges, me lad.

(CONRAD *puts the trunk on a rack below and behind the* COACHMAN's *box and begins to tie it there.*)

HANS: Make sure you tie it good and tight.

(*The great door again opens.* VICTOR, ELIZABETH, *and* LOUISE *emerge. Seeing the Master and Mistress,* HANS *pushes* CONRAD *aside and takes over the job of securing the trunk.*)

ELIZABETH: Good evening, Hans.

HANS: Good evening.

ELIZABETH: It was such a magnificent evening, Victor. We're so lucky to have such friends. Did you see how shamelessly that little Baroness Von Auslin was flirting with Henry? By the way, where is Henry?

VICTOR: My guess is that he's in the garden. (*To* CONRAD) Conrad, would you go to the garden and see if Mr. Clerval is there, please? (*To* HANS) You may as well fetch the other trunk.

CONRAD: (*triumphantly to* HANS) You heard what the master said . . . me lad.

(CONRAD *gives the satchel to* HANS *who gives it to* LOUISE *as he exists up the stairs.* CONRAD *goes Upstage into the garden.* HANS *goes back into the Great Hall.*)

VICTOR: I imagine Henry is out there meditating on the *Bhagavad-Gita* or some other piece of Asiatic moonshine.

(LOUISE *crosses to coach and puts satchel down.*)

ELIZABETH: Victor, that is unkind.

VICTOR: It wasn't meant to be. I've come to think that Henry may be wiser than I am. You're cold. (*To* LOUISE) Louise, fetch your mistress a cloak, please.

LOUISE: Yes, sir.

(*She goes up the stairs.*)

VICTOR: Darling, I have no right to such happiness. (*They kiss.*) But I love you more than I could ever tell you.

ELIZABETH: Victor, I feel so privileged to be your wife. Our children will grow up in the world that you're helping to create. Oh, the world will be beautiful for them; thanks to men like you the twentieth century will be a new Golden Age—an age in which there will be no poverty, no sickness, no war.

VICTOR: I wish I were as sure of that as I used to be. Elizabeth, I have a confession to make. I have done something shameful.

(LOUISE *enters with a furpiece.*)

ELIZABETH: Oh, darling, you don't have to implore my forgiveness for your past infatuations. I don't care about that.

(*The maid adjusts the furpiece around* ELIZABETH'S *shoulders.*)

VICTOR: It's nothing like that. (*Turning away*) Elizabeth, there are sins of the flesh, sins of the mind, and sins of the spirit. Christians worry most about the sins of the flesh. Henry tells me that Hindus believe that the most terrible sins are those of the mind; if they're right I may have committed the ultimate, unforgivable sin.

(HANS *enters with a trunk.*)

ELIZABETH: Victor, I don't believe you're capable of doing anything wicked. You question your own motives too much. You must learn to laugh more.

(CONRAD *returns from the garden.*)

CONRAD: I couldn't find hide nor hair of Mr. Clerval in the garden, sir.

VICTOR: If we don't get on the road soon we'll have to take tomorrow's boat.

ELIZABETH: Henry would never forgive us if we left without saying goodbye to him.

VICTOR: Ah, he said something about the study. I'll look. (*To the servants*) Do we have all the bags now?

HANS: There's still three or four of the smaller ones and the Mistress's hatboxes, sir.

VICTOR: Bring them out as quickly as you can.

HANS: Right, sir. (*Exits with* CONRAD.)

ELIZABETH: (*Laughing to* LOUISE) You'd better carry my hatboxes, Louise. I don't trust the men with them.

LOUISE: Of course, ma'am. (*Exit.*)

VICTOR: (*On the stairs*) I don't like leaving you alone.

ELIZABETH: I'm not alone, my darling; our good coachman is here.

VICTOR: I'll be back in a moment, then.

(VICTOR *exits up the stairs;* ELIZABETH *crosses left, listening to the music from the hall. Behind* ELIZABETH, *the* CREATURE *stirs and then descends from the box. The scarf is now so arranged that it conceals the face. Hearing something behind her,* ELIZABETH *suddenly turns.*)

ELIZABETH: Coachman, you startled me.

CREATURE: (*Hiding its face and bowing*) I beg your forgiveness, madam.

ELIZABETH: (*Laughing*) It isn't as serious as all that. You must be freezing. Sitting up there all evening. You should have gone inside to keep warm.

CREATURE: I am accustomed to being outdoors, madam. The cold does not bother me. But you have not said if you forgive me.

ELIZABETH: There's nothing to forgive.

CREATURE: Nevertheless, it would comfort me greatly.

ELIZABETH: (*Laughing, crossing right*) What a sensitive coachman you are! Of course, you are forgiven. Think no more about it. (*There is a silence.*)

CREATURE: Madam is very beautiful. Such beauty must have given you great happiness. (*Moves closer to her*)

ELIZABETH: I am not at all sure that I am beautiful. To myself, I am simply Elizabeth. I would be the same Elizabeth whether I was beautiful or ugly.

CREATURE: (*Looking up the stairs*) You jest. If you were ugly, the Baron Frankenstein who now professes to love you would long ago have driven you out of this house with a curse.

ELIZABETH: (*Crossing to go up the stairs*) Coachman, I think you had better look to your horses.

(*As the* CREATURE *reaches out for her she starts to cry out, but the sound is stifled by its hand over her mouth.*)

CREATURE: It will be over quickly. There will be almost no pain. (*It smothers her in her furpiece.*) You see, I told you it would be over quickly. (*It puts its hand to* ELIZABETH'S *face and strokes it almost lovingly.*) So very, very beautiful. (*It puts her body on the foot of the stairs, returns to the coach, takes up* CLERVAL'S *body, carries it to the stairs and places it beside* ELIZABETH'S. *The* CREATURE *crosses to the couch, groaning with remorse at its horrible deeds. After a pause it turns to the entrance and screams*) Victor! Victor!

(VICTOR *enters with the servants behind him.*)

CREATURE: Victor, behold my wedding gift!

(VICTOR *screams and the* CREATURE *exits.*)

Scene 2

Same setting as for Act One, Scene One. We hear the sound of the Arctic wind. To facilitate the quick change, VICTOR'S *speech may be taped and played over during scene change.*

VICTOR: There is little more to tell. I have been pursuing him ever since that night. Down the Alpine passes into Italy, across the Mediterranean and the Black Sea, through the wilds of Tartary and Siberia. I have endured hunger and cold; I have gone days without sleep. I have been attacked by beasts and brigands. Time and again I have been so exhausted that I would have been content to die had it not been for my hatred of him—my determination to destroy him as he has destroyed everything that I loved. (*Lights come up and tape out.* WALTON *is seated on stool, beside* VICTOR *lying on the bed.*) Then three days ago I saw him, a speck in the distance, across the mountainous ice of the ocean. He was no more than a mile ahead of me. But at that moment a tumultuous sea rose between my enemy and me and I was left drifting on a cake of ice.

WALTON: When you began your story I thought that you were delirious. But later I kept thinking of that figure we saw racing across the ice. Even at a distance it seemed unnatural. The crew sensed that more clearly than I did.

VICTOR: Captain Walton, if I should die . . .

WALTON: You're not going to die.

VICTOR: If I should die and he should appear—swear that you will not let him live.

(*Enter* FIRST *and* SECOND SEAMEN.)

SECOND SEAMAN: Captain, we want a word with you. (*He hesitates.*)

WALTON: Well, speak up.

SECOND SEAMAN: You might say we was a delegation.

WALTON: (*Getting angry*) A delegation? What kind of nonsense is this?

FIRST SEAMAN: It's not that we got anything against you, sir. You're as good a master as we ever served under.

WALTON: Come to the point.

SECOND SEAMAN: We want to turn back. The men voted and we're all agreed. They elected us to come and tell you.

WALTON: This isn't Parliament. I'm the master here. I'll decide when it's time to turn back.

SECOND SEAMAN: (*Challenging*) Maybe you will and maybe you won't.

WALTON: Damn it, are you threatening me?

SECOND SEAMAN: Call it what you like. We're not going to let you kill us. If we keep sailing northward the ice is going to tear the ship apart.

FIRST SEAMAN: For the love of God, sir, we've got to turn back!

SECOND SEAMAN: (*To* FIRST SEAMAN) We didn't come here to beg. The fact is this ship is going to turn south. (*To* WALTON) You can come with us or you can stay here. That's up to you. (*He turns to exit.*)

WALTON: You know the penalty for mutiny.

SECOND SEAMAN: (*Turning back*) I'd a damn sight rather be hung by the neck than crushed by the ice.

(*Enter* WILLIAMSON)

WALTON: Mr. Williamson, it would seem that we have some damned mutineers aboard.

WILLIAMSON: (*Trying to keep the peace*) I don't think we ought to get excited, Captain. These are good men. You can't blame them for not wanting to die.

WALTON: You knew about this, then?

WILLIAMSON: I've heard talk. (*To the* SEAMEN, *strongly*) You men should have come to me first. You had no right to approach the Captain. (*To* WALTON) But they're right. It would be suicide to go on.

WALTON: (*Turning away*) Whose side are you on?

WILLIAMSON: I hope it doesn't come to that. You're a pretty fair seaman. I think you'll do what's right by the men.

VICTOR: (*Sitting up*) Don't go back to your families in disgrace! If you go back now you'll be branded as cowards.

WALTON: Don't excite yourself, Baron.

VICTOR: If you go on, you'll be hailed as the benefactors of your race.

WALTON: (*Forcing* VICTOR *to lie down*) The men may be right. I can't sacrifice them to my pride.

VICTOR: Then give me a boat and some supplies. I must follow him.

WALTON: (*To the* SEAMEN) Go back to your duties. We'll discuss this later.

(*The* SEAMEN *hesitate*.)

WILLIAMSON: You heard what the Captain said.

(*Exit* FIRST, SECOND SEAMEN)

WILLIAMSON: (*With kindness*) I think you should know that they'll kill both of us if they have to.

WALTON: So it's as bad as that.

WILLIAMSON: (*Going over to the bunk where* VICTOR *has fainted*) It was him that tore the mains'l as far as the crew was concerned. (*He pauses, waiting for a decision.*) Well, I best go on deck and keep an eye on things. The mood the men are in, anything could happen.

WALTON: (*To* WILLIAMSON) Mr. Williamson. Summon all hands on deck. I'm going to make an announcement. We're turning back.

WILLIAMSON: (*Relieved*) Good. (*Then, with affection*) I'm damned sorry for your sake that it had to end this way.

WALTON: Thank you, Mr. Williamson.

(*Exit* WILLIAMSON. WALTON *crosses to the door with his stool, takes his coat off the hook where it hangs.*)

VICTOR: (*Who has regained consciousness, watching* WALTON) It's strange but I don't hate that thing I created. Not any more. Now I wish that he were dead for his sake rather than for mine. (*A pause*) I am almost content now.

WALTON: I have to leave you for a little while, Victor. Try to sleep.

(*Exit* WALTON)

(*The* CREATURE *enters through the window at the right.*)

CREATURE: Victor.

VICTOR: Have you come to watch me die?

CREATURE: Victor, I do not wish you to die. Time after time as you pursued me I could have let you starve. Instead I left you food. Because I pitied you and abhorred myself.

VICTOR: I thought you did it to taunt me.

CREATURE: (*Softly and logically*) Am I to be thought the only criminal when all mankind sinned against me?

VICTOR: No, you are not the only criminal.

Frankenstein

CREATURE: Oh, Victor, do you think that the groans of Clerval and Elizabeth were music to my ears? I was the slave of an impulse I detested.

VICTOR: Yes, we are all slaves of impulses that we detest. We do not do the thing we love but the very thing we hate.

CREATURE: I could not allow you to enjoy the companionship of your mate while I had none.

VICTOR: Poor Elizabeth. We killed her, you and I. We destroyed them all. Nothing can undo what we did. Death is the great simplifier. I wish for you a speedy death. Because I pity you.

CREATURE: (*Stretching out its hand*) Victor, take my hand. Please.

VICTOR: (*He makes a feeble and unsuccessful attempt to raise his arm*) You must help me.

CREATURE: No, that would not be the same. I do not ask that you forgive me. I ask only that you reach out and touch me. No living creature has ever done so.

VICTOR: I would, I swear it. But all my strength is gone.

CREATURE: Victor, please.

VICTOR: (*Softly and prayerfully*) Oh God. (*With enormous effort he takes the* CREATURE'S *hand in both of his. He sinks back dead.*)

CREATURE: (*Embracing him*) Thank you, Victor. May your maker be as merciful to you. Now, at last, you are at peace and soon I will follow you. No one could understand what has passed between us. I have made peace with my maker. You are the last human being who will ever see me. I will leave this vessel on the ice raft that brought me here. (*Music under is climax of immolation scene from Gotterdammerung.*) Soon I will die and what I feel will no longer be felt. I will build a funeral pyre and consume into ashes this miserable frame so that it will afford no light to any unhallowed wretch who would create another such as I. I will exalt in the agony of the flame and the wind will sweep my ashes into the sea. My spirit will sleep in peace with my maker.

(*During this speech the ship starts to move off on its pivot and the* CREATURE *steps off the ship and crosses the centre. All lights fade except the body spot on the* CREATURE.)

After Words

1 In your journal, respond to the play, and reflect again on issues in science and technology of interest to you.

2 Summarize each scene of the play. Then, consider:
   - What were Victor's motivations?
   - What did the creature seek from its creator?
   - Why was Victor not willing to accept his creation?
   - How is the conflict resolved?

3 In a group, consider what functions the following serve: Elizabeth; Clerval; Fritz; De Lacey; Conrad, Hans, and Louise; Walton, Williamson, and the seamen.

   How do they illuminate the main characters, the conflicts among these characters, and the themes of the play?

4 Write a journal entry from the creature's point of view describing his final voyage.

5 In a small group, discuss the reasons for the creature becoming a feared and hated outcast. What modern parallels can you find? Share your findings with the class.

6 Choose scenes from the play to dramatize in groups—one scene per group. In your group, discuss, rehearse, and revise your performances. (You might want to simplify and/or modernize the production.) Present the scenes in the order they appear.

7 Evaluate Victor's motivations and actions. Support your evaluation with references to the play, examples from contemporary life, and, perhaps, personal experience. Share your evaluation with the class.

Death Seat

A stage play by JOAN MASON HURLEY

JOAN MASON HURLEY was born in Victoria in 1920 and has spent most of her life in British Columbia. She has written plays such as *Passacaglia, The Grandmother, Parents' Day*, and a documentary drama about Jane Austen, to whom her family is linked. Under the name Joan Austen-Leigh, she has also written a novel. She won the 1973 Best Original Play award in the British Columbia Drama Association Festival and the Burnaby Centennial Trophy for her contribution to drama in the province. *Death Seat* was first performed in 1972 by the Gallery Players at the Art Gallery of Greater Victoria. In this symbolic play, which poses questions about life and death, nameless characters and a seedy bar setting take on greater meaning.

Prelude

1 In your journal, reflect on how various people respond to illness, an accident, and/or the death of a loved one. What attitude toward life and death does one of these responses suggest?
2 In this play, the playwright uses a fairly simple setting symbolically. Brainstorm 2-3 places (e.g., the mall, the moon). Suggest—for a film, music video, play, story, or poem you might create—what you could use each place to represent (e.g, *mall* for greed, modern town square, *moon* for dreams and ambitions, the last frontier).

Death Seat

Characters

    Bartender: wearing black turtleneck, black pants

    A **Woman**: well-dressed

    A **Housewife**: casually dressed, slightly dishevelled

    A **Customer**: a chronic alcoholic

    A **Nurse**: in uniform

    A **Teenage Boy**: in jeans and T-shirt (non-speaking)

Scene: *Sunset Bar. A strange forbidding place with an unusual atmosphere.*

> *Sombre music which fades as the curtain rises on a bar, dimly lit. A door, the entrance to the bar, centre back. Another door downstage right. Beside this door, the bar itself, behind which the* **Bartender** *sits motionless, his back to the room. Several small tables. At one, the* **Customer**, *his head down, lies in a semi-stupor. In the centre of room sits* **Woman** *wearing dark glasses, her right hand encloses the stem of a wine glass. She stares straight in front of her. Silence.* **Housewife** *enters nervously. She looks at* **Customer** *with repugnance, hesitates, seats herself at a table next to* **Woman**. *She fumbles in her bag for a cigarette, puts one in her mouth, discovers she is without matches.*

Housewife: (*To* **Woman**) Excuse me, do you have a light?

> (*Without speaking,* **Woman** *picks up folder of matches out of ashtray on her table and hands it to* **Housewife**.)

(*Reading*) Sunset Bar! That's this place, isn't it? I noticed the sign when I came in. Cigarette?

Woman: No, thank you.

Housewife: Mind if I keep these? (**Woman** *inclines her head.*) You come here often? (**Woman** *does not answer.*) Well, I can tell you this is the first time I've been here. Normally, I wouldn't dream of going into a bar alone. Oh, no offence meant, of course. But today hasn't been normal. Today has been the worst day of my life. To tell you the truth, I just had to have a drink.

Funny, I've driven along this road for years, and I've never even noticed this place before. The entrance isn't very inviting, is it? And the name . . . you don't even see the sign until you get right up to the door. But it's convenient. I mean, being near the hospital and all. I guess mostly doctors and nurses come here. (*Pause*) You don't work at the hospital, do you?

WOMAN: No, indeed.

HOUSEWIFE: Say, where is the bartender? How does a person get a drink around here?

CUSTOMER: (*Lifting his head*) Don't worry. He'll come.

HOUSEWIFE: Oh? (*Raising her voice unnecessarily*) Waiter! (BARTENDER *turns so that she can see him. She appears to recognize him. Hand over her mouth, she gasps.*) Oh!

BARTENDER: (*Coming forward*) Anything wrong, madam?

HOUSEWIFE: Sorry. Just for a moment, seeing your face, I thought you were Dr. Walters. (*Laughs nervously*) I could have sworn you were the doctor.

BARTENDER: That's all right, madam. I am often mistaken for someone else.

HOUSEWIFE: (*Still nervous*) And yet you're not really like him.

BARTENDER: No?

HOUSEWIFE: In fact, I've never seen you before. Never in my whole life. In fact I can hardly see you now, it's so damn dark in here.

BARTENDER: Just as well.

HOUSEWIFE: What do you mean?

BARTENDER: Most people hate to see my face.

HOUSEWIFE: Go on! Well, you're not conceited, I'll say that much for you.

CUSTOMER: (*Shouting belligerently*) Not me!

HOUSEWIFE: What?

CUSTOMER: Not me, I said. I think he's great. I like it here. (*Points to door by bar*) But I want to get through that door. (*Hysterically*) That's what I came for. To get through that door.

HOUSEWIFE: Where does it lead?

CUSTOMER: (*Shouting*) I don't know. I don't care. I just want to get through it.

HOUSEWIFE: You're drunk. Waiter, a double rye on the rocks, please.

BARTENDER: Yes, madam. (*Returns to bar*)

CUSTOMER: Now, who's talking?

HOUSEWIFE: There are special circumstances. You don't know anything about it.

(CUSTOMER *laughs rudely, then yawns, puts head down on arm*)

HOUSEWIFE: (*To* BARTENDER) Have you got the evening paper? I'm anxious to see it.

BARTENDER: (*Matter of fact*) The account of the accident. One dead, two critically injured.

HOUSEWIFE: (*Astonished*) How in the world did you know?

BARTENDER: (*Bringing drink*) I know.

HOUSEWIFE: Being so near the hospital, I guess news gets around.

CUSTOMER: (*Opening eyes*) Anyway, he always knows.

(HOUSEWIFE *attempts to pay* BARTENDER, *but he is not interested.*)

HOUSEWIFE: Say, waiter?

BARTENDER: (*Approaching*) Yes, madam.

HOUSEWIFE: You own this place?

BARTENDER: No.

HOUSEWIFE: Just work here, huh?

BARTENDER: In a manner of speaking.

HOUSEWIFE: I was telling this lady, I haven't been in here before.

BARTENDER: I know, madam.

HOUSEWIFE: You been around long?

BARTENDER: Yes, a very long time.

HOUSEWIFE: (*Laughs*) Since the year one, I suppose?

BARTENDER: Precisely the case. (*He goes back to bar.*)

HOUSEWIFE: (*To* WOMAN) He's a strange guy.

WOMAN: Yes.

HOUSEWIFE: Know anything about him?

WOMAN: All I want to know.

HOUSEWIFE: Well, he's sure strange.

WOMAN: You get used to him in time.

HOUSEWIFE: In time! I'm not coming here again. Not to this dump. That's certain.

WOMAN: Most people come only once. Not many come twice. Some linger a while, like me. Others pass through quickly. I envy them, passing through quickly. (*Suddenly vehement*) I hate it here.

HOUSEWIFE: It is pretty depressing. But why stay if you don't like it?

WOMAN: You don't think it's my choice?

HOUSEWIFE: You're waiting for someone?

WOMAN: Just waiting . . . (*Pause*) Why did you come?

HOUSEWIFE: Because I had to have a drink. Had to. Though I'm not an alcoholic, understand—nothing like him. (*Looks with distaste at* CUSTOMER)

WOMAN: Ah, him.

CUSTOMER: They're not particular, lady. They take all sorts. Even me, even you.

HOUSEWIFE: (*Shifting chair so her back is to customer*) I wish he'd leave.

WOMAN: Not him. Alcohol is poison to him. But he can't keep away from it. Keeps drinking. (*Resigned*) It'll kill him one of these days.

HOUSEWIFE: Well, I guess I can put up with anything, just so long as Chris is all right. They're operating now. I heard Dr. Walters say—mind you, he was talking to the nurse, he didn't know I could hear—I heard him say it could be hours. That's why I'm here. There was nothing I could do. I had to have a drink. Couldn't carry on any longer. (*To herself*) Please, don't let him die.

(WOMAN *says nothing.* HOUSEWIFE *looks at empty glass. Change of mood. Calls out boldly*)

Hey, what's-your-name!

BARTENDER: Yes, madam.

HOUSEWIFE: (*Coyly*) You don't object to being called What's-your-name?

BARTENDER: They call me many names.

HOUSEWIFE: They do, huh? Who's they?

BARTENDER: Everyone.

HOUSEWIFE: The customers, I suppose?

BARTENDER: Call them that if you like.

HOUSEWIFE: What do you mean?

BARTENDER: This is your first opportunity.

HOUSEWIFE: Opportunity?

BARTENDER: To meet me.

HOUSEWIFE: To meet you? Opportunity! You aren't half conceited, are you?

BARTENDER: Well, perhaps we should say a nodding acquaintance. Or do you prefer the expression "ships that pass in the night?"

HOUSEWIFE: I haven't the slightest idea what you're talking about? Bring me another drink.

BARTENDER: Another transfusion?

HOUSEWIFE: Transfusion! (*Laughs*) Oh, so that's it. Medical terminology picked up from the hospital, huh? Well, whatever you want to call it, bring it anyway. (*To* WOMAN) So you know about the accident?

WOMAN: Only what he said just now. One dead, two critically injured.

HOUSEWIFE: He didn't tell you more? Before I came in here, I mean.

WOMAN: Certainly not. I never speak to him.

HOUSEWIFE: Don't you?

WOMAN: (*Staring defiantly at* BARTENDER) No.

(BARTENDER *meets her gaze. Brings drink for* HOUSEWIFE, *puts it on table.*)

HOUSEWIFE: (*To* WOMAN) I've got to talk to someone.

WOMAN: The accident?

HOUSEWIFE: Yes, involving my son Chris, his friend Roland, and me. At least I was in the car, in the back seat, you know.

WOMAN: Yes?

HOUSEWIFE: It goes round and round in my head. I'm dizzy thinking about it. It's so awful, so awful. (*Breaks down*) Without this drink I'd go crazy.

WOMAN: Yes.

HOUSEWIFE: It was such a beautiful day. I suppose it still is a beautiful day out there. Anyway, Chris, my son, came home for lunch and said, "Mum, Roland and me want to go up to the lake for a swim." I never can resist that kid, anything he wants to do, I'm a sucker for it. And if only I'd said no, it would all have been different. But how could I tell? You never know what's coming, do you? Roland's parents are an older couple, much older. They say Mrs. Phillips had Roland when she was over forty. He was their only child. He would have graduated this year from high school. It's kind of ironic, isn't it, us all living in the same block? I've been thinking . . . if I were at home now I could see right down the street, right to the Phillips' house. I guess the sun is still shining, the little kids still playing hopscotch, the big ones pitching ball, and a few mothers wheeling their babies. I wonder if Mrs. Phillips is watching them from her window, watching those kids enjoying themselves just as if nothing had happened. I mean, it all goes on the same, doesn't it?

WOMAN: But why should it change? There's nothing different on your street except that Roland isn't there. That is, I guess from what you say that Roland is dead.

HOUSEWIFE: Oh, he's dead, all right, and Chris is badly injured. God, I hope Dr. Walters can do something. It's terrible, terrible. I blame myself. How will I ever face Mrs. Phillips? What will I say? There'll be a trial, dangerous driving. Oh, God. (*Pause*) Of course Chris was driving too fast. What sixteen-year-old doesn't drive too fast. It was my car. (*Laughs wryly*) "Was" is the right word for it. Chris is learning to drive. He has his learner's licence. He's allowed to drive if I'm in the car. It was lovely spinning along the country roads. I was sitting beside Chris in the front seat, what they call the death seat, you know, with Roland in the back. Then the kids wanted to stop for Cokes. When we got back in the car, we changed places. Somehow I got in the back and Roland got in the front. To think that Roland's dead because of a bottle of Coke. You never know, do you? We came over the crest of a hill and there was this huge truck pulling out of a farm. There was nowhere to go. It must have happened in a split second of time. But in my head it's a horrible, slow-motion movie. Roland went right through the windscreen, and the steering wheel smashed into Chris's chest. There was blood everywhere. I was pretty shaken up, I can tell you.

WOMAN: And now they're operating on your son?

HOUSEWIFE: Yes. Hours it will be. That's why I'm here. I couldn't stand waiting. I had to have a drink. (*Pause*) There's one comfort, Roland died instantly. Never knew what hit him. My Chris is the one to worry about. Dr. Walters is the best surgeon in town. If anyone can save Chris, Dr. Walters can. Oh, God, they've got to save my boy.

WOMAN: (*Pause*) If it isn't sudden and unexpected, it's slow and painful. Which would you choose?

HOUSEWIFE: (*Continuing her own train of thought*) I'm not a religious person, never have been, but I said to myself, if Chris gets better, his life has been spared for a reason. Oh, I'm sorry for Mr. and Mrs. Phillips. Desperately sorry. I keep wondering . . . wondering . . . Was it my fault? Was it fate? Why did it have to happen? Chris wasn't really driving so very fast. The Phillips worshipped that boy. Worshipped him. Brilliant and clever, he was. He had a great future, I know. Oh, it sounds awful, awful . . . selfish even, but I've got to say it, I've got to. I'm glad it wasn't Chris.

WOMAN: I beg your pardon?

HOUSEWIFE: I said, I don't want to sound selfish, but . . .

WOMAN: (*Violently, passionately*) You don't want to sound selfish! Would you rather be unselfish and have Chris dead? Such hypocrisy makes me sick. What's selfish about wanting to live? Doesn't the fact of our being born presuppose a desire to live? (*She stands for the first time, she drinks.*) To life! (*She drains her glass and hurls it defiantly at the bar. It shatters.* BARTENDER *remains unmoved.* WOMAN *sits.*)

CUSTOMER: (*Drunkenly from seat*) To death! (*Drinks*)

HOUSEWIFE: (*To* WOMAN). Why did you do that?

WOMAN: (*Savagely*) To drain the cup.

HOUSEWIFE: Aren't you afraid of him?

WOMAN: Not any more.

HOUSEWIFE: He's a pal of yours, then?

WOMAN: I've learned to accept him.

HOUSEWIFE: I thought you never spoke to him.

WOMAN: I don't. But he keeps after me.

HOUSEWIFE: You mean for a date?

WOMAN: Yes. I won't be able to resist much longer.

HOUSEWIFE: (*Pause*) He hasn't moved.

WOMAN: It makes no difference to him. He knows we have to pay in the end.

HOUSEWIFE: I don't understand.

WOMAN: (*Passionately*) Don't try. Listen to me. I also have a son. Is it selfish if I say, I'm glad he is alive? If it's selfish, then let me be selfish. As soon as we're born, we begin to die. But not too soon, God, not too soon. (*Pause. She begins again, calmly, almost conversationally.*) Yesterday in the paper, did you notice? An infant suffocated in its crib. The grandmother was baby-sitting. Poor woman, how must she have felt, permitting death to enter that home and gather in the child? And did you read that out in the country a six-year-old boy drowned in his own swimming pool? Do you suppose his parents will ever want to swim in that pool again once death has visited there?

HOUSEWIFE: I don't know. There are all sorts of terrible things in the paper.

WOMAN: And last week, a ferry near Hong Kong sank in a typhoon. Fifty school children and their teachers were lost.

HOUSEWIFE: A ferry? Hong Kong? What are you talking about? What has that to do with us?

WOMAN: You think it doesn't matter if it's Hong Kong? From Hong Kong to the country, to your street, to your house, to your car, to the seat you are sitting in.

HOUSEWIFE: I know, I know. Five minutes earlier and I would have been sitting in that seat. But the point is, I wasn't.

WOMAN: So it doesn't matter about Hong Kong?

HOUSEWIFE: I didn't say that.

WOMAN: And Roland is dead. Sixteen was he? Then he's had more life, a larger share than these other children who died. Tell his mother be grateful, be glad.

HOUSEWIFE: Be grateful! Glad! Are you crazy? Sixteen! He might have had seventy, eighty years.

WOMAN: But sixteen is more than six weeks or six years.

HOUSEWIFE: I don't care. People who live on our street aren't killed in accidents every day.

WOMAN: Aren't they? But who knows who may be next? And if you're not ready, you'll say, "Why should it be me? I have things to do. Let me wait." But if death has touched you, he won't wait.

(CUSTOMER *stretches his arms. Yawns. Picks up his empty glass and carries it over to the bar. Slams it on counter. Grabs bottle out of* BARTENDER'S *hand, fills glass.*)

CUSTOMER: (*To* BARTENDER) I'm not waiting. I'm not waiting for you to serve me. I'll serve myself. A drink, (*Quickly swallows it*) and another, and another.

(CUSTOMER *reels toward door beside bar, tries to pass through it.* BARTENDER *obstructs, but does not touch him.* CUSTOMER *retreats.*)

BARTENDER: Not yet.

CUSTOMER: (*Shrugs shoulders. To* WOMAN) I heard you arguing. What's life for? Life feeds death. Then let death be satisfied. I see them, the suckers who come in here. They've spent their lives working. They mow their grass, wash their cars, keep up their life insurance, and if they're lucky, before they die, they can pay off the mortgage. (*Points to* HOUSEWIFE) What's the reason? To raise children? So you change their diapers and take them to swim practice, and argue with them about who gets the car, and then what? Grandchildren! Then their kids have kids. And they repeat the same cycle. And will they have enough for their old age? You live to work and you work to live, and you live to die. So you might as well die anytime, because when you're dead no one will care or even remember your name.

HOUSEWIFE: What a horrible outlook. Life would be pointless if everyone thought like you.

CUSTOMER: Life is pointless, lady.

WOMAN: (*Passionately*) Life is not pointless. Life is love. (*To* CUSTOMER) Have you never known love?

CUSTOMER: (*Hesitates*) Once . . . once . . . . before I was like this . . . once . . .

HOUSEWIFE: (*To* WOMAN) You're right. The poor devil is drinking himself to death.

WOMAN: And why? Why is he doing it? (*To* CUSTOMER) Why? Why do you choose this slow death, why when others long for another hour of life?

CUSTOMER: (*Stubbornly*) It's my life. It's my death.

(WOMAN *stands, points straight at audience.*)

WOMAN: Have you looked out the window? Have you ever seen such beauty? The clouds . . . great grey umbrellas with frills of pink and orange sunset. The sky, a crystal bowl, and the mountains, royal purple where they meet the sea.

HOUSEWIFE: The view is pretty. I suppose that's why it's called Sunset Bar.

CUSTOMER: (*To* WOMAN) You're crazy. There's no view. There isn't even a window there.

WOMAN: There is a view. Once . . . once . . . even you must have seen it.

CUSTOMER: (*Laughs coarsely*) Once! It was a long time ago, lady. (*Drains glass, staggers uncertainly towards* BARTENDER'S *door*) Now I don't care about any view. I want one thing. (*Shouts*) I want to get through that door! (*Tries again to pass, once again is prevented*) I'm a regular customer. Why don't you let me through? (*Giving up*) Well, one day I'll make it. You'll see.

(*He staggers back to his table, puts his head down and passes out.*)

HOUSEWIFE: A sad case, evidently. A wasted life.

(*Pause*)

WOMAN: The view often comes too late. Too late to be seen, to be appreciated.

(*Another pause.* HOUSEWIFE *lights a cigarette.* WOMAN *stares in front of her.*)

WOMAN: (*Suddenly*) Do you ever travel by bus?

HOUSEWIFE: No, never.

WOMAN: But you've seen people waiting for it?

HOUSEWIFE: Of course.

WOMAN: Have you noticed how pitiful they are? All their heads turned in one direction, gazing down the road . . . staring into the distance as if they could observe the whole route of the bus. Where it started, how far it has progressed, when it will turn the corner. As if by watching in this way, they could ever guess when it will arrive at the point where they are standing. Yet, in spite of this anxiety, this obsession, the bus comes no sooner, no later, than the time at which it would always have come. (*Pause.* HOUSEWIFE *smokes, looks bored.*) Don't you see, just as it is true that ten thousand years ago you were going to inhale your cigarette at this very moment, so it is also true that ten thousand years ago the bus was going to arrive at the moment it does.

(HOUSEWIFE *stubs out cigarette.*)

HOUSEWIFE: (*Yawning*) How interesting.

WOMAN: I find it very interesting.

(*A pause.* HOUSEWIFE *drinks.* WOMAN *stares in front of her.*)

HOUSEWIFE: It's getting dark.

WOMAN: Yes.

HOUSEWIFE: The sun is setting.

WOMAN: Yes.

HOUSEWIFE: There's something creepy about this place.

WOMAN: Of course.

HOUSEWIFE: I think it's him. (*Indicates* BARTENDER)

WOMAN: I'm sure of it.

(*A silence*)

HOUSEWIFE: If it's not a personal question, is there something wrong with your eyes?

WOMAN: No.

HOUSEWIFE: I was wondering why you wear sunglasses. Don't you want to be recognized?

WOMAN: I don't want to recognize.

HOUSEWIFE: Oh. (*Pause*) It's chilly in here. I'm cold. So cold. The doctor should be finished soon. Hours, he said. Oh, Chris, Chris, you've got to be all right. (*Pause*) Your son, I suppose he takes the bus to school?

WOMAN: He's at boarding school.

HOUSEWIFE: Boarding school! He's a problem then?

WOMAN: A problem! At ten years old. (*Smiles*) He's been the best thing in my . . . life.

HOUSEWIFE: You and your husband must be terribly busy. I mean, I suppose you don't have time for a child.

WOMAN: I have no husband. No relatives at all.

HOUSEWIFE: And you send your son away to school?

WOMAN: Yes.

HOUSEWIFE: I'd never send Chris from home. I'd sooner die. (*Pause*) Does your little boy like boarding school?

WOMAN: He hates it.

HOUSEWIFE: Hates it! How cruel you are.

WOMAN: Not cruel. Kind.

HOUSEWIFE: Doesn't he miss you?

WOMAN: (*Distressed*) As much as I miss him. (*Fiercely*) He must learn to miss me.

HOUSEWIFE: Poor little fellow, only ten years old!

WOMAN: (*Angrily*) Will you stop tormenting me! It's for his own good. He has to learn to be without me. Don't you understand? He must live his own life. You don't think I do it from choice, do you?

HOUSEWIFE: I'm sorry. It's none of my business.

(BARTENDER *gets up, unasked he brings* WOMAN *a glass of wine. She does not touch it.* BARTENDER *returns to his place.*)

That was nice of him.

WOMAN: Another transfusion. It wasn't nice at all.

HOUSEWIFE: Aren't you going to drink it?

WOMAN: No. He flirts with me. I don't know when he'll come to the point.

HOUSEWIFE: He flirts with you? I don't understand.

WOMAN: Indeed, you don't. (*Pause. Points out front*) Look, the sun has gone down. The mountains and sea have almost disappeared in blackness.

HOUSEWIFE: We don't have much view on our street.

WOMAN: It isn't always the street . . .

HOUSEWIFE: If I had this view, I could look at it forever.

WOMAN: Forever? Yes, years. Years to look at the view. Years to do anything. Tomorrow and tomorrow and tomorrow.

HOUSEWIFE: Shakespeare, isn't it? I saw the movie. (WOMAN *does not answer.* HOUSEWIFE *looks at watch.*) Time is passing. Oh, Chris, keep fighting, sweetheart. (*She shivers.*) I'm so cold. It's freezing in here. (*To* WOMAN) Do you think Dr. Walters will let me know as soon as it's over?

WOMAN: Yes, I would think so.

(*Silence. A* BOY *of about sixteen appears in the doorway. He is very calm, very still. He walks through the room and towards the door by the bar.* BARTENDER *holds it open for him, touching him on the shoulder as he passes through.* HOUSEWIFE *and* WOMAN *do not see* BOY, *though* HOUSEWIFE *shivers again.*)

HOUSEWIFE: I'm shivering. I can't stop shivering.

(BARTENDER *approaches her.*)

BARTENDER: Madam?

HOUSEWIFE: (*Sharply*) What do you want?

BARTENDER: I have a message for you. Your son . . .

HOUSEWIFE: (*Gasps*) My son! Oh, Chris, Chris . . . (*Suspiciously to* BARTENDER) A message? What message? Where did it come from?

BARTENDER: The hospital, madam.

HOUSEWIFE: How could it have done? I never heard any phone. (*Mounting anger*) Nobody's come. You've never left the room. (*To* WOMAN) He's been listening to our conversation. If there is a gag, it's in the worst taste, and he deserves to be . . .

WOMAN: Look at him!

HOUSEWIFE: (*Stares at* BARTENDER. *Shudders*) How horrible. How dreadful.

(BARTENDER *turns and walks back to bar.*)

WOMAN: It always comes as a shock.

HOUSEWIFE: (*Horrified*) It's a wonder he can find work . . .

WOMAN: There's always plenty of work.

HOUSEWIFE: Especially here, meeting the public.

WOMAN: That's what he does. Meets the public.

HOUSEWIFE: Who employs him? Who owns this place? Why does he have to be here?

WOMAN: We don't know. Nobody knows. We wish we did.

HOUSEWIFE: I must go to Chris. Back to the hospital. What is the matter with me?

What am I doing drinking when my son is in danger? (*Goes to bar*) Waiter, the check.

BARTENDER: There is no charge, madam.

HOUSEWIFE: No charge! But I had two double ryes.

BARTENDER: (*Leans towards her*) Another time you will be required to pay.

HOUSEWIFE: (*Frightened*) Get away. Don't touch me.

(*She backs away from him.*)

BARTENDER: (*Advancing*) Ah, who is it I will not touch?

HOUSEWIFE: Not me. You won't touch me. I'll scream.

BARTENDER: They often scream. It does no good.

HOUSEWIFE: Help!

(NURSE *appears in doorway.* BARTENDER *moves away from* HOUSEWIFE. NURSE *does not enter room, but speaks with compassion, as if to a very ill person.*)

NURSE: Here I am, dear. Here I am.

(*At the sound of her voice,* HOUSEWIFE *stretches out her hand.*)

HOUSEWIFE: Oh, it's you, Nurse. How glad I am to see you. I thought you'd forgotten me.

NURSE: Not for an instant.

HOUSEWIFE: How is he? How is my son? Tell me, please tell me. Is Chris going to live?

NURSE: (*Gravely*) Everything possible has been done.

HOUSEWIFE: Oh, God, they can't let him die. They can't.

NURSE: Come, come along. Rest is what you need. Rest and quiet.

HOUSEWIFE: I've been so cold, Nurse. But I'm warmer now. I've had two drinks. (*Nods at* WOMAN) Transfusions, she calls them.

NURSE: That's right.

HOUSEWIFE: My head is not so dizzy. It's you, Nurse. I feel better when you are with me. (*To* WOMAN) Won't you come, too? Come away from here.

WOMAN: I can't. It's too late.

NURSE: (*To* HOUSEWIFE) Come now, you've been here long enough.

(BARTENDER *turns, raises his hand in silent greeting to* NURSE)

HOUSEWIFE: (*Surprised*) Is he a friend of yours?

NURSE: Sometimes a friend, sometimes an enemy. I see him all the time at work.

HOUSEWIFE: He frightens me.

NURSE: I know.

HOUSEWIFE: I feel a little stronger now.

NURSE: You'll need all your strength for the ordeal ahead.

HOUSEWIFE: No ordeal could be worse than staying here. (*To* WOMAN) But you're staying? Why?

WOMAN: I must. (*Pleadingly, she seems to be addressing* BARTENDER) I'd give anything to be able to write to my son. If only I could send him a word, tell him I loved him.

BARTENDER: There's not time.

WOMAN: (*Taking off her dark glasses and speaking to* HOUSEWIFE) You see, one never knows about time. You use it like a spendthrift, suddenly to find you're bankrupt. Goodbye. I hope your son will survive. I hope you both live to be a hundred.

HOUSEWIFE: Aren't you afraid of being left alone with him?

(NURSE *and* HOUSEWIFE *are already on their way out.* WOMAN *speaks to their retreating backs.*)

WOMAN: Don't worry. He has already touched me. In fact we have a date, he and I, quite soon.

(WOMAN *stares straight in front of her.* BARTENDER *is motionless. Light fades.*)

After Words

1. In your journal, note your feelings and associations in response to the play. Comment on the Housewife's experience and on her future.

2. Describe and give reasons for the view of life and death as held by each of the following: the Customer, the Woman.

3. a) Discuss the symbolic value of the following: the play's title, the bar, the bartender, the view from the bar. How does the playwright develop each symbol?

   b) Discuss whether a bar setting is appropriate. What other settings would be suitable? Why?

4 The playwright does not name the characters but only identifies them in the script with labels. What is the effect? What would the effect have been if she had used alternative labels such as proper names? Try out some options.

5 In a small group, discuss and decide how you would produce the play. Consider in detail:
- directions to each of the actors regarding his or her role
- costume and make-up
- set design, including how you would present the front window
- lighting and music

Present your decisions in writing and visuals.

6 Give a sequel, offer an alternative ending, recall a related event, or explore a theme in a manner you choose. You might do so in drama, visuals, or writing.

Glossary

Act A major division in the action of a play. Modern full-length plays are usually three acts, although some are two or four. Shakespearean plays are divided into five acts.

Adaptation The redevelopment of a work in one medium to fit another—e.g., a short story to film, a stage play to radio drama.

Aside In theatre (rarely in TV and film), a brief comment made by an actor directly to the audience.

Backdrop In theatre, back of the stage onto which a setting may be painted or projected. In early film and TV, actors sometimes performed scenes in front of blank backdrops with settings projected onto them, e.g., scenery outside a "moving" car.

Beat A very brief pause in speech.

Biz/Business Dialogue, movements, and/or sound appropriate to action of the drama. In theatre, for example, a character may fumble with clothing or pretend to talk with another while the main action takes place away from them. In radio drama, "biz," such as the sound of paper tearing to represent a character ripping up a contract, is usually distinguished from other sound effects, such as the sound of applause.

Blocking/Blocking diagram Blocking refers to the positions and movements of actors on the stage. The director creates a blocking diagram to direct the actors.

Camera cues In film and TV, camera cues direct the **camera shots**—a single piece of exposed film in uncut frames—and **sequences**—groups of related shots. Directions are given in the screenplay and/or during the direction and production, and relate to the following:

    camera distance from subject—long, medium, short, close-up

    camera angle in relation to subject—low (from below), high (from above), normal or flat (on the same level), etc.

    camera movement—e.g., pan (horizontally across the screen), tracking (following the action), zoom in (with a special lens moving smoothly, closer to subject)

    type of shot—e.g., exterior (EXT) shot (showing the outside of a house, a landscape, etc.), interior (INT) shot (showing the interior of a building, the character's room, a kitchen, etc.), establishing shot (such as a landscape to establish visually a setting), stock shot (shot from newsreel footage or film archives)

    editing of the frames, shots, and sequences—e.g., fade in (dark screen brightens to image), fade out (the reverse), cut to (transition from one shot to another with no blackout or break)

Chorus character A character who voices concerns the audience might have or who comments on the main action of the drama.

Comedy of manners A humorous drama that comments on behaviour peculiar to a particular time; often depends on witty dialogue.

Credits List of people involved in the production: actors, director, camera personnel, technicians, etc. In TV or film, most credits are included in the closing titles.

Curtain In theatre, sometimes hung to conceal the stage from the audience. Usually, the curtain rises to open the play, falls to end the play. It can also be used to open and close acts. Sometimes action, as in a sub-plot, may take place in front of the curtain.

Dialogue In all drama, the spoken words; in scripts, the lines to be spoken as opposed to the cues or directions.

Docudrama A work dramatizing or based on historical fact.

Episode In TV or radio, one complete portion in a series of connected dramas.

Fade, Fade in, Fade out In radio, indicates a change in the sound's volume; also used for sound and lighting in stage and screen productions.

Farce A very obvious, unsubtle comedy designed to create simple, hearty laughs.

Foil A character employed as a deliberate contrast to another.

Melodrama A drama—such as a TV or radio "soap opera"—with exaggerated plot, character, and acting; similar to farce, though not comic.

Narrating commenting upon or describing the action and characters, or simply telling the plot. Narration is often used in radio and, as "voice-over" in TV or film.

One-act play A short play about 20–30 minutes long. Two or three one-acts are often staged consecutively to provide a full evening of theatre.

Pause A definite silence in mid-speech; may be deliberately long, "a dramatic pause."

POV Point of view, either physical or mental.

Props/Properties Articles of costume, furniture, etc. used in the production of a drama.

Prelude A performance serving as an introduction; similar to the opening act for the main attraction in music.

Recitation Actor reading from a text or reciting from memory.

Scene A division within drama, indicating a single action or dramatic situation; in theatre, a subdivision within an act; in film and TV, a series of shots using one location. In radio, sound effects may open and close scenes. "Scene" can also refer to the set or setting.

Script, Screenplay The script is the written representation, record, or basis of drama, including dialogue, cues, etc. Screenplays are scripts for film and TV—in other words, for the "screen."

Sketch/Skit A very short, self-contained scene.

Stage directions Instructions, usually given in the script in brackets and/or italics, to the actors and to sound and lighting technicians. Stage directions sometimes refer to the **stage positions**, which are given from the actor's point of view:

down stage (DS): front of stage, closest to audience

up stage (US): rear of stage, closest to any backdrop, farthest from audience

stage left (SL), stage right (SR), centre stage (CS): respectively, to the left or right, or in the centre of the stage when facing audience

off stage (OS): literally "off the stage"—usually refers to sound effects or a voice from the **wings** (the area just off stage, out of sight of the audience)

More detailed directions might be given, e.g., **down stage left (DSL), up stage right (USR)**. Directions for **spotlights** (intense, focused lights) and other lighting effects may be given using stage positions.

Storyboard A series of drawings to represent or plan the shots and their sequence in TV or film.

Teleplay A drama written for TV.

Title In film or TV, a printed heading, usually used to indicate time and place, such as "Berlin 1944."

Voice-over (VO) In film and TV, speech recorded "over" the image, often narrating the action onscreen.

Additional Selection Groupings

The scripts in this collection may be experienced, grouped together, and combined with other materials in a myriad of ways. The following chart presents some additional options to the groupings of Identity, Relationships, and Power.

Quests/Journeys
> Eve
> Frankenstein
> Death Seat

Finding Ourselves
> Eve
> Medicine River
> To Set Our House in Order

Family
> Eve
> Medicine River
> To Set Our House in Order

Romance
> Eve
> Medicine River
> A Marriage Proposal
> On the King's Birthday

Death and Reconciliation
> The Interview
> To Set Our House in Order
> Compensation Will Be Paid
> Death Seat

Individuals and Society
Community
> Medicine River
> A Marriage Proposal
> Compensation Will Be Paid

Bias
> Eve
> The Interview
> The Exhibition
> On the King's Birthday
> Frankenstein

Alienation
> The Man Who Turned into a Dog
> The Exhibition
> Frankenstein

Current Issues
> Eve
> The Interview
> The Man Who Turned into a Dog
> The Exhibition
> On the King's Birthday
> Compensation Will Be Paid
> Frankenstein
> Death Seat

Historical Settings/References
> The Interview
> The Exhibition
> A Marriage Proposal
> On the King's Birthday
> To Set Our House in Order
> Compensation Will Be Paid
> Frankenstein

Adaptations
> Eve
> Medicine River
> To Set Our House in Order
> Frankenstein

Docudrama
> On the King's Birthday
> The Exhibition

Humour
> Eve
> Medicine River
> A Marriage Proposal

Additional Selection Groupings

Film connections
>The Exhibition
>Medicine River
>To Set Our House in Order
>Frankenstein

Canadian
>Eve
>Medicine River
>On the King's Birthday
>To Set Our House in Order
>Compensation Will Be Paid
>Frankenstein
>Death Seat

Credits

Every effort has been made to trace the original sources of materials contained in this book. The publisher would be pleased to hear from copyright holders to rectify any errors or omissions.

ANTON CHEKHOV: *A Marriage Proposal* translated by Theodore Hoffman. Reprinted by permission.
Inquiries about performing rights of all kinds are to be addressed to: Samuel French (Canada) Ltd., 80 Richmond Street East, Toronto, Ontario M5C 1P1. No kind of performance, even those defined as 'private,' partial or complete, in any medium, may be given without written permission in advance and proper payment of royalty.

OSVALDO DRAGÚN: *The Man Who Turned Into a Dog*. This work originally appeared as *The Man Who Turned Into a Dog* by Osvaldo Dragún in *Selected Latin American One-Act Plays*, Francesca Colecchia and Julio Matas, editors and translators. Published in 1973 by the University of Pittsburgh Press. Adapted and reprinted by permission of the publisher.

LARRY FINEBERG: *Eve*, a play by Larry Fineberg, based on the novel *The Book of Eve* by Constance Beresford-Howe. Reprinted by permission of the author. Changes in *Eve* have been made at the publisher's request which do not apply to the acting edition.

THOMAS GIBBONS: *The Exhibition*. © Copyright, 1980, by Thomas Gibbons, © Copyright, 1978, by Thomas Gibbons as an unpublished dramatic composition under the title *The Elephant Man*.
CAUTION: The reprinting of *The Exhibition* included in this volume is reprinted by permission of the author and Dramatists Play Service, Inc. The amateur performance rights in this play are controlled exclusively by Dramatists Play Service, Inc., 440 Park Avenue South, New York, NY 10016. No amateur production of the play may be given without obtaining, in advance, the written permission of the Dramatists Play Service, Inc., and paying the requisite fee. Inquiries regarding all other rights should be addressed to the author, care of Dramatists Play Service, Inc.

HILDA MARY HOOKE: *On the King's Birthday* is reprinted from *One Act Plays from Canadian History* (Longmans, Green and Co., 1942)

JOAN MASON HURLEY: *Death Seat* from *Four Canadian One-Act Plays*, A Room of One's Own Press, 1990. Reprinted by permission of the author.

THOMAS KING: *Medicine River: The Radio Play*, copyright by Thomas King. Used by permission of The Bukowski Agency, Toronto.

ALDEN NOWLAN and WALTER LEARNING: *Frankenstein, The Play* (Toronto: Clarke, Irwin and Company, 1976). Reprinted by permission of Stoddart Publishing Co. Limited, Don Mills, Ontario.

GWEN PHARIS RINGWOOD: *Compensation Will Be Paid* from *The Collected Plays of Gwen Pharis Ringwood*, Borealis Press, 1982. Reprinted by permission of the publisher.

PETER SWET: *The Interview*. Copyright © 1975 by Peter Swet. All rights reserved.
CAUTION: Professionals and amateurs are hereby warned that *The Interview*, being fully protected under the Copyright Laws of the United States of

America, the British Commonwealth, including the Dominion of Canada, and all other countries of the International Copyright Union and the Universal Copyright Convention, is subject to royalty. All rights, including professional, amateur, motion picture, recitation, lecturing, public reading, radio and television broadcasting, and the rights of translation into foreign languages, are strictly reserved. Particular emphasis is laid on the question of readings, permission for which must be secured from the author's agent in writing. All inquiries concerning rights should be addressed to the author's representative, Lois Berman, 21 West 26th Street, New York, NY 10010.

ANNE WHEELER: Film script of *To Set Our House in Order* by Margaret Laurence. Reprinted by permission of Anne Wheeler.